Financially Focused Project Management

Thomas M. Cappels

J.ROSS
PUBLISHING

ISBN 1-932159-09-6

Printed and bound in the U.S.A. Printed on acid-free paper
10   9   8   7   6   5   4   3   2   1

Library of Congress Cataloging-in-Publication Data

Cappels, Thomas M., 1953-
    Financially focused project management / Thomas M. Cappels.
      p. cm.
    ISBN 1-932159-09-6
1. Project management. 2. Project management—Finance. 3. Project management—
Cost effectiveness. I. Title.
    HD69.P75C37 2003
    658.4′04—dc21

                                                                    2003007671

    Direct all inquiries to J. Ross Publishing, Inc., 6501 Park of Commerce Blvd., Suite 200, Boca Raton, Florida 33487.

                            Phone: (561) 869-3900
                             Fax: (561) 892-0700
                            Web: www.jrosspub.com

CONTENTS

CASE STUDIES

FOREWORD

As we move through the 21st century, it has become even more important than ever to monitor the bottom line. This, of course, calls for knowledgeable management teams to address the many financial, quality, ethical, and stakeholder-related issues that face domestic and global organizations today and tomorrow. Further, in the wake of the blunders of organizations such as Enron, WorldCom, and others, it is imperative that proven quality management and financially focused techniques be instilled into an organization's culture.

As is the case today, the "New Economy" is providing organizations with many challenges. These challenges include — but are not limited to — downsizing, increased global competition, and managing change. In order to ensure that a substantive portion of a project is delivered on time, within budget, and meets customer requirements, an organization must now employ proven financially focused project management tools and techniques. Moreover, the project manager of the 21st century must have a varied skill set. The project manager of today must be able to identify a problem, frame the problem, seek alternatives, choose the best alternative, and implement the solution.

These skills are a necessity and must be obtained through formal education, seminars, and on-the-job training. This book is a valuable piece of the puzzle as a reference for obtaining these skills. In fact, as in his other publications, the author, Tom Cappels, provides a wealth of information on the topics of project management, quality, and financially focused measurement and analysis. He has worked hard to ensure that the book is not just another look at project management, quality, and financial analysis, but an in-depth look at how these functions can work together to ensure project success.

As a former journeyman of Lockheed Martin Missiles and Space, he has a very impressive track record. Furthermore, his proven techniques saved Lockheed Martin millions of dollars and aided in efficient project management functions. In addition, as an educator, he is in touch with the pedagogical requirements of writing a text for today's student, whether it is at a traditional or nontraditional institution of higher learning. His ability to make practical use of these techniques is what makes the book a success.

I would also like to say that having worked directly with Tom, he is a very experienced, knowledgeable, and dedicated project manager, educator, and quality guru. He is continually updating his skill set by keeping abreast of the latest trends and even starting some trends himself. So, it is my privilege to recommend this book for its exceptional topical coverage of key project management concepts and practices.

Robert W. Key
MAEd, MBA, PMP
University of Phoenix

PREFACE

Project management is described as the formal usage of principles and methods in the planning and control of projects. Although this definition emphasizes formality, it should also emphasize the goal of effective project management: *profitability*.

In today's highly competitive global economy, bottom line financial performance has become more important than ever. Rightsizing and technology improvements created efficiencies and productivity enhancements that led to lower costs and improved earnings, but the aftermath of September 11 and continued distrust of corporate executive management have reinforced and heightened expectations on the part of shareholders, investors, and lenders to unprecedented levels.

When a company fails to meet Wall Street's earnings expectations, even by a few cents, the stock is often savagely punished by the market. In today's world, understanding the bottom line and the importance of increasing shareholder value is not just a requirement for the finance organization; it is a prerequisite for all employees and disciplines within a company.

A recent article in the *Business Times*[1] discusses how project management leadership has become a highly sought-after skill. The increasingly competitive global marketplace demands that businesses complete new projects, services, and business developments quickly, on time, and within budget.

No businesses in the 21st century can escape these demands. Small companies, web-based businesses, and giant global corporations alike need project managers to fuel much of the successful development of exciting new business enterprises.

Project managers do this by delivering projects that have consistent value and help increase profits. Talented, educated, and knowledgeable project managers are the business leaders, entrepreneurs, and global citizens of tomorrow, proving their value to any organization competing in today's fast-paced marketplace.

Regardless of how much demand there is, good project managers are not born, but rather are created through a combination of education, experience, time, and talent. The fast-changing technology available today further complicates matters as plans become obsolete or outdated with ever-increasing speed.

Thus, a good project manager must not only be proficient at managing, he or she must retain that proficiency as the circumstances change. Fast-speed adaptability is not an option, but rather an absolute requirement of the job.

Clearly, the job of "project manager" is not for the faint-of-heart. When faced with a first project, many project managers are worried that they do not yet know what they should know.

Historically, project management had a reputation for always being late and over budget. Even under the best of circumstances, project management is not easy. The project manager is continually faced with changing conditions, technology, resources, requirements, and schedules.

Good preparation and knowledge about what the job entails are hugely valuable and key to the success of the project. Outstanding organization skills are a prerequisite for the project manager, but so are other key attributes, such as the *financially focused mindset*,[2] which also needs to be developed.

In the past, most of this development occurred on the job, so few individuals who were promoted to the role of project manager ever felt fully ready to take on the challenges offered to them.

The imperative for successful implementation of every project that a company undertakes must remain at the forefront of the project manager's objectives. After all, managing projects that lead to providing customers the value they are seeking is the key to long-term business success and a major determinant in beating the competition.

The challenge that companies face today is how to focus their businesses on producing quality products, while at the same time achieving the bottom line performance that shareholders and the investment community demand. It is exactly this challenge that financially focused project management (FFPM) tackles head on.

This text formally introduces FFPM to the academic and business worlds. The FFPM management science has been evolving over the years at such companies as Lockheed Martin Missiles and Space and Litton Applied Technology and has been documented to save these companies millions of dollars.

FFPM takes the latest project management tools one critical step further by ensuring an education that offers the inclusion of a thorough financial viewpoint at the beginning of a project. This allows the integration of cost recognition in each step of the process.

This book presents methodologies for company-wide and scholastic education on key financial considerations. Project management principles are clearly presented. Related basic financial concepts are explained. The FFPM elements and their use in making and implementing business decisions are introduced. Case studies are presented that show successful FFPM applications. Readers will be equipped to implement FFPM in their work environments, offering the prospect of improving the translation of project implementation to the bottom line.

- FFPM successfully couples formal and professional education with the hard knocks of the real business world.
- The approaches presented result from benchmarking the best practices of hundreds of companies. Hundreds of millions of dollars have been saved, and billions more will be, as the worlds of project management and finance unite.

FFPM provides business and project management professionals with a financial foundation in the form of the basic business concepts that are vital for success in the 21st century. FFPM offers terms, definitions, and instructions that will enable these professionals to talk the talk and walk the walk of FFPM.

FFPM effectively deals with one of the greatest challenges that businesses face today. It helps all members of the working class, from board members to first-line employees alike, to better understand the relationship and balance between managing projects and meeting the demanding challenges of the bottom line. Our futures depend on it.

THE AUTHOR

Thomas M. Cappels is the Controller for the San Mateo County (California) Office of Education and also serves as an Adjunct Professor and course developer for the University of Phoenix. He has over 20 years of industrial and financial management with Lockheed Martin, serving as a project manager on such prestigious programs as the Hubble Space Telescope and Space Station Freedom. Educated at the University of California at Los Angeles (UCLA) and San Jose State University (SJSU), he has earned his BA and MBA. With over 100 publications, he has authored texts on quality control, product liability, and financial administration.

As a project manager, Tom Cappels experienced the evolution of quality and project management firsthand. He lived the life of statistics, quality circles, suggestion systems, awards, MRP2, total quality management, and executive management proclamations. He stays in tune as a member, author, speaker, and former officer for the American Society for Quality. He has seen how an analytical, prudent, and informed financial viewpoint can reap tremendous benefits. Tom Cappels accentuates his years of hands-on project management and financial experience as a graduate-level project management and finance professor and is President of the International CA-VIA. He has built his reputation through 30+ years of studies and publications, which culminate here in *Financially Focused Project Management*.

™ Web Added Value

Free value-added materials available from
the Download Resource Center at www.jrosspub.com

At J. Ross Publishing we are committed to providing today's professional with practical, hands-on tools that enhance the learning experience and give readers an opportunity to apply what they have learned. That is why we offer free ancillary materials available for download on this book and all participating Web Added Value™ publications. These online resources may include interactive versions of material that appears in the book or supplemental templates, worksheets, models, plans, case studies, proposals, spreadsheets and assessment tools, among other things. Whenever you see the WAV™ symbol in any of our publications, it means bonus materials accompany the book and are available from the Web Added Value Download Resource Center at www.jrosspub.com.

Downloads available for *Financially Focused Project Management* consist of PowerPoint slides. a project management software guide, and an extensive glossary of project management terms.

UPDATE ON PROJECT MANAGEMENT

INTRODUCTION

You are a contestant playing the television game show "Wheel of Fortune." You have had pretty good luck so far, winning the preliminary rounds, and advancing to the final spin.

"We know you've got a lot of fans out there in the studio audience." Pat Sajak is as charming as ever. "They'll all be rooting for you as we take a look at the final puzzle!"

Vanna White glides onto the stage, wearing a gorgeous Versace gown, as the following puzzle appears:

_ _ _ _ _ _ _ _ _ _   _ _ _ _ _ _ _

_ _ _ _ _ _   _ _ _ _ _ _ _ _ _

"The category is Business Buzzwords." announces Pat. "And now let's see those letters R, S, T, L, N, and E. There's a little something there. Might be a good start for you."

As Vanna walks, the letters magically appear:

_ _ N _ N _ _ _ L L _   _ _ _ _ S E _

_ R _ _ E _ T   _ _ N _ _ E _ E N T

You like what you see so far, and already have an idea for the answer.

"What letters would you like to add?" questions Pat.

You hesitate, but only for a moment. "Pat...I'd like an M, G, an F, and the letter A!"

"I think you are going to like what happens when we add those letters!" approves Pat. "Vanna, are there any Ms, Gs, Fs, or As?"

A few members of the audience gasp as the letters begin to appear, and when the last letter is added, the audience bursts into applause.

F _ N A N _ _ _ L L _   F _ _ U S E _

_ R _ _ E _ T   M A N A G E M E N T

Pat cautions the audience with "No help, please." Then he turns to you with resigned anticipation. "I think you know it...."

"Do I ever!" you exclaim. "It's Financially Focused Project Management!" The puzzle fills in with the answer.

F I N A N C I A L L Y   F O C U S E D

P R O J E C T   M A N A G E M E N T

"Of course that's right," Pat says, shaking his head. As he begins to open the prize envelope he adds, "Let's see what you won...."

Even Pat looks surprised as he shows you the award — $150 million cash! You are instantly surrounded by family members running down from the audience. Even Vanna gives you a big hug.

"Financially Focused Project Management," says Pat knowingly. "Don't go away. We're taking a short break."

Thank goodness you work for a company that recognizes the need to focus fully on the financial aspects of project management activities. The recent company-sponsored training you attended put financially focused project management (FFPM) in the forefront of your mind. FFPM is the next step in the evolution of the project management science.

EVOLUTION OF THE PROJECT MANAGEMENT SCIENCE

The science of project management has been evolving at an ever-increasing pace since the turn of the 19th century. Denise Romberg[3] notes that, despite sophisticated software, half of all projects are delivered late or over budget. A classic case of poor project management is Casa Loma, a 98-room estate built in Toronto, Canada, for Sir Henry Mill Pellatt, a wealthy, decorated military hero. Begun in 1911, Casa Loma took 3 years, 300 men, and $3 million of imported materials to complete.

When the project was finished 3 years later, Pelatt was nearly bankrupt! His odds of completing the project on schedule and on budget would have been greatly increased had he employed any number of the many project management tools, systems, computer programs, and philosophies available today.

He also could have come in on schedule and under budget had he established a much more lenient schedule and a much higher budget!

But the fact remains, had Pellatt's project manager made use of current systems and technology, he may have more readily anticipated the problems and reacted more quickly to situations leading to schedule delays and increased costs.

In the 1980s and 1990s, project management started to be viewed as a trend-setting business discipline used in budgeting and allocating resources. Around the time that mainframe computers began moving to Macs and PCs, the art of project management began to become a science. The technological advance in distributed computing revolutionized project management and permitted desktop users access to manipulating what-if scenarios. Teams of experienced operators once required to manage the most complex engineering and construction projects gave way to multiuser systems managing multiple projects in complex environments.

While word processing, spreadsheet, and presentation software dominate software sales, project management accounted for U.S. sales of $900 million in 1999, and has been growing by 20% annually, according to the Gartner Group. Microsoft Project represents approximately a third of the market, outselling all other applications in this field.

Romberg[4] also offers that sophisticated software tools will not ensure project management success. She cites a 1998 benchmark survey performed by the Standish Group of Dennis, Massachusetts. This study found that project managers were successful in only 26% of the 23,000 projects surveyed; 46% of the projects were time and cost challenged and 28% were deemed failures. The survey found the retail industry enjoyed the best project results with 59% of projects successfully meeting deadlines, budgets, and user expectations. Health, financial, manufacturing, and software projects all achieved close to 30% or better success rates, while government projects were rated least successful at 18%.

Romberg suggested another approach to acquiring project management skills. This was a computer-based simulation environment entitled Project Challenge, developed by the creators of SimCity for use as an internal Systemhouse training tool and retail product. The game, offered at three levels of difficulty, creates a set of parameters, deliverables, and people to manage.

"If you are not successful in keeping up morale and delivering on time, you get yourself fired," explained Jim Hughes, vice president of software development at SHL Systemhouse in Toronto.

Hughes worked on Project Challenge and now advises the Integrated Justice consortium, in which Systemhouse is the integrator, in a 5-year project aimed at improving communication and eliminating redundancy throughout Ontario's justice system.

Hughes noted that the project actually consists of 6 projects that will team people from the combined ministries of the Attorney General and Solicitor General and accommodate about 300 points of integration. Hughes seemed to acknowledge that government projects do not fare as well as industry ones. The project payment schedule for the consortium deviates from the standard time and materials contract, "forcing us to discipline ourselves to deliver something that works or we don't get paid," Hughes explained.

EVOLUTION OF THE CORPORATE WORLD: WHERE IS TODAY'S CORPORATE FOCUS?

The 1990s and early 21st century found most businesses retreating to short-term emphasis on profits.

Today's corporate culture continues to embrace the latest trends in project management. Just a few of such trends are listed below, all of which are discussed in this text.

- Project management office
- Portfolio management
- FFPM
- Human aspects of project management
- Network of relationships
- Virtual teams
- Work package to network
- Responsibility matrix (planning and resource management)
- Resource plan
- Task duration table
- Project network diagram
- Gantt (bar) chart
- Financially focused quality
- Knowledge management
- Activity-on-arrow network
- Activity-on-node network

- Arrow diagram method
- Balanced matrix
- Bar chart
- Groupthink

And while the focus of project management continues to evolve, projects continue to complete beyond schedule and over budget. Such results impact the bottom line, and it does not appear to be getting better. Companies are resorting to "re-engineering, restructuring, downsizing, and outsourcing." While such actions will often reduce costs (exclusive of severance expenses) in the short term, other related impacts (e.g., substandard quality, increased training, decreased employee morale) can have significant negative impacts on profitability.

Listed below are just a few time periods in the recent past where dramatic head count reductions were made at major companies.

During in the fourth quarter of 1997, the following actions were taken:

- Citicorp (CCI) said it would dismiss 9,000 of its 90,000 employees worldwide as part of a massive restructuring designed to cut costs and improve the efficiency of back-office operations. The layoffs, which were to take place over 18 months, would be offset by the creation of 1,500 new jobs, bringing total cutbacks to 8.3% of the bank's workforce.
- Silicon Graphics, Inc., the high-end graphic computer concern, announced it would be firing up to 1,000 workers.
- Fruit of the Loom gave 60-day layoff notices to nearly 4,200 Louisiana workers and another 1,035 in Kentucky, and announced it was closing its plant at Abbeville, Louisiana. This was part of a nationwide employment cutback in an effort to send more jobs to Central America, where there are more competitive wage levels.
- Cadbury Schweppes's U.S. beverage unit, Dr. Pepper/Seven Up, Inc., announced it would cut 10% of its U.S. workforce, about 110 workers, by the end of 1998.
- Levi Strauss & Company, the blue jeans manufacturer, said it would shut down 11 of its 37 plants and cut 34% of its North American labor force. The layoffs at the clothing concern were expected to total 6,395 people out of a global workforce of 37,500.
- Imaging giant Eastman Kodak Company said it might cut 14,000 jobs, slash costs by as much as $1.0 billion, consolidate several businesses, and expand joint ventures.
- Deutsche Bank AG announced plans to acquire Bankers Trust Corporation for $10.1 billion, forming the world's biggest financial-services company and promising to boost profits by cutting 5,500 jobs, or

5.7% of staff. One week later, Citigroup (formed by the merger of Citicorp and Travelers Group) announced that it would cut another 1,400 jobs, bringing the total to 10,400, or 6.5% of its workforce.

The Bloomberg News Service reported that U.S. companies announced more than 574,000 job cuts in the first 11 months of 1998. Rightsizing (e.g., downsizing and layoffs) continues. Virtually every company is now looking for new approaches to achieve financial goals. Restructuring, re-engineering, out-sourcing, and rightsizing are popular terms being used in corporate boardrooms.

News stories running during 2002 and 2003 again reflected significant layoff actions, including the following:

- Navistar International Corp. announced it officially would make 1,100 layoffs, as the truck and engine manufacturer struggled to regain profitability.
- Boeing Wichita gave notices to the final 56 workers as officials said the company was nearing the twilight of a plan to eliminate up to 5,200 jobs in Wichita and 30,000 in the company's commercial airplanes division.
- IBM Corp. had laid off about 15,600 employees through the first half of the year — about 7,000 more than expected — according to filings with the U.S. Securities and Exchange Commission.
- WorldCom, Inc. began laying off 17,000 workers worldwide.
- Data storage company EMC Corp. reported a preliminary quarterly loss and revenue that were worse than expected and said it would cut 1,350 jobs due to dismal spending on technology.
- Fidelity Investments said it would lay off 1,695 employees, or 5.4% of its workforce, to cut costs.
- Bombardier announced layoffs of another 1,980 people from its aerospace division because of continuing weakness in the airline industry.
- SBC Communications, Inc. said it would eliminate 11,000 more jobs, or 6% of its workforce.
- Circuit City Stores announced plans to eliminate about 2,000 jobs, or 4.8% of its workforce, and absorb $16 million in severance costs. The Richmond, Virginia–based consumer electronics chain also said it is converting to a single hourly pay structure for its store employees.
- Bank of America said in February 2003 that it would cut about 1,000 technology and operations jobs, or 1% of its workforce, to reduce costs, according to Bloomberg News Service. The Charlotte, North Carolina–based bank laid off about 900 such workers in November and December of 2002.

Obviously times are still tough. Many projects are put on hold until financial resources become available. When funding does exist, the key to successful project management is incorporating an educated financial focus in the process.

FFPM

The next step in the evolution of the project management science leads to FFPM. Applying the tools and principles of FFPM with the latest project management concepts greatly enhances the opportunities for increased productivity and profitability, keeping projects on schedule and under budget.

Corporate executives justify cost-cutting measures by focusing on the cold cruel world of balance sheets and the bottom line. Head count reductions and other actions designed to improve the business are dictated and budgets are slashed prior to thoroughly understanding total impacts to profitability. It is now paramount that management, administrative, and technical employees everywhere understand from an educated, financial perspective how their activities and decisions affect the bottom line. FFPM offers the means to achieve this understanding.

Total Improvement Management

Total improvement management (TIM) was originated by a team of authors led by H. James Harrington, International Quality Advisor for Ernst & Young. TIM blends elements of total quality management, total productivity management, total cost management, total resource management, total technology management, and total business management methodologies.

At the heart of Harrington's model is the TIM pyramid, arranged as follows:

- Tier 1 — Direction: Top management leadership, business plans, environmental change plans, external customer focus, and quality management systems
- Tier 2 — Basic concepts: Management participation, team building, individual excellence, and supplier relations
- Tier 3 — Delivery process: Process breakthrough, product processes, and service process
- Tier 4 — Organizational impact: Measurements, organizational structure
- Tier 5 — Rewards and recognition

The Financially Focused Blueprint

FFPM adds a new element to the TIM pyramid, creating a modified design called the financially focused blueprint[2] (Figure 1.1) for total enterprise success.

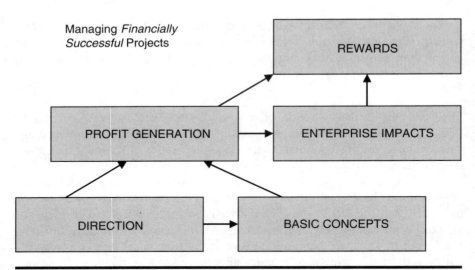

FIGURE 1.1. Financially Focused Blueprint. (Reprinted with permission from Cappels, T.M., *Financially Focused Quality*, CRC Press, 1999. Copyright CRC Press, Boca Raton, Florida.)

The major addition is educational training and other FFPM tools to ensure that all improvement activities are performed with the financially focused mindset. Also, while in the middle of the TIM pyramid are the processes by which products are delivered, the financially focused blueprint labels this component "profit generation." After all, the processes can run as beautifully as possible, but if they do not generate profits, the business will not operate for very long.

Brief descriptions of financially focused blueprint components are presented below.

Component #1 — Direction

The primary purpose of a for-profit enterprise is to make money. Top management must establish systems and exercise the leadership skills to accomplish this purpose. Direction is exhibited in the following six elements.

1. The project manager: Direction begins with two-way communication of goals and expectations.
2. General management leadership: Leading is more than supplying the resources for the latest improvement process or latest technological gadget. It includes participating in the project design and being part of the process.
3. Business plans: Giving direction requires that business plans be completely thought out and communicated clearly to all employees.

4. Environmental change plans: Valid implementations of new processes will usually require changing the work environment. Successful FFPM necessitates a financially focused environment, achieved via financial training.

5. External customer focus: Profitable enterprises have an excellent understanding of, and a close working relationship with, their external customer/consumer.

6. Quality management systems (e.g., ISO 9000): Harrington calls these systems the "blocking and tackling" of the improvement process and the essential building blocks for the rest of the structure.

Component #2 — Basic Concepts

1. Management participation: Management's active participation will be facilitated when management feels comfortable in its leadership role.

2. Team building: Synergies are achieved when employees unite in teams with common goals.

3. Individual excellence: Each employee must be motivated, empowered, and provided the proper tools (e.g., financial training) to make a difference and spark positive impacts.

4. Supplier relations (partnerships): Both the organization and its supply organizations should work together to achieve mutual success.

Component #3 — Profit Generation

Note that this is the only component that is linked to all the others. Profit generation is the central theme. The elements contained in this component are designed to generate profit through delivery of products and services.

1. Process breakthrough: Benchmarking, process improvement teams, just-in-time manufacturing, and outsourcing are just a few of the approaches utilized to improve processes and the output that its customers receive.

2. Product processes: The process in place to deliver products and manage projects to completion must operate at a peak level of excellence. This means the processes themselves are well designed and documented, and effort is undertaken to continually improve the product/project delivery process with a financially focused mindset.

3. Service process: The delivery process for services varies from the process for completion of projects and delivery of products. This element focuses on the design, documentation, and continual improvement of project management and the service delivery process with a financially focused mindset.

Component #4 — Enterprise Impacts

With the improvement process well underway, the next component of the financially focused blueprint is addressing how changes impact the enterprise. There are two elements to examine:

1. Measurements: Only when the improvement process documents positive measurable results can management be expected to embrace the newly implemented methodology as a way of life. This measurement process should apply the basic financial concepts touted by FFPM.
2. Organizational structure: Large organizations need to give way to small business units that can react quickly and effectively to changing business needs.

Component #5 — Rewards and Recognition

This component is the result of a well laid out financially focused blueprint. The employees are rewarded with job security and good pay. Employees and teams may also receive recognition with special awards and pats on the back. Company owners are rewarded with increasing profits, dividends, and stock value.

SELF-STUDY/DISCUSSION QUESTIONS

1. Have you or someone you know been party to any layoff actions? Discuss.
2. How does the threat of layoffs affect a company and its employees?
3. What are some of the projects undertaken by your company?
4. What is the average cost of these projects?
5. Who were the customers (internal/external)?
6. Of projects with which you have been involved or of which you have been aware, which have finished on schedule? On budget? Both? Late? Over budget? Both?
7. Have you ever contracted for a major project in your home (e.g., swimming pool, addition of room, another story, another bathroom, kitchen remodel)? What was the outcome as far as schedule and budget? What lessons did you learn?
8. What are the components of the financially focused blueprint? Describe and discuss each as it applies to your place of work. Which is the most important? The least important?

2

PROJECT MANAGEMENT OVERVIEW

INTRODUCTION

One of the very first projects in history to be documented was Noah's Ark.[5] This project had a very tight schedule with a dramatic incentive to stay on or ahead of schedule. The schedule was fairly simple: The ark had to be built before the flood. The consequences of delivering the project behind schedule include:

- Noah would lose his job.
- Every pair of animals intended to sail on the ark would drown.
- Noah and his family would drown.
- Mankind would be decimated, and no one would be alive today.

While terms of many contracts in the 21st century contain significant negative incentives for completing behind schedule and/or over budget, the terms of Noah's contract gave him perhaps the greatest incentive of all time to be on schedule.

THE ENVIRONMENT OF PROJECT MANAGEMENT

A review of the case studies in the back of this book makes it clear that project management tools and techniques may be applied to a wide range of situations. The environment of project management includes the following:

- Virtually any business venture (e.g., setting up a lemonade stand or developing a missile defense system)
- Technological environment
- Socioeconomic environment
- Legal environment
- Business cycle environment
- Environmental impact of projects

Technological Environment

It is amazing to consider all the technological advancements that have taken place over the last 10 years. The popularity of the Internet has certainly led to remarkable benefits to the project management field. It was reported that the Overland Park (Kansas) Public Works Department developed a web-based manual to guide city engineers and technicians through the administration process for capital improvement projects.[6] By using the manual, the city streamlined and standardized its project management procedures.

Development of the web-based manual was accomplished as follows:

1. The department first compiled a paper version of its project management procedures, few of which had ever been written down.
2. The manual documented the process for completing capital improvement projects, from conception through construction and inspection.
3. The manual also outlined project tasks to help engineers set and meet schedules.
4. The city management staff and the Kansas Department of Transportation approved the content of the manual.

The manual became available and the department began actively using it in the fourth quarter of 1997.

Soon after obtaining approval, the Public Works Department's computer management group, working with Kansas City, Missouri–based HNTB, incorporated the manual into an electronic project management system — Project Expert System. The software allowed users to search the manual and a comprehensive library of project documents by keywords.

Included in the project management software was a "wizard" that helped users develop project schedules. The wizard asked users a series of questions that coordinated directly with the procedures in the manual. By answering the questions, users generated project schedules with prepopulated task lines that saved engineering time and ensured projects follow approved procedures.

The computer management group did not stop there. They also added some of their own enhancements to the software. For example, they expanded the program's capabilities to create a folder for each capital improvement project and subfolders corresponding to phases in the procedures manual.

Bob Lowry, director of the Public Works Department, was quoted to say, "The electronic manual has provided a great time-savings. By better managing a project from design through construction, we have more control over the schedule and cost. We have found that we can execute projects significantly faster than in the past, and time is money."

The project manager of the 21st century must be aware of every technological advancement and capability that could lead to similar savings on projects.

Socioeconomic Environment

Project managers need to recognize that interactions with the environment often have far-reaching effects. Such interactions include, but are not limited to, such things as: (1) construction projects that alter the physical landscape, (2) establishing a theater complex in an urban shopping area, or (3) developing civilian radioactive waste management sites.

To go a step further, any of the following socioeconomic models can influence the activities of the project manager:

- Anarchism
- Capitalism
- Colonialism
- Communism
- Consumer lifestyle
- Control techniques
- Decentralization
- Democracy
- Economics
- Fascism
- Imperialism
- Militarism
- Multiculturalism
- Nationalism
- Neoliberalism
- Philosophy
- Populism
- Sneetchism
- Socialism
- World government

Consideration of a project's impact on the socioeconomics of its affected region may yield tremendous benefits, and substantial project interruptions may be avoided.

Legal Environment

As with a project's socioeconomic environment, so too must allowances be made for the legal environment. The legal environment necessitates an understanding of the legal system.

- Social, ethical, and judicial foundations
- The nature of law and views on jurisprudence
- The relationship between law and ethics
- The framework of the U.S. legal system
- The creation and interpretation of law

The experienced project manager should be aware of potential trials and tribulations, such as:

- Resolving disputes in and out of court
- Types of courts and how they function
- Jurisdictional framework of the federal and state judicial systems
- How a civil case moves through the judicial system, from filing a complaint to collection of a judgment
- How "alternative dispute resolution" differs from "dispute resolution" in the judicial system

Other areas where an understanding of the legal environment could provide benefits include:

- Intentional torts
- Negligence and strict liability
- Business torts and employer liability
- Fraud
- Unfair competition
- Property and environmental torts
- Employer liability for the torts of employees and other agents
- Contract law, including legal and equitable remedies for breach of contract
- Uniform commercial code
- Consumer law
- Product liability
- Employment law, including workplace safety, job security, employment-at-will, individual employee rights, and employment discrimination

Lastly, the legal environment includes consideration for "doing the right thing: business ethics and social responsibility."

Current Drivers

The 21st century finds the science of project management continuing its evolution toward financial focus and profitability. The primary drivers effecting this evolution are (1) increased competitiveness, (2) speed of change, and (3) corporate resizing.

Increased Competitiveness

There is no doubt that the heat has been turned up as fierce competition unfolds among industry leaders. The following factors have led to increased competitiveness:

- More skills: More skills lead to increased competitiveness. Education, education, education, throughout the world! Policy makers are being persuaded that the route to economic advantage is through upskilling (i.e., improving employee skills). Increasingly, the rhetoric of global competition has been to push a policy agenda in which a highly skilled workforce becomes the linchpin of success.
- Lower labor costs: Many companies are outsourcing, or establishing manufacturing plants in areas with substantially lower labor costs. Lower labor costs allow the company to lower the price of its products and/or increase its profit margin.
- Increasing productivity: The first company to implement the latest technological advancements has an edge over its competition. State-of-the-art upgrades (e.g., MRP2 system implementation, just-in-time manufacturing) lead to lower manufacturing costs.

Speed of Change

The 21st century has brought about a new economy. Welcome to the new economy — a world where the rate of change is so rapid it is only a blur. There were no personal computers 25 years ago. Just 15 years ago, cell phones were a novelty, while the World Wide Web came into being less than 10 years ago. Today, many people cannot imagine doing business without cell phones, e-mail, or the global connectivity of the Internet.

Project managers have to stay on top of the latest developments to ensure their project has every possible advantage, enhancing the opportunity to come in on schedule and on budget.

Corporate Resizing

One of the big money savers talked about in corporate boardrooms 10 years ago was "downsizing," which led to the more politically correct term "rightsizing."

Rightsizing implied that, after performing a thorough analysis of the work to be done in a company, the head count would be adjusted either upward or downward to ensure the "right" or most efficient number of people were assigned to the tasks at hand. It appears that in every case in which rightsizing was employed, there was a reduction in head count (e.g., layoffs).

The next step in the evolution of the various "sizing" activities is "corporate resizing." This term has been catching on worldwide, and expands the topic to include other unfortunate business activities. These activities are covered quite well in the December 2002 text titled *Resizing the Organization: Managing Layoffs, Divestitures, and Closings.*[7]

So there is downsizing, rightsizing, resizing. What is next? Some say *cap*sizing, but time will tell.

MANAGING PROJECTS

George Pitagorsky[8] offers considerable insight into the advantages of utilizing a well-founded project management approach. He has found that many organizations recognize the need for a formal approach to project management to improve their performance. It is important to realize that project management is both a science and an art.

Effective project management necessitates flexibility within structure. It is the formal application of principles and techniques to the planning and control of project work. This reference to it as formal means putting plans, decisions, objectives, requirements definitions, change requests, etc. in writing — clearly defining roles and responsibility to promote accountability and following a pre-established, repeatable process. Formality connotes discipline most effectively, self-disciplined adherence to structures that add value.

There have, however, been instances where the "formality aspect" can be taken too far. For example, one company was implementing an MRP2 system.[9] It utilized program management software and found itself identifying hundreds of very small work packages that were updated almost on a daily basis. As a result, hundreds of pages were being printed every week, and were outdated by the time they were distributed to project team members. The lesson to be learned here is that it is important to understand the benefits derived from *all* program management activities. A cost analysis (sometimes termed "cost–benefit trade-off") should be performed when there is doubt about their value. Cost analyses are discussed in Chapter 12.

Pitagorsky offers some ancient wisdom about how to keep horses. If you put a horse in a tight pen, either it will kick its way out, or it will become too docile. If you keep the horse in an open, unfenced area, it will wander away. If you keep a horse in an area that gives it enough space to exercise and have a sense of freedom, it will be satisfied. When it reaches the fence it will turn and go in a different direction, because it is not worth the effort to jump the fence.

Project management disciplines work similarly. If the rules are too rigid, there will not be enough space for the adaptation that performers and managers need to succeed. If the rules are too loose, there is inefficiency. The goal is to strike the right balance — no excess, no insufficiency.

Formality without flexibility leads to bureaucracy. Bureaucracy is too costly and too slow for today's fast-moving, fast-changing world. Flexibility without formality is chaos. It is also too costly and inappropriate given the complexity and impact of projects.

Financially focused project management (FFPM) offers the tools to calculate and determine what is "too costly." Flexibility means that project managers must be able to tailor project management to the type of project being performed.

Balancing formality and flexibility allows for creativity, adaptation to undefined situations, and continuous improvement while having a clearly stated set of standards, procedures, and guidelines that promote best practices.

Essential Definitions

Project Management

Project management is distinct from project execution, which is specific to the project and results in the project's deliverables. Project management is performed to ensure that the project is optimally executed.

Project management ensures that:

- Goals, objectives, and acceptance criteria are defined.
- A plan is developed.
- The correct amount and type of resources are available.
- A formal plan is followed when work is performed.
- All activities are coordinated and designed to achieve a specific goal.
- Intermediate results are toward the original end result.
- Interested parties are informed of project performance.
- The original goal is the main target, which may be updated as required.
- The plan is adjusted to take into account unplanned circumstances.
- The final result is acceptable, and meets project expectations and specifications.

Project Success

Generally speaking, a successful project meets its objectives within time and budget constraints, while fulfilling the needs of stakeholders, including project sponsors, product users, product managers, product support people, project performers, and participants. Project sponsors and users should be satisfied that project results add value.

Product

A product is the result of a project. It might be a new or upgraded software product, a business process, or service. Product success depends on the usefulness and marketability of the product, typically related to reducing operating costs, improving customer service, making a profit, etc.

Project objectives should be measurable, linked to strategic initiatives, prioritized with respect to one another and the objectives of other projects, clearly understood by project stakeholders, and expressed as a few major objectives that may be subdivided into more detailed objectives.

The Key to Success

There is a tale about a wise, old, gentleman named Edgademer. One evening, he was on his hands and knees under the street lamp in front a friend's home in Las Vegas.

A jogger stopped by and asked him what he was doing. Edgademer gazed softly into the jogger's eyes. He explained, "I'm looking for my car keys. I dropped them as I was unlocking the door to my car."

The jogger, being a very helpful soul, dropped to his knees and assisted Edgademer in the search. Before long they had covered every inch of ground under the street lamp. After a while, the jogger asked, "Are you sure you dropped the keys here?" and was surprised when Edgademer whispered, "Oh, no, I dropped the keys over there on the front lawn. But it's very dark there, so I thought we could look here where the light is much better."

This story is intended to point out that if the light is not aimed in the right direction, it will be virtually impossible to achieve your goal. Even a comprehensive set of project management procedures will not solve problems that are rooted in inadequate judgment, interdepartmental warfare, lack of effective communications, illogical problem solving/decision making, fear- and blame-based politics, or any other common causes of project performance ills. Group dynamics, communication skills, and problem-solving processes should be examined. This is where many of the keys to successful project management are found.

Project Management Process

A project may be divided into the following processes (see Figure 2.1):

1. Potential opportunities
2. Selection
3. Initiation
4. Planning and organizing
5. Proposal (if applicable)
6. Budgeting
7. Execution
8. Reporting and controlling
9. Termination/closing
10. On-going process and cross-project improvement

Connecting these processes, and providing the foundation on which they all work, is communication: candid, concise, complete, clear, clever, copious, controlled, and mutually understood. Communication is the critical factor that gives project stakeholders the ability to negotiate, plan, solve problems, keep one another informed, and reach consensus.

The processes use techniques and principles associated with scope management, time management, cost management, communications management, design management, human resource management, quality management, risk management, and procurement (contracts) management.

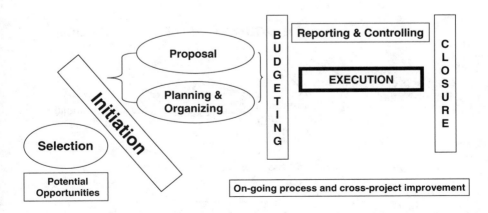

FIGURE 2.1. Project Management Processes.

The Relationships of FFPM Processes

The processes involved in project management are inter-related as shown in Figure 2.2.

From the onset, the project concept must be evaluated with a financially focused mindset. Fundamental financial analysis necessitates that projections and assumptions be made utilizing a conservative posture. These projects should show the likelihood of a profitable return prior to investing significant funds in the planning and organizing process.

As planning and organizing is performed, the related processes are:

- Controlling: The project manager and project office establish a performance measurement system and begin tracking activity to planned schedules and costs to budgets.
- On-going process and cross-project improvements: The project manager begins maintaining records that reflect the success and efficiencies as the project progresses. When appropriate, various analyses and benchmarking studies are conducted to ensure that operations are flowing as smoothly and efficiently as possible.
- Financial focus: As is the relationship with all project management processes, the financial focus ensures that all activities contribute to the bottom line. Cost analyses drive determination of the most cost-effective actions.

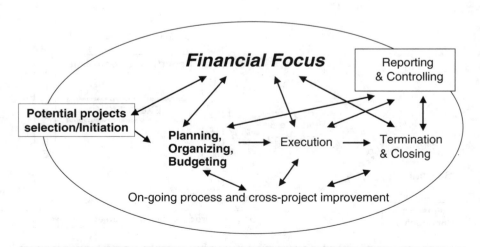

FIGURE 2.2. Financial Focus and Project Management Processes.

The execution process and the termination and closing process are similarly tied to controlling, on-going process and cross-project improvement, and the financial focus.

Potential Opportunities, Selection, and Initiation

The first step in managing a project is its origination. An idea becomes a concept, which eventually takes shape with a firm purpose and potential benefits. In a successful firm, many ideas emerge. Sources for such ideas include: ideas from customers (e.g., focus groups, marketing surveys), recommendations from employees, and successes in the research and development organization.

A formal analysis needs to be determined to decide which projects to select. One technique is portfolio project management. For more information, see Overview of the Portfolio of Projects below and Chapter 5.

Project initiation defines the business objectives and the product in terms of its features, functions, and performance criteria. Project initiation defines the scope of the project, identifies key participants, and determines if the desired outcome warrants the time, effort, risk, and resources necessary to produce the product.

Initiation may be a relatively short process or one that is extended over time and performed repeatedly, as the product and its costs and expected benefits are further defined in detail. Work is incrementally authorized, in work packages or at checkpoints, to obtain greater assurance that assumptions, and the estimates based on them, are correct before committing resources.

Planning and Organizing

Proper planning helps ensure that results are in keeping with expectations, and that work efforts are efficiently and effectively performed. Planning makes it possible to model the way the project will be performed, who will perform it, when interim and final results will be ready, and how much risk and uncertainty there is. Planning also gives insight into how to deal with uncertainty, how much the plan is subject to variance, how many and what kinds of resources will be needed, when, and how much the project will cost.

The project plan consists of:

- Objectives
- A clear description of the product and its acceptance criteria
- A detailed task list with descriptions of each task, including a description of the concrete outcome of the task, dependencies among the tasks, resource requirements and effort, and duration estimates
- A schedule (with contingencies addressed)

- A well thought out budget plan (with contingencies and management reserve in place)
- Assignment of roles and responsibilities
- Standards and procedures for project planning, control, and performance

Planning is performed throughout the life of a project. Iterative plan refinement uses the information that results from an increasingly detailed description of the product and from project control. As assumptions are proven by actual experience, confidence in the plan's accuracy increases. As assumptions are proven to be erroneous, the need for replanning is identified.

The only thing that is certain is the uncertainty of project plans. The longer and more complex the project and the more uncertain project sponsors are of the nature of the product, the greater the potential variance, or difference between the actual outcome and the original planned outcome of the project.

Project planning includes an assessment of risk and uncertainty. Planners identify contingency plans and reserves to protect the sponsors and users of the project outcome from false expectations and unacceptable losses. Risk assessment is a significant factor in the decision to perform a project.

Budgeting

Overlapping with planning and reporting, and the primary tool used for controlling, is budgeting. Budgeting is a most critical element for the success of a project. During the budgeting process, managers agree that their staffs will accomplish their milestones in accordance with predetermined, time-phased budgets.

Reporting and Controlling

Project control monitors the performance against the plan, so as to evaluate progress and provide data for plan refinement and on-going improvement. Project control consists of progress control, information control, quality assurance, change control, and issue control.

Progress control collects data and reports on compliance to the schedule and budget. These data include task completions, effort and cost expenditures by task, and the occurrence of and cause of any variances between actual performance and the plan.

Periodic reports clearly and candidly give the status of the project with respect to the plan. These are used by management to decide if any redirection is needed. Progress control and reporting can be as simple as reports that show expected vs. actual completions of tasks, or may use earned value analysis and other sophisticated techniques to show integrated data regarding budget and schedule performance. Earned value is discussed in Chapter 9.

Information control deals with the flow of communication and maintains the documentation that describes the product and the project process. Requirement definitions, designs, marketing materials, training materials, etc. make up the product documentation. The plan, status reports, issues and resolutions, and changes and their disposition make up project process documentation. Communication includes reporting, problem and issues resolution, and the exchange of information among project stakeholders to execute the project.

Quality assurance establishes the methods for project performance and assesses the acceptability of both interim results and the final product. Interim results are assessed to catch errors and omissions as early as possible so as to reduce their impact on the project.

Change control manages the changes that are inevitably made to the definition of the business objectives, product definition, and plan. The goal is to minimize disruptions to project performance by postponing as many changes as possible. Uncontrolled change in product specifications is a primary cause of project overruns.

Change control also issues control records, documents problems as they arise, and ensures the problems are addressed.

Termination/Closure

Closing the project includes validating and accepting that project objectives have been achieved, or otherwise deciding to terminate. Resources, human and other, must be redeployed. Budget lines must be formally closed, and the documentation that represents the project history and product description must be archived.

Finally, a postimplementation review should be held to assess the success of the project and highlight lessons learned to improve the performance of future projects.

On-Going Improvement — Learning from Experience

Organizations learn in much the same way people do, and project management includes a learning process. Each project performed is an experience for learning how to perform the next project more effectively. This is achieved by evaluating performance periodically throughout the project, and on the project's completion, by publishing the results to inform others of pitfalls and best practices. Over time, best practices are carried forward, poor practices are discarded, and estimates are made increasingly accurate because they are based on past experience.

Accountability

The culture that supports an effective project management process must value and promote clear accountability. Project management principles require that commitments be made and documented, and that status with respect to those commitments be reported with ruthless candor and regularity — nothing is hidden.

Blaming should be replaced with acceptance coupled with a disciplined analysis of cause to promote continuous improvement. Teamwork should be cultivated by rewarding people for overall project success, as well as for success in their own activities. Team values should be continuously reinforced and employees reminded of the big picture and the need for collaborative efforts. Role definitions should be expanded to include partnering with others and not just working as individuals.

Being Firm: Limiting the Workload — Denying Some Requests

An effective project manager must be able to say "no" or at least "not now" when warranted. It is not uncommon for people to become overwhelmed by an unlimited flow of work. Saying "no" to clients and senior managers who make what they see as reasonable and necessary demands and requests is not easy. Yet, to really satisfy clients and management and to successfully grow and survive as a project-performing organization, there must be a reasonable flow of work, not a flood. The flood mode leads to constant priority shifts and overwork. These lead to an inability to fulfill commitments to deliver quality products within time and cost constraints. Late and poor quality products cost money and loss of customer confidence. Constant overwork costs the organization in burnout and high turnover of the most valuable people.

There are thousands of ways to creatively say "no." Among the more effective are: "Your deadline is understandable. Let's see how we can work together to free up the resources to get it done." "It would be terrific to be able to deliver the product for that price in that schedule. Let's see what features we can eliminate to make it possible." These tend to lead to more successful outcomes than using dismissive comments such as "Are you joking!?" or "There's no way."

Project Office

The project office is an administrative function that collects project plans and performance data, provides information to management for use in coordinating resources across projects, and provides project history for use in on-going improvement of project planning and performance. A master schedule is maintained to identify all committed projects and the allocation of resources.

Project Management Benefits

Project management adds value by eliminating unreasonable deadlines and budgets, making estimating more accurate and easier. It promotes best practices across projects while eliminating the repetition of known errors and omissions, giving stakeholders clear, concise, and accurate information about project status and the prognosis for completion. And, it ensures that the "right" projects are done in the "right" way.

To quantify the value of project management, identify the costs of project overruns, poor quality products, chronic overtime, and the other symptoms of poorly managed projects.

Implementing project management disciplines in an organization requires a concerted effort over a protracted period of time. The difficulty of the effort depends on the degree to which the organization is currently using a nonbureaucratic, disciplined approach in performing its business and on the resolve of management and staff to improve the way they work.

In discipline-averse and bureaucratic organizations alike, the effort to implement project management is more difficult. When all effort is being devoted to firefighting and handling a never-ending flow of current work, and no effort is being devoted to on-going improvement, implementing project management is impossible.

Improving project management is a process improvement project. Like any project, it requires effective initiation, planning, control, and closure. Its critical factors are clearly understood objectives, sufficient resources, sustained commitment from senior management, patience, and effective communications.

FUNCTION OVERVIEW — PROPOSALS

Budgeting

The budgeting process generally begins after a contract has been awarded. However, from time to time, a go-ahead may be given prior to finalization of the contract terms. Uncertainty regarding forward pricing rates, escalation factors, specific contract requirements, or a myriad of other situations could result in the lack of a signed agreement.

A detailed discussion of budgeting is presented in Chapter 7.

Reporting

The organizations that have signed the agreement and accept the funding are required to monitor their performance on a periodic basis and provide status reports to the project manager.

These reports contain the following information:

1. Variances between budgeted costs and actual costs for the report period
2. Schedule variances
3. Reasons for variances
4. Management action taken to correct the variances (if necessary)
5. Variances forecasted at completion of effort

By alerting program management to potential problems, steps may be taken to correct the situation (e.g., management reserve may be designated to cover overbudget situations).

PROJECT LIFE CYCLE PARAMETERS

There are five phases to the project life cycle (Figure 2.3), as follows:

1. Definition phase
2. Planning phase
3. Execution phase
4. Delivery phase
5. Termination phase

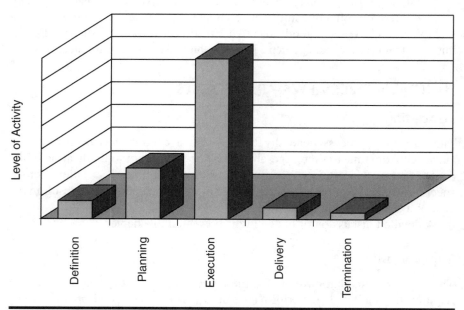

FIGURE 2.3. Project Life Cycle.

Definition Phase — Identification of a Need or Opportunity

The definition phase (approximately 5 to 10% of the total effort) includes the "initiation" component. The major steps in the definition phase are:

- Identifying a **NEED** or opportunity: Sometimes this can be as simple as becoming aware of an RFP (Request for Proposal) from a buyer with which the company has previously worked. Needs can also be identified by any employee in the company who observes or thinks up the opportunity for improvement or a new product.
- Developing the **GOALS** for the proposed solution to the opportunity, and ensuring the goals correlate with the goals of the organization.
- Laying out the **TASKS** necessary to complete the project.
- Assigning **RESPONSIBILITIES** to the managers and organizations carrying out the tasks.
- Creating the **TEAMS** performing in the organizations and cross-functional groups.
- Designing to **SPECIFICATIONS** of the project: This is more than just the who, what, where, and why, but also precise requirements and measurements that the completed project can be measured against. Such detail is termed the **SCOPE** of the project, which includes:
  1. Objectives
  2. Deliverables
  3. Milestones
  4. Technical requirements
  5. Exclusions

Planning Phase — Detailed Development of the Proposed Solution

The planning phase (5 to 15% total effort) is critically important to the financials of the project. This is the stage that addresses:

- Schedules
- Budgets
- Resources
- Risks
- Staffing

The planning phase is very critical. Chapter 7 of this text is devoted to project planning.

Execution Phase — Delivering the Project — Implementing the Solution

Generally speaking, the execution phase accounts for roughly 70% of the total effort on a project. This phase includes the following:

- Status reports
- Changes
- Quality (see Chapter 13)
- Forecasts

Delivery Phase

Depending on the project, the delivery phase may account for 1 to 15% of the total effort. The activities in this phase include:

- The physical delivery of the product to the customer's site
- Final inspection and test at the customer's site
- Training the customer
- Honoring the warranty period (e.g., service calls, replacements)

Termination Phase

This final phase usually begins during the delivery phase, and may account for 2 to 10% of the total effort.

In the routine termination phase, the company performs the following:

- Releases unused/unnecessary residual materials
- Reassigns staff
- Performs contract closure activity
- Develops lessons learned documents

If a project is terminated prior to completion (e.g., the customer cancels the project), additional (and sometimes costly) activity may be required, including:

- Prematurely closing down production
- Unloading/finding an economical use for excess materials
- Canceling subcontracts

Chapter 10 provides greater detail on the termination phase and project closure.

OVERVIEW OF THE PORTFOLIO OF PROJECTS (SEE CHAPTER 5 FOR MORE DETAIL)

A cutting-edge concept in project management is the formation of project-based organizations. They replace the vertical, hierarchical structure with one in which a project management office (PMO) coordinates resource providers (the accounting department, the marketing department, etc.). These resource providers furnish the critical resources for projects, in alignment with corporate policy and strategy.

Trane Corporation, for example, a provider of industrial and commercial air-conditioning systems headquartered in Lacrosse, Wisconsin, has highly skilled technical employees whose unique skills are a scarce resource. The company's PMO manages all projects and the various components of each work breakdown structure (WBS) in order to maximize those skilled resources at the critical time and place within each project. Laying out a company's entire portfolio of projects facilitates visibility across different projects and their tasks. Without this strategy, resource conflict can escalate to upper levels of management where they waste executives' effort and time. Like a well-balanced financial portfolio, a portfolio approach to project management allows the most effective use of constrained resources.

Contradictions between the needs of individual projects and the project portfolio can wreak havoc with a project unless senior management is committed to shaping an overall vision and setting and communicating priorities. "The triple constraints of projects are time, cost, and performance," explains Vail.[10] "Extending a project's schedule may raise costs. Cutting the schedule may affect performance or quality. One of the three constraints is usually the primary driver of the project. Some projects are cost-driven, others are time- or performance-driven."

The principles of portfolio project management are applicable to any enterprise. The key to getting started is to identify the current projects, break them down with a WBS, and manage them as a portfolio for the total return of the company, not just individual returns within projects.

Directing the Orchestra

Project management techniques and the WBS bring a consistent recognition of priorities across the organization, helping everyone focus on a strategic result and move forward while reducing the feeling of chaos and time pressure. To be successful, project management must be part of a company's culture, part and parcel of the work effort.

The convergence of tasks made possible by a WBS is vital, for example, in new product development from R&D to customer utilization. Aligning the many segments — development, marketing, sales training, advance purchase of advertising space, etc. — ensures a smooth product launch. Ads are in place, major networks are featuring the product, the sales force is prepared to answer questions, and the product is ready to go. As part of a comprehensive project management effort, a WBS orchestrates the entire launch strategically so everything comes to fruition at the same point and place to maximize the strategic returns for the organization.

Because projects are finite by definition, project teams are constantly coming together and disbanding. They must be able to get up to speed quickly, perform, and then move on to another project. Successful project teams are made up of people who are adequately trained, encouraged, and nurtured so they can steer clear of the fog of confusion. "A WBS is best done in a project team environment," recommends Dobson.[10] "It engenders a greater sense of ownership and thus brings added benefits. This means every team member should be familiar with the process, though not necessarily all at the highest level of sophistication. Project management is too valuable and too important for its knowledge to be limited to the project managers."

When Trane Corporation introduced integrated project management skills using WBS, it significantly improved its customer service. Performance increased by about 6% or $19 million over a period of 18 months. Providing solutions to clients utilizing project management enables Trane personnel to make realistic delivery estimates. A solid project plan presented to clients outlines and schedules the project's components and milestones leading to eventual installation.

"We streamlined our processes through project management and by providing project management training not just for our engineers, but across the organization for our sales, support and fulfillment staff," says Trane's corporate service fulfillment leader, Lou Zaccone. "It created tremendous value to our clients and brought a significant increase in gross margin."

Clarity and Control

When projects are decomposed using project management and the WBS, they are much less confusing. Individual segments can be managed, tracked, and measured, and a critical path developed, all contributing to the ultimate successful completion of the project on time and on budget. A project management program improves communication, enables more accurate accounting, keeps work on schedule, identifies responsibilities with greater clarity, and allows better control. Project management training utilizing a WBS can re-energize an enterprise's projects, make the multitude of tasks a little easier, and manage the confusion of change and complexity.

THE PROJECT AND ITS RELATIONSHIP TO THE MISSION AND VISION STATEMENTS

Unless a company is considering a broad shift in its composition, any project undertaken should conform to the company's goals.

Vision Statements and Mission Statements

Potential new projects should always be reviewed in light of the enterprise's core business. Sometimes what appears to be a great opportunity could result in a shift in business strategy that could be detrimental to operations elsewhere in the company.

Most companies have developed vision and/or mission statements, the purpose of which is to keep all employees focused on core values.

Vision Statements[2]

Many companies have been adopting "vision statements" to help focus all employees in the same direction. A vision statement presents a view of what the company should be like 10 or 20 years into the future. It could be as simple as that established by the Des Moines City Government:

A friendly and safe waterfront community.

A vision statement can also be more detailed, as is the following vision statement for the California State University, Monterey Bay:

California State University, Monterey Bay (CSUMB) is envisioned as a comprehensive state university, which values service through high-quality education. The campus will be distinctive in serving the diverse people of California, especially the working class and historically under-educated and low-income populations. It will feature an enriched living and learning environment and year-round operation. The identity of the University will be framed by substantive commitment to a multilingual, multicultural, intellectual community distinguished by partnerships with existing institutions, both public and private, and by cooperative agreements which enable students, faculty, and staff to cross institutional boundaries for innovative instruction, broadly defined scholarly and creative activity, and coordinated community service.

The University will invest in preparation for the future through integrated and experimental use of technologies as resources to people, catalysts for learning, and providers of increased access and enriched quality learning. The curricula of CSUMB will be student- and society-centered and of sufficient breadth and depth to meet statewide and regional needs, specifically those involving both inner-city and isolated rural populations (Monterey, Santa Cruz, and San Benito). The programs of instruction will strive for distinction, building on regional assets in developing specialty clusters in such areas as the sciences (marine, atmospheric, and environmental); visual and performing arts and related humanities; language, culture, and international studies; education; business; studies of human behavior, information, and communication, within broad curricular areas; and professional study.

The University will develop a culture of innovation in its overall conceptual design and organization, and will utilize new and varied pedagogical and instructional approaches including distance learning. Institutional programs will value and cultivate creative and productive talents of students, faculty, and staff, and seek ways to contribute to the economy of the state, the well-being of our communities, and the quality of life and development of its students, faculty, and service areas.

The education programs at CSUMB will:

- *Integrate the sciences and the arts and humanities, liberal studies and professional training;*
- *Integrate modern learning technology and pedagogy to create liberal education adequate for the contemporary world;*
- *Integrate work and learning, service and reflection;*
- *Recognize the importance of global interdependence;*
- *Invest in languages and cross-cultural competence; and*
- *Emphasize those topics most central to the local area's economy and accessible residential learning environment.*

The University will provide a new model of organizing, managing, and financing higher education:

The University will be integrated with other institutions, essentially collaborative in its orientation, and active in seeking partnerships across institutional boundaries. It will develop and implement various arrangements for sharing courses, curriculum, faculty, students, and facilities with other institutions. The organizational structure of the

University will reflect a belief in the importance of each administrative staff and faculty member, working to integrate the university community across "staff" and "faculty" lines.

The financial aid system will emphasize a fundamental commitment to equity and access. The budget and financial systems, including student fees, will provide for efficient and effective operation of the University.

University governance will be exercised with a substantial amount of autonomy and independence within a very broad CSU system-wide policy context.

Accountability will emphasize careful evaluation and assessment of results and student learning goals.

Our vision of the goals of California State University, Monterey Bay includes a model, pluralistic, academic community where all learn and teach one another in an atmosphere of mutual respect and pursuit of excellence; a faculty and staff motivated to excel in their respective fields as well as to contribute to the broadly defined university environment. Our graduates will have an understanding of interdependence and global competence, distinctive technical and educational skills, the experience and abilities to contribute to California's high-quality workforce, the critical thinking abilities to be productive citizens, and the social responsibility and skills to be community builders. CSUMB will dynamically link the past, present, and future by responding to historical and changing conditions, experimenting with strategies which increase access, improving quality, and lowering costs through education in a distinctive CSU environment.

University students and personnel will attempt analytically and creatively to meet critical state and regional needs and to provide California with responsible and creative leadership for the global 21st century.

The California State University vision statement above can actually be broken down into several vision statements, with different statements applying to different departments and organizations within the university.

Mission Statements[2]

Mission statements are very similar to vision statements, and much overlap exists. While the vision statement presents a forward-looking view of what the company wants to become, the mission statement will contain similar wording, though frequently not as detailed as the California State University vision statement above. For example and for contrast, the mission statement of the Des Moines City Government is:

> *To enrich residential living by providing leadership, administration, and community services that reflects the pride and values of Des Moines.*

The mission statement for hamburger giant McDonald's is:

> *To satisfy the world's appetite for good food, well served, at a price people can afford.*

PROJECT MANAGEMENT AND THE IDEAL PROJECT

As can be seen from this overview, there is much to the science of project management. Projects must be selected, defined, planned, executed, delivered, and terminated. It is easy to lose sight of the main reason projects are undertaken: to contribute to the long-term financial success of the enterprise. The forthcoming chapters present the detail regarding state-of-the-art project management approaches, techniques, systems, and tools. They also offer students of the project management science the opportunity to ensure that project management activities yield the desired financial success.

SELF-STUDY/DISCUSSION QUESTIONS

1. In relation to a project with which you have been involved, describe the project initiation process. How could the project have gotten a better start?
2. How does the government contracting process compare with the process conducted by a homeowner? What is similar? What is different? What are the advantages of each?
3. Explain the project life cycle parameters. Discuss each phase.
4. What is the vision and/or mission statement of your company? If it were up to you, what improvements would you make in the wording?

Free value-added materials available from the Download Resource Center at <u>www.jrosspub.com</u>.

HUMAN ASPECTS OF PROJECT MANAGEMENT

INTRODUCTION

One of the biggest challenges project managers face is balancing, organizing, winning, overcoming, placating, supporting, guiding, leading, and as appropriate, modifying the human aspects involved with the project. The key areas to be addressed include:

- Project sponsorship and leadership
- The organization structure and culture
- The project team
- Communication

THE NETWORK OF RELATIONSHIPS

Figure 3.1 presents the hierarchy needed for smooth operations and to enhance the opportunity for profitability.

Top Management/Stockholders/Stakeholders

Generally speaking, those at the top level of management in a company have a high level of intelligence, education, experience, and interpersonal ability that qualifies

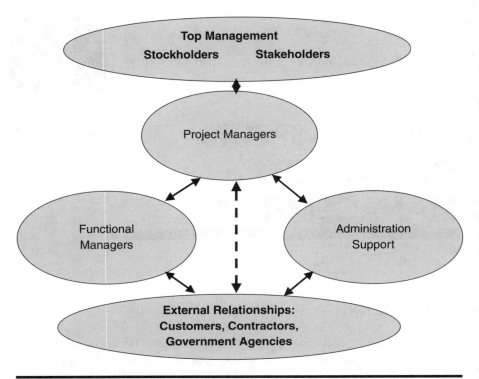

FIGURE 3.1. The Network of Relationships.

them for their positions. They are usually proven leaders and command the respect of their subordinates. And thank goodness that respect exists, because the loyalty of a company's workers is an integral trait of successful projects.

Senior corporate officials must thoroughly support the project before it gets off the ground. Often, before significant funds are allocated to initiate a new undertaking, a detailed presentation must be made to and a formal approval received from the company's board of directors, who are elected by the shareholders. Top management with the support of stockholders/stakeholders needs to continue in the oversight capacity, holding the project manager accountable to schedule and cost requirements. Periodic status meetings are held, where the project manager presents details regarding progress. At these meetings, and also on an occasional informal basis, executives interrogate the project manager to ensure the full story is being presented and there are no hidden problems that could possibly appear.

Project Managers

Project managers are the only component of the network of relationships that touches all other components. This is because the project manager is the heart of the organism, and must have direct contact to function efficiently. (See below for a more in-depth discussion about the skills necessary for a project manager.)

Functional Managers

The organizations that actually perform the hands-on project work are termed *functional organizations*, and they are governed by *functional managers*.

Administrative Support

All groups that indirectly support a project are termed *administrative support*, and include such departments as human resources, legal, and marketing.

External Relationships

Customers, contractors, government agencies, and professional societies are some of the external relationships with which a project manager may interact.

The customer may look to the project manager to provide periodic status reports. Contractors must stay in contact with project management, particularly when problems impacting cost and schedule occur. Government agencies perform periodic audits and need to be apprised of potential impacts to society. Professional societies (e.g., the American Society for Quality, Computer Associates Visual Information Association) may have a professional standards point of view.

Project Sponsors

Another component of the network of relationships is the project sponsor. This is the person or group that helps obtain the resources. Financial resources are granted by management with budgetary control. Necessary human resources are at the command of organization heads. Project sponsors are usually situated at or near the top of the network.

CORE TRAITS/SKILLS REQUIRED FOR A SUCCESSFUL PROJECT MANAGER

In his article "Realistic Criteria for Project Manager Selection and Development," Jurgan Hauschildt[11] examined five types of project managers. He determined the level of success of each and its frequency of occurrence in the project manager

Leadership vs. Management

Personal Integrity

Full Cycle Mindset

Systems Thinker

Good Communication Skills

Proactive

Skilled Politician

Optimist

High Tolerance for Stress

General Business Perspective

FIGURE 3.2. Core Traits/Skills Required of Successful Project Managers.

sample. When refined through further research, this typology holds the promise of more effective project manager selection and development tools and the possibility of maintaining a population of project managers in an organization that is optimum for the needs of that organization. Some of these findings are summarized below.

One approach to finding a good project manager begins with generating a list of characteristics that the ideal project manager should have (Figure 3.2). Then, select people who have these characteristics and/or design training programs that develop them.

Some of the more important traits a project manager needs include the following:

- Flexibility and adaptability
- Significant initiative
- Leadership skills
- Aggressiveness
- Confidence
- Persuasiveness

- Verbal fluency
- Ambition
- Activity
- Forcefulness
- Effectiveness as a communicator
- Effectiveness as an integrator
- Broad scope of personal interests
- Poise
- Enthusiasm
- Imagination
- Spontaneity
- Ability to balance technical solutions with time, cost, and human factors
- Well organized
- Disciplined
- A generalist rather than a specialist
- Ability and willingness to devote most of his/her available time to planning and controlling
- Ability to identify problems
- Willing to make decisions
- Ability to maintain a proper balance in the use of time

One study[12] reviewed 44 empirical investigations of the determinants of project success and found that project managers do make a difference. In this study, 257 successful and 191 unsuccessful projects were examined. Results showed that the success of a project is much more dependent on human factors (project leadership, top management support, project team) than on the technocratic instruments of project management such as planning, processing information, and communication. Furthermore, it was found that the importance of the human factor increases when projects have greater complexity, risk, and innovation.

Various combinations of the characteristics listed and discussed above were analyzed. Results generated the following list of preferred abilities of a project manager:

- **Organizing under conflict:** The abilities to delegate and manage time are linked with conflict tolerance and ability to handle criticism. This emphasizes the ability to organize, but in situations in which there is some conflict and/or criticism.
- **Experience:** This directly includes experience or years of employment and knowledge of procedures. The knowledge comes, presumably, from years of experience.

- **Decision making:** Skills relating to judgment, thinking, and decision making are linked to systematic, analytical thinking. The thrust is decision-making and related cognitive processes.
- **Productive creativity:** Creativity is similar to the generation of specific, beneficial idea generation, which in turn includes the ability to carry out those ideas.
- **Organizing with cooperation:** The ability to plan and organize is included with items having to do with the ability to include others in a positive way through learning, sensitivity, and team orientation. These organizational abilities are carried out in a much more positive interpersonal context than are those listed under "organizing under conflict."
- **Cooperative leadership:** The ability to motivate others is associated with the ability to cooperate and communicate with others.
- **Integrated thinking:** The ability to think analytically is associated with the ability to attend to the ideas of others, which should involve analysis using disparate ideas that must be integrated.

The traits discussed below merit particularly close attention.

Expertise and Education

In addition to the personality traits and skills listed above, project managers need a certain level of expertise and education. Some believe the ideal project manager should have at least 8 years of graduate-level education, earning doctorates in engineering, business, and psychology, and at least 10 to 15 years experience with 10 different companies in a variety of project office positions, and would be about 25 years old. Of course, it is not always possible to find an "ideal" project manager. In fact, most often it is necessary to look for people with only some of these qualifications. So which are the most important?

Systems Thinker[13]

Technology is science, not religion. The people who make technology are engineers, not priests. Technology is ultimately knowable. How does simulation work? What are optimization models or linear programs? How are results generated — the strengths and weaknesses of the various approaches?

Only a guru who really knows how simulation technology works can explain exactly when it does not. Only an expert in optimization theory or linear programming can truly grasp the limitations of those problem-solving approaches.

It is not practical for the project manager to understand all the detail of a project's technology. However, he or she must possess the skills of a "systems thinker" and be able to communicate with the "gurus" and "experts" that are employed.

Personal Integrity[14]

Victor Parachin* writes that one of the most popular and amazing small aircraft is the Lear Jet. It was created by Bill Lear, an inventor, aviator, and business leader. Lear was quite an engineer, holding more than 150 patents, including those for the automatic pilot, car radio, and the eight-track tape (the what??). In the 1950s he sensed the need and potential for a small corporate jet. It took him several years to turn his dream into reality, but in 1963 the first Lear Jet made its maiden voyage and in 1964 he delivered his first jet to a client. Bill Lear's success was immediate and he quickly sold many aircraft.

However, not long after he got his business rolling, Lear learned that two of his jets crashed under mysterious circumstances. He was devastated. At the time, 55 Lear Jets were privately owned, and Lear immediately sent word to all the owners to ground their planes until he could determine what caused the jets to crash. He was very concerned and worried that more lives might be lost. This thought was far more important to him than any adverse publicity that would result from his action. He tirelessly researched the ill-fated flights and eventually identified the likely cause but could not verify the technical problem on the ground. There was only one way to know whether he had diagnosed the problem correctly and that was to recreate it personally — in the air.

This was, of course, a very dangerous proposal, but that is what Bill Lear did. As he flew the jet, he nearly lost control and almost met the same fate as the other two pilots, but he managed to make it through the tests and was able to verify the defect. Lear developed a new part to correct the problem and fitted all 55 planes with it, eliminating the danger.

Think about the *integrity* it took for Bill Lear to follow that course of action. Grounding the planes cost him a lot of money. Further, it planted seeds of doubt in the minds of future customers. As a result, he needed 2 years to rebuild his business. Yet, he never regretted his decision. He was willing to risk his success, his fortune, and even his life to solve the mystery of those crashes. He was not willing to risk his *integrity*. By responding as he did, Lear simultaneously maintained and rebuilt his credibility. He is an outstanding example of the wisdom contained in this Latin proverb: "A good name keeps its brightness even in dark days." *Integrity* is the most important trait to cultivate for both *personal* and *professional* success. Here are some ways to develop the vital virtue of *integrity*.

---

* In addition to being an ordained minister, Victor M. Parachin is a free-lance journalist and author of several books.

Write a Personal Integrity Statement

Many corporations utilize mission statements (see Chapter 2) to outline their goals and commitments. Anyone can do the same by taking time to think about and write out his or her own brief, tightly written *integrity* statement. Abraham Lincoln, America's most popular president, guided his life and presidency by this *personal* credo: "I am not bound to win, but I am bound to be true. I am not bound to succeed, but I am bound to live by the light that I have. I must stand with anybody that stands right, stand with him while he is right and part with him when he goes wrong." A simple *integrity* statement could be like this one: "I seek, in all of my dealings — both *personal* and professional — to be a person of *integrity*, credibility and character. If I must choose between profit and *integrity* or between compromise and *integrity*, I shall always choose *integrity*." After writing the *integrity* statement, copies can be printed, placed in one's wallet, in one's workstation, and in one's home so that it can be routinely reviewed.

Remain 100% Committed

Individuals should always stand by their convictions. It is not possible to be 70 or 80% committed to *integrity* and credibility. The commitment must be a full 100%. Consider the sterling example of Leonard Roberts. He became CEO of Arby's, the fast-food restaurant chain, when it was losing money. He made Arby's profitable but then resigned from the board of directors when Arby's owner threatened to withhold bonuses for Roberts' staff and not to give promised help to Arby's franchisees in order to further increase profits. In retaliation for his ethical stand, Roberts was fired as CEO.

Roberts landed on his feet when he was hired as CEO of another restaurant chain, Shoney's. However, to his dismay he discovered the company was the subject of the largest racial discrimination suit in history. Believing the company was in the wrong, Roberts promptly promised the suit would be settled fairly. The owner of Shoney's agreed to pay and settle, but only if Roberts would resign afterward.

"My stand on *integrity* was getting a little hard on my wife and kids," Roberts said. "However, I knew it had to be done. There was no other way. You cannot fake it. You must stand up for what is right regardless. You cannot maintain your *integrity* 90 percent and be a leader. It's got to be one hundred percent."

Ultimately Roberts became CEO of RadioShack and a year after that CEO of Tandy, which owns RadioShack. In 1987, President Ronald Reagan presented Roberts with the Presidential Private Sector Initiative Award. In 1991, Roberts was honored with the annual Business Leadership Award presented by *Restaurant Business Magazine*. He also received the B'nai B'rith International

Distinguished Achievement Award and the 1991 Multi-Unit Foodservice Chain Operator's Award. In 1992, Roberts received the Wall Street Bronze Critics Award. Roberts was named Brandweek's Retailing Marketer of the Year in 1996. In February 1997, Roberts was named Sales & Marketing Executive of the Year by the Sales & Marketing Executives of Fort Worth, Texas. In May 1999, Roberts was honored as Father of the Year by the Dallas/Fort Worth Father of the Year Committee. He was recognized by *Texas Business Magazine* as one of the top 25 most influential Texans in Technology in March 2000.

Choose the Harder Right Over the Easier Wrong

Babe Zacharias was one of the most gifted female athletes of the 20th century. A champion amateur golfer in the 1932 Olympics, she later became a professional golfer. On one occasion she penalized herself two strokes when she accidentally played the wrong ball. "Why did you do it?" a friend asked. "No one saw you, no one would have known the difference." Zacharias's reply was simple and succinct: "I would have known." With that response she revealed herself also to be a champion of *integrity*.

Adhere to the Spirit of Your Principles

It is not enough to merely stick to the letter of the law when it comes to agreements made. An individual should place on oneself a higher standard, that of adhering to the spirit of one's principles. John Wareham, founder and chief executive of Wareham Associates, tells of a dilemma he faced recently. One of his long-time employees who directed a field office took out a 10-year lease. Without consulting Wareham, he gave his *personal* guarantee to secure what appeared to be a favorable term. A few years later the office relocated and, with the landlord's permission, assigned the lease to someone else. Unfortunately, the business climate soured and the sublessee fell into bankruptcy. The space could not be sublet, and, contrary to his earlier assurances, the landlord used the *personal* guarantee clause to leverage damages from Wareham's colleague. The issue went to court and Wareham's codirector, a man now retired, was suddenly liable for nearly $100,000 in back rent and legal fees. (This was a substantial amount of money a decade ago.)

Since Wareham did not give the *personal* guarantee, he was legally and personally off the hook. No one could extract that money from him. The only individual who could be legally held responsible was his former employee, so action was taken to collect the money from his home and pension. However, Wareham understood his responsibility was not to the letter of the law but to the spirit of the agreement. He explained: "Once you've given your word, stick to it

— taking care to remind yourself of the spirit of the understanding. That was how I came to shell out the $100,000 for which my codirector was technically liable. We'd never discussed the matter, but he knew he had my permission to act on my behalf in any way he felt best. He also knew me well enough to know that I'd likely have given my *personal* guarantee, albeit reluctantly, to secure that particular piece of office space at that particular time. I just wasn't around and he had to move quickly, so he selflessly put his name and signature on the line. I also so greatly respected my colleague's *personal integrity* that I could never have held up my head in his presence had I reneged on our tacit contract to look out for each other."

Be Truthful

Always speak the truth. Promises should not be made if there is any doubt about one's ability to follow through. Broadcaster Edward R. Murrow noted that credibility is founded on truthfulness: "To be persuasive, we must be believable. To be believable, we must be credible. To be credible, we must be truthful."

Practice Generosity of Spirit

The simple process of living and working means that rivals, challengers, opponents, and even enemies will be encountered. One should practice generosity of spirit with each of those as well as toward those who have different opinions. Stephen Carter, Yale University law professor and the author of numerous books on ethics, clerked for U.S. Supreme Court Justice Thurgood Marshall from 1980 to 1981. During that year, Carter was deeply impressed and impacted by Marshall's *personal* conduct. The African-American justice had seen, firsthand, the ugliness of racism yet he believed in the basic goodness of people, an attitude he often conveyed to Carter. The justice spoke of John W. Davis, his old litigation foe during the Brown v. Board of Education case, as "a great man, a wonderful man. He just believed in segregation," he told Carter. Marshall's generosity of spirit toward opponents left an indelible imprint on his young law clerk.

Admit Mistakes and Accept Responsibility

Finally, if an individual makes a blunder, commits a major error of judgment, or acts or speaks unwisely, it is important to admit the mistake and accept responsibility for it. Learning from one's mistake and doing what one can to make amends is a critical part of integrity. "If we have made obvious mistakes, we should not try, as we generally do, to gloss them over, or to find something to excuse them," wrote the philosopher Arthur Schopenhauer. "We should admit to ourselves that we have committed faults and open our eyes wide to all their enormity, in order that we may firmly resolve to avoid them in time to come."

Financially Focused Mindset[2]

A key to successful project management is acquiring and maintaining the *financially focused mindset*. This mindset requires that all significant financial implications be considered before significant project management activities. In a company where financially focused project management has been properly implemented, all employees receive financially focused training. This training increases the probability that their decisions and actions result in improved profitability.

The project manager should spend a good deal of time maintaining a consciousness of the financial aspects of his or her organization. Perhaps the biggest factor contributing to this concern is the fact that project managers negotiate or are given budgets for accomplishing tasks.

Good Communication Skills

It is essential that a project manager be skilled in most if not all modes of communication, including:

- Clear/concise writing skills (e.g., letters, reports, bulletins, memos)
- E-mail correspondence
- One-on-one conversations
- Meeting administration
- "Brown-bag" (lunchtime) sessions
- Anticipating questions
- Proper formality

Skilled Politician

Wouldn't it be nice to be able to please all of the people all of the time? For there never to be a loser, and everyone to be a winner? A realistic project manager knows this is not possible, but a skilled politician can come very close to achieving this harmony.

One successful technique employed by politicians is getting disagreeing points of view to agree via a consensus. A consensus is possible on most cases, but often requires compromise on the part of participants.

Another approach is helping employees to come to the desired answer on their own. Successful project managers find that task leaders are more apt to embrace changes in project plans if they recommend the actions themselves.

Optimist

The positive, upbeat personality of an optimist is infectious. Project managers surround themselves with "up" personalities, and it is difficult not to want to be part of a team that exudes confidence. The power of positive thinking is very real, and project team members get caught up in the momentum of the optimistic project manager.

Leadership vs. Management

Do not be surprised if someday while you are interviewing for a management position, the interviewer asks you: "What is the difference between leadership and management?" It is not an uncommon interview question, and the answer can be a big factor in determining whether or not you get the job.

The correct answer acknowledges that both skills are critical to success, but it is true that leadership is perhaps the most difficult skill to master. While management involves budgeting, statusing, performing appraisals, and following specific procedures, rules, and regulations, the characteristics of leadership are much more difficult to ascertain.

A "leader" is the captain of the football team or the U.S. president. A leader does not push, but encourages and leads the team by example with charisma and enthusiasm. The leader visualizes the goal for the team and makes everyone aware of their role, motivating them to accomplish their part of the overall plan.

ORGANIZATION STRUCTURE AND CULTURE: IMPACT ON PROJECT MANAGEMENT

There are three basic project management structures used by enterprises to administer their projects: (1) functional organization structure (Figure 3.3), (2) dedicated project team (Figures 3.4 and 3.5), and (3) matrix organization structure (Figure 3.6).

All of these structures are quite common, and in some of the larger companies, different versions of one or more may be employed simultaneously. Lockheed Martin, for example, has used the functional structure for missile programs, while using the matrix organization structure for major internal software development and implementation projects. Gray and Larson[15] provide discussions of these structures and of their advantages and disadvantages below.

Functional Organization

A fundamentally sound method for organizing projects is within the existing functional organization of the enterprise. The functional organization structure is very common. It displays in hierarchical fashion from top to bottom the flow of management in an organization. Instructions and coordination are maintained through the usual management chain of command. Figure 3.3 presents the functional organization of the finance and accounting organization within a very large company. Both the compliance (audit) and financial services departments report to the manager of audit and financial services, who in turn reports to the controller. Similarly, the budgeting and pricing functions report to the manager of budgets and pricing, who answers to the controller.

The finance and accounting organization has undertaken a software upgrade project. The assistant controller, whose job is primarily assisting the controller with special needs, has been given the added responsibility of managing the upgrade in financial software. There is no need to establish a formal project team for this activity, as the assistant controller has direct access to the managers involved in the upgrade and will deal directly with the required individuals. The people who perform tasks in support of the project are still responsible for performing their usual responsibilities.

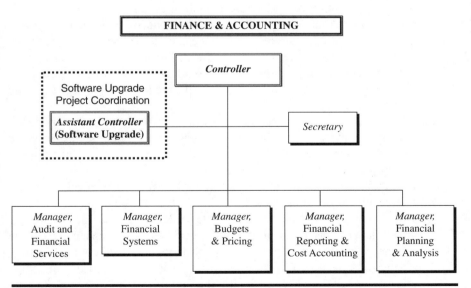

FIGURE 3.3. Functional Organization Structure.

The administration of projects within the functional organization structure offers the following advantages:

- If the scope of the project is very refined and the appropriate functional unit is assigned primary responsibility, then the personnel with the essential expertise will be in the right place at the right time to ensure that the critical areas of the project are carried out.
- There is little or no disruption in normal operations, as projects go from start to finish within the basic functional structure of the organization.
- The functional organization structure allows maximum flexibility in the use of staff. Appropriate experts in the different functional departments can temporarily be assigned to work on the project and then return to their normal home organization. Having a wide range of technical personnel available within each functional unit allows employees to switch among various projects quite easily.
- By offering specialists the opportunity to make significant contributions to projects, but still stay in their home organization, they find that their opportunities for professional growth are not hampered.

Offsetting these advantages are several disadvantages:

- Projects will often lack focus. Each functional unit has its own core routine work to do; sometimes project responsibilities get pushed aside to meet primary obligations. This difficulty is confounded when the project has different priorities for different units. For example, the marketing department may consider the project urgent while the operations folks consider it only of secondary importance. There could be considerable tension if the marketing people wait for the operations people to complete their segment of the project before they proceed.
- There may be poor integration across functional units. Cross-functional communication and coordination are slow and limited at best in most hierarchical organizations. Furthermore, there is a tendency to suboptimize the project with respective functional specialists being concerned only with their own segment of the project and not the total project.
- It generally takes longer to complete projects through this functional arrangement. This is in part attributable to slow response time — project information and decisions have to be circulated through normal management channels. Furthermore, the lack of horizontal, direct communication among functional groups contributes to rework as specialists realize the implications of others' actions after the fact.
- Motivation may be weak for individuals assigned to projects. Often, if employees already have a full-time job, they may look upon the added responsibility of serving on a project team as an additional burden.

Dedicated Project Teams

Now we take a look at a very large project. This project requires that a dedicated project team (Figure 3.4) be established.

The goal of this project is to implement a new finance and accounting software package throughout a company and its many remote sites located across America, including such diverse areas as Denver, Colorado; New Orleans Louisiana; Orlando, Florida; and Memphis, Tennessee. There are many different systems currently in use, because most of the locations joined the company due to mergers and acquisitions. The new software will replace existing packages at remote sites, and all systems will operate from one centrally located server. The project manager for "software consolidation" hires his own dedicated staff of financial systems specialists to work with the various functions and representatives at each site.

The structure for Prestige Productions (Figure 3.5) sets up dedicated project teams for many on-going projects. Each project is a film that is intended for commercial release. The team is comprised of screenwriters, actors, lighting and sound technicians, and set and costume designers. The producer is the project manager, with responsibility for hiring the director and other major parts of the project team.

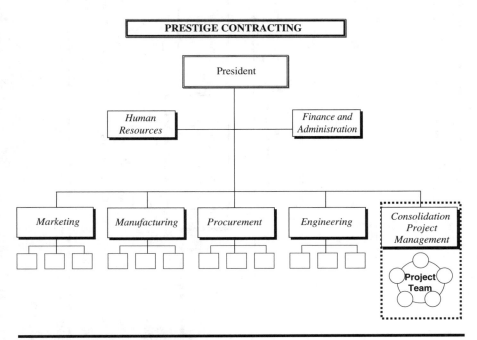

FIGURE 3.4. Dedicated Project Team.

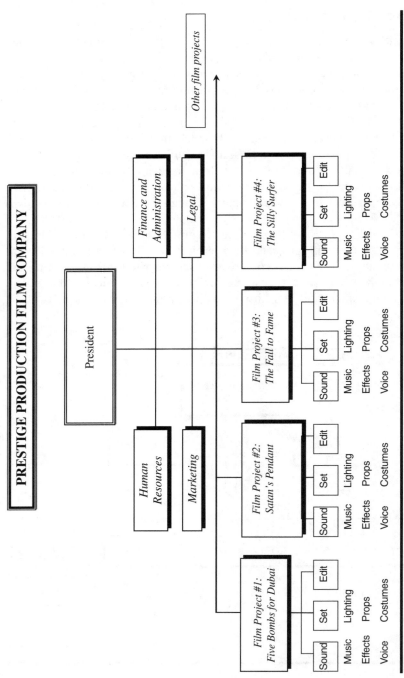

FIGURE 3.5. Project Organization Structure.

The advantages of administering projects with dedicated teams include:

- It is fairly simple to complete a project that does not directly disrupt on-going operations. Other than taking away resources in the form of specialists assigned to the project, the functional organization remains intact with the project operating independently.
- A concentrated project focus is often missing in the functional approach. The project manager has full authority over the project. Although the project manager reports to senior management in the parent organization, there is a dedicated workforce whose sole function is to complete the project.
- Generally speaking, projects are completed in a more timely manner. Team participants devote their full attention to the project and are not distracted by other obligations and responsibilities. In addition, response time tends to be quicker under this arrangement because most decisions are made within the team and are not deferred up the functional hierarchy.
- Participants are on "the team," sharing a common goal and personal responsibility for the projects success. This results in a high level of motivation and cohesiveness.
- With the right personnel assigned to the project team, a high level of cross-functional integration occurs. The experts from different parts of the company work closely together and, under a skilled project manager, become committed to optimizing the project.

The following disadvantages should be noted when considering implementation of a dedicated project team:

- It is costly! It requires the creation of self-contained project teams comprised of full-time personnel. In addition to creating a new management position (the project manager), resources are also assigned on a full-time basis. This may result in duplication of efforts across projects and the loss of some economies of scale.
- "Projectitis," i.e., sometimes a project team takes on an adversarial relationship with the parent organization. Rather than realizing the project team is part of the total company team, projectitis results when team members begin complaining about such issues as insufficient resource allocation. This divisiveness can undermine not only the integration of the eventual outcomes of the project into mainstream operations, but also the assimilation of project team members back into their functional units once the project is completed.
- The creation of self-contained teams may inhibit maximum technological expertise being brought to bear on problems. Technical expertise is limited

somewhat to the talents and experience of the specialist assigned to the project. While nothing prevents the specialist from consulting with others in the functional division, the we–they syndrome and the fact that such help is not formally sanctioned by the organization discourage this from taking place.

■ One of the biggest problems with the dedicated project team occurs when the project is complete and it is time to figure out where the team members go next. If other project work is not available, then the transition back to their original functional departments may be difficult due to their prolonged absence. They need to catch up on recent developments, and someone may have already taken their place.

Managing Project with Matrix Organization Structures

In a matrix organization structure, the normal vertical functional hierarchy is superimposed with a project management structure. This imposes two chains of command: (1) the traditional hierarchy imposed by the functional structure and (2) the command of the project manager over those performing on the project team and/or those in the functional organizations.

In Figure 3.6, Spacely Manufacturing has a traditional functional hierarchy, but also has an organization titled "project administration," which houses the project management responsible for Spacely Projects. A project manager may administer more than one project, and other staff within the project administration group may provide support in such areas as scheduling and resource management. However, the hands-on members of the project team actually reside in the functional organizations. Budgets dictate how many employees from each functional organization will serve on the project team. For example, Project A may require a full-time project manager and a total of 12 functional employees (e.g., 7 from manufacturing, 4 from engineering, and 1 from marketing). A smaller Project B may require only 2.5 employees (e.g., a half-time project manager, 1 from manufacturing, 0.75 person from engineering, and 0.25 person from marketing).

One of the most difficult problems with matrix structures is the chain of command. Usually an employee has only one "real" boss — the individual who gives the annual performance appraisal and pay increases. In most cases, that is NOT the project manager. As a result, the employee is apt to be more loyal to the functional manager when the employee must determine priorities.

To address this issue, there are many different kinds of matrix systems, the two most common of which appear below:

■ **Functional matrix:** Similar to a functional approach, except there is a formally designated project manager responsible for coordinating. The

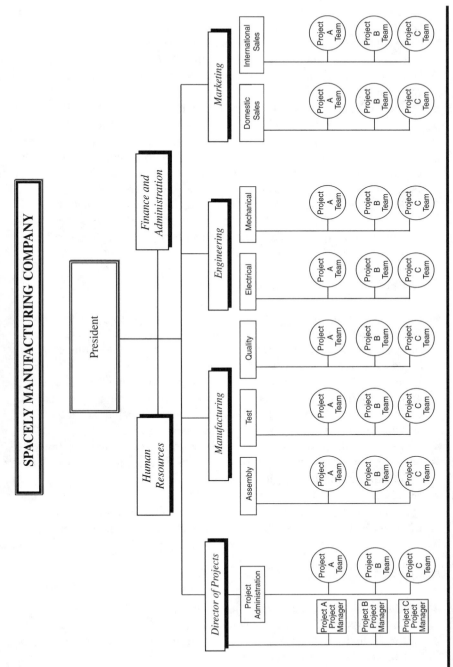

FIGURE 3.6. Matrix Organization Structure.

functional managers manage their portion of the project, while the project manager performs as a staff assistant who prepares schedules and check-lists, collects information on status of the project, and facilitates completion of the project. The true power rests with the functional managers, who make most of the decisions and decide who performs specific tasks and when they are to be done.

■ **Balanced matrix:** More to the project manager's liking, here the project manager is responsible for defining what needs to be done while the functional managers are responsible for how it will be done. The project manager establishes the overall plan for project completion, integrates the contribution of other functions, sets schedules, and monitors progress. Functional managers are responsible for assigning personnel and executing their segment of the project according to the specification (schedules/ standards) established by the project manager. Both parties must work closely together to ensure all functions flow smoothly together and jointly approve technical and operational decisions.

The advantages of matrix organizations include:

■ Personnel expertise can be shared across multiple projects as well as within functional divisions. Individuals can divide their energy across multiple projects on an as-needed basis. This reduces the duplication that is required in a pure project team structure.

■ With a formally designated project manager, responsible for coordinating and integrating contributions of different units, a strong project focus is provided. This also helps sustain an all-encompassing approach to problem solving that is often missing in the functional organization.

■ The project has reasonable access to the entire reservoir of technology and expertise of functional divisions, because the project organization is superimposed on the functional structure.

■ Matrix arrangements provide for flexible utilization of resources and expertise within the firm. In some cases functional units may provide individuals who are managed by the project manager. In other cases, the contributions are monitored by the functional manager.

The disadvantages include:

■ Any situation in which equipment, resources, and people are being shared across projects and financial activities lends itself to conflict and competition for scarce resources. Infighting can occur among project managers, who are primarily interested in what is best for their own project.

- Matrix management causes friction because functional employees must answer to two bosses: their functional manager and one or more project managers. Working in a matrix structure can be very stressful. It would be very difficult to have three different managers asking you to do three different things.
- The presence of a project manager to coordinate the project should accelerate the completion of the project. However, the decision-making progress sometimes slows as agreements need to be reached across multiple functional groups. This is especially true for the balanced matrix.

The goal of organization structures is to help establish an effective framework for the interaction of human beings. There are many options, and it is not uncommon for an enterprise to always be on the lookout for a way to make improvements.

ORGANIZATIONAL CULTURE

Avan Jassawalla and Heman Sashittal[16] studied how the organizational culture influences a firm's economic consequences. They recognize its important role in shaping product innovation processes. Highly innovation-supportive cultures are credited with fostering teamwork and promoting risk taking and creative actions that seem directly linked to effective new product development.

The *Jakarta Post*[17] offers the following research on the value of a corporation's culture. Nissan, the second-largest automotive manufacturer in Japan, recorded a loss of $5.7 billion, adding to its already huge debt of $5.3 billion. A year later, however, Nissan achieved one of the greatest turnarounds in Asia, raking in a profit of $2.9 billion that is still continuing.

Much of the credit was given to *organizational culture*–related improvements, e.g., building in clearer profit orientation; increasing focus on customers and less on chasing competitors; instilling a culture of working together across functions, borders, or hierarchical lines; and nurturing a shared vision.

In another example, profit has been generated every year for 28 consecutive years by medium-sized Southwest Airlines. From the second year after its inception, the company never recorded a year of loss, for which Herb Kelleher, its cofounder and chairman, gives unquestionable credit to the company's unique corporate *culture*.

Nissan and Southwest Airlines are just two examples of organizations that adopted strong, positive *organizational culture*, the essential ingredient to successful operations and for-the-long-term turnarounds in companies everywhere.

It is imperative that when an organization is at the low point of its life cycle it reconsider its foundations: corporate vision and *culture*. They are the solid ground, glue, and compass that more than ever support, hold together, and direct the modern organization. Nevertheless, these two basic elements tend to be overlooked, and instead, top management commonly focuses on the quality of management, organization restructuring, business process re-engineering, the installation of new corporate systems, or the like.

Poorly performing organizations should look into realizing a change solution that is deeper and longer lasting in its impact, a solution in which the organization sets itself up to prevent the possibility of "firefighting" in the future. As corporate vision has been much discussed, I would like to focus here on the solutions that derive from organizational culture change.

Organizational culture is the foundation of the organization on which it stands and from which it grows. Thus, the relevance of rethinking an organization's culture should not be overlooked. Organizational culture and its process can be observed in real life cultural change, just as the examples above have resulted in dramatic turnarounds in global business history.

Although a strong culture is important in driving the organization to success, it is, however, important to ensure that it is one that encourages healthy adaptation to its external environment. A strong culture that is unadaptable may be more damaging than a weak one.

SUMMARY OF HUMAN ASPECTS OF PROJECT MANAGEMENT

Much of the project manager's success results from his or her mastery of the related human aspects. It is the people that make or break a project. To operate at maximum efficiency the project manager needs to obtain supportive project sponsorship and should possess the following characteristics:

- Expertise and education
- Be a systems thinker
- Possess personal integrity and the financially focused mindset
- Have good communication skills
- Be a skilled politician and an optimist
- Understand the nuances of leadership vs. management
- Utilize the organization structure and culture to ensure positive impacts on the project

The project team is just as important (if not more so) than the project manager. It is necessary to assemble an effective team of qualified professionals and motivate them to work together. The project team is discussed at length in Chapter 4.

Effective use of open communication and meetings is also key, as is ensuring adequate training.

Employing the strategies related to the human aspects discussed above has been shown to enhance employee effectiveness, and increase motivation. Enhanced effectiveness and properly channeled motivation offer the prospect of making an organization more profitable. This prospect is heightened when financially focused project management is used to evaluate the true costs and benefits during each step of the process.

SELF-STUDY/DISCUSSION QUESTIONS

1. Which of the core traits of a project manager presented in this chapter do you feel are most important? Why? Which are the least important? What important traits were omitted from this chapter? Discuss.
2. What organization structure is employed at your company? How are project teams developed? How could your company's organization structure be modified to potentially improve efficiencies in operations? Discuss.
3. For projects you have been a part of, who were the project sponsors? The project manager? The customers? The team members?
4. How has ethics played a role in the projects of which you have been a part?
5. What are the various methods available to project leaders to communicate with the following:
   - Project sponsors
   - Senior management
   - Customers
   - Team members
   - Functional managers
6. In question 5 above, which methods work the best? Why? Which may not be so effective? Why?
7. Share some horror stories regarding meetings at your company. Share some successes.

Free value-added materials available from the
Download Resource Center at www.jrosspub.com.

4

THE PROJECT TEAM

INTRODUCTION

The project manager is NOTHING without the project team. Part of the challenge is assembling a team of qualified professionals, and then getting them to work together like a finely tuned machine.

Members of the Project Team[18]

The members of a project team will vary of course, depending on the project on which the team is working. In a generic sense, the following leaders may serve on the team:

1. Project manager: The project manager is the coordinator, the leader, the administrator, the motivator, the heart and brains for the team, and the soul of the project. If the project is successful, the project manager is the hero. If the project fails, the project manager is fired, or at best is assigned to another project.
2. Lead project engineer: The individual in charge of product design and development, with responsibility for functional analysis, specifications, drawings, cost estimates, quality/reliability, engineering changes, and documentation is the project engineer.
3. Lead manufacturing engineer: The task of this engineer is to ensure the efficient production of the product or process that has been designed by the project engineer. This includes having the responsibility for manufacturing engineering, design and production of tooling/jibs/fixtures, production scheduling, and other production tasks.
4. Contract administrator: The administrator is responsible for all official paperwork, keeping track of customer changes, billing, questions, com-

plaints, legal aspects, costs, and other matters related to the contract authorizing the project. Not uncommonly, the contract administrator also serves as project historian and archivist.

5. Field manager: For projects involving the installation of a product at a remote site, the field manager is responsible for installation, testing, and support once it is delivered.

6. Project controller: The controller keeps daily account of budgets, cost variances, labor charges, project supplies, capital equipment status, direct and indirect costs, and the like. The controller also prepares periodic reports and keeps in close contact with both the project manager and the company controller. If the contract administrator does not maintain an historical database, the controller can perform this function.

7. Support services manager: This person is in charge of most functions providing product support. Such functions include subcontractors, data processing, general management support, and training.

The project team may also have any number of scientists, engineers, technicians, clerks, and training and publications staff, all of whom may play vital roles on the team.

Stages in the Life of a Project Team

Gido and Clements[19] presented several stages of team development and growth, which have been augmented here for the application of financially focused project management (FFPM) (Figure 4.1): forming, adorning, storming, norming, performing, and adjourning.

Forming

The first stage in the life of a project is *forming*. This is how the process might work in a functional organization structure.

Imagine that you are the project manager. You are meeting with the project sponsor, who is also a member of executive management, and the challenge of the new project is presented to you. The executive says something like, "That's it in a nutshell. Now it's up to you to decide who you want on your team. You have 6 months to finish the project, and you'll have budget to support about a three-person level. Now you can take the ball and run with it."

By nature of your many years with the company and your previous experience managing teams, you already have an idea of what the composition of the team will be. You will have to recruit your team members from functional organizations. Since the people you will want are critical to their home organizations, you will be lucky to get them any more than half time, so your budget will support four to six people at most.

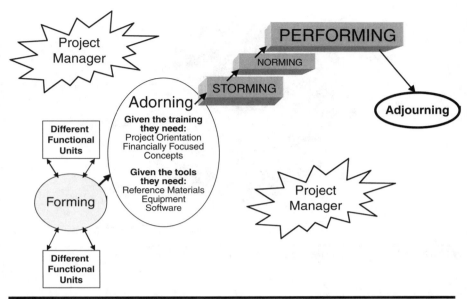

FIGURE 4.1. Stages in the Life of a Project Team.

Team Make-up

You decide your project requires people with the following skills:

- Financial reporting systems engineer
- Financial accounting systems engineer
- Project controller/administrator
- Documentation/trainer

Team Budget

With budget to carry a three-person man level for 6 months, you calculate roughly 18 months of budget. You know you will be spending 6 months of the budget, so you only have about 12 months left. Based on that, you budget accordingly:

- Financial reporting systems engineer (half time for 6 months) = 3 months of budget
- Financial accounting systems engineer (half time for 6 months) = 3 months of budget
- Project controller/administrator (quarter time for 6 months) = 1.5 months of budget
- Documentation/trainer (quarter time for 6 months) = 1.5 months of budget

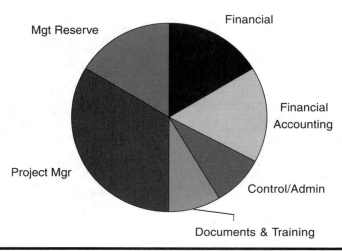

FIGURE 4.2. Project Team Budget Allocation.

That means, including yourself, you have budgeted 15 months, leaving you with 3 months of budget for a management reserve. Management reserve is a funding buffer you can fall back on just in case you need extra funding downstream. Your budget allocation is displayed graphically in Figure 4.2.

Next you need to do your recruiting. You know some outstanding engineers with whom you have worked in the past. The only problem is that these individuals are already working 40-plus hours a week. But you know that old saying: "If you want to get something done, assign it to the busiest person." The trick is to be as organized as possible when you meet with your recruits. Make them realize that you will not waste their time. Assure them that their home organization takes priority, but if they do join the team, you expect them to put forth a sincere effort to accomplish their tasks. Explain to them exactly what you expect, the designated times they will be required to participate in team meetings, and get a commitment.

One by one you recruit your four team members. All are enthusiastic about the project on which they are serving. They look upon this project as a new challenge, something fun, and they are excited about being on your team.

Adorning

Adorning is the next phase. In a very short time, you must equip your team members with everything they will need to be successful. The most important is to conduct a short half-day (4-hour) financially focused training session (see also Chapter 11).

At a second half-day training session, give your team members a complete overview of the project. Ensure they all know their roles and the roles of the other team members. This is also the meeting in which real team bonding takes place. This meeting is also used to determine exactly what they will need to accomplish their responsible tasks. It is important to identify early in the project the following:

- Specific tools
- Reference materials
- Equipment
- Computer software and hardware

Then do it. Go to you project sponsor and request the items that have been identified as essential to the project. By "adorning" your team members with everything they need, you build their loyalty to the project, and you have completed the second stage of developing a successfully team.

Storming

The third stage in the life of a project team has been termed *storming*. Just as adolescence of the youngster is a tough phase in family growth, so too is storming a difficult time for most team members.

By the time the team is formed and adorned, the project objective should be fairly clear in everyone's minds. This is when the team members actually begin applying their skills to work on the activities for which they are responsible. A short time after the ball gets rolling, some team members may begin to lose their enthusiasm for the project. Certain aspects may be more difficult than first anticipated, and they begin to feel an increasing level of dissatisfaction with the project, and the project manager may feel the brunt of this reaction. Dissatisfaction can become frustration, which can lead to anger and even hostility.

Team members begin asking for more resources and for expanded schedules, and often conflicts emerge. This is when members begin to express their individuality and may not give the leader the respect required. Just as a 14-year-old may become upset when his parents disallow his plans to go sky diving, so too may team a member exhibit contempt when the project leader disallows the continuance of unnecessary overtime.

As in all stages of project team development, the project leader needs to maintain control of the team, but perhaps not as directly as in other stages. This is when team members must be allowed enough freedom to make and learn from their own mistakes. Caution must be exercised, however, to ensure such mistakes are only cosmetic.

The project manager has to provide guidance and foster conflict resolution. No sides should be taken. Instead, the parties to the unrest should be encouraged to resolve such situations on their own. These problems must be resolved in a timely manner. The storm should not be permitted to last very long.

Norming

As many parents know, the terror of storming often gives way to the wonder of *norming*, when their child suddenly begins to act *NORMAL*! This is sometimes displayed when the child gets his or her first full-time job, enters college or graduate school, or is no longer embarrassed to be seen with the parents. This is when children realize their parents are not so dumb after all.

The same phenomenon happens in team development. After the initial struggle ends, the project team progresses into the stage known as norming. The petty conflicts have been resolved for the most part, the level of dissatisfaction has significantly been reduced, and most conflicts have subsided. Members' expectations have now aligned with the reality of the situation. There is a general acceptance of the resources available, constraints, and the other team members. The operating environment has become comfortable, the project procedures are fairly well understood, and process improvement can begin.

By this time, the project manager has successfully transferred much of the control and decision making to the subteam leaders and the members themselves. Aside from attending the periodic status meetings and asking the necessary probing questions, the project manager can begin falling into "automatic pilot" mode and take a more supportive role.

The project manager and key team members should maintain records of unexpected problems that have arisen. This information covers "what went right" and "what went wrong" to use in the adjourning stage for a "lessons learned" white paper.

Team cohesion and trust blossom. A true feeling of camaraderie envelops everyone as a greater sharing of ideas and feelings occurs. The project team members may plan a special event (e.g., luncheon) to recognize the project team for the progress being made.

Performing

The second to the last stage in the life of a project team is *performing*. At this stage, the team is highly committed, truly motivated, with a high sense of success. There is a sense of unity and pride, as every team member understands their role, and all are operating at the peak of efficiency. During this stage, all the traits of a successful team should be visible:

- Commitment is strong.
- Confidence is high.
- Communication is open, frank, and timely.
- Individuals work independently or in temporary subteams, as needed.
- There is a great degree of interdependency.
- Members frequently collaborate and willingly help each other.
- The team feels fully empowered.
- There is a feeling of satisfaction as progress is made.
- Team members are experiencing professional growth.
- Team members continue to maintain records of "what went right" and "what went wrong" to use in the adjourning stage for a "lessons learned" white paper.

In this stage, the project manager should perform the following actions:

- Fully delegate responsibility and authority, further empowering the team.
- Focus on helping the team execute the project plan and give recognition to team members for their progress and accomplishments.
- Concentrate on project performance with response to the budget, schedule, scope, and plan.
- Facilitate and support the development and implementation of corrective actions when necessary.
- Act as a mentor, supporting the professional growth and development of the team members.

Adjourning

The sixth and final stage in the life of the project team is its demise, affectionately known as *adjourning*. In New Orleans, the death of a loved one is often marked by rejoicing in the life of the departed. So too should the ending of the project team be filled with celebration.

Ideally, the project manager throws a big celebratory bash, complete with awards to team members, a delicious feast, open bar, and entertainment. All team members find themselves welcomed back to their home organizations or are assigned to another exciting project. Unfortunately, it does not always work this way. Sometimes team members are unable to find work within the company. Sometimes projects are terminated before the project is complete, and the entire team is given pink slips. This of course is very rare, and it is an unfortunate project manager who must deliver the bad news.

Appraising the Attributes of a Project Team

The stages in the life of a project team are fairly constant. What is not fairly constant are the attributes or characteristics of the team and its members. There have been many studies in the attempt to determine the composition of a successful project team.

Ammeter and Dukerich[20] interviewed project team members in an effort to clearly identify factors that lead to high levels of team performance. A survey was given to 151 project teams in the engineering and construction industry that focused on project team leader behaviors, use of team building, and team member characteristics as predictors of project cost and schedule performance. Results of this survey revealed that the following factors had the most impact on project cost performance:

- Making an effort to utilize industry best practices
- Specific behaviors of the project manager

Best Practices

Best practices are determined via a process improvement tool known as *benchmarking*. With respect to project teams, benchmarking measures and compares the structure and operations of a particular project team with the structure and operations of similar teams in other departments within the same company or other companies in the same industry. The goal of benchmarking is to increase your project team's performance by adopting the best practices of other project teams with similar goals. Since best project teams' practices are always evolving, benchmarking should be applied at least annually.

Project Manager Behaviors

The behaviors of the project manager should reflect the "core traits/skills required for a successful project manager" discussed in Chapter 3.

While Ammeter and Dukerich found the characteristics of best practices and project manager behaviors most important, one cannot deny the importance of the team members themselves.

Team Member Considerations

The following factors should be considered when selecting members of the project team:

- "Unsuccessful" team members: Consider the individual's history of performance. If a potential team member has been on quite a few unsuccessful teams, this may be more than just a coincidence.
- Characteristics of effective team members: The ideal team members will have the following skills:

1. Problem-solving ability: Every team needs "can do" people with the skills to overcome significant obstacles.
2. Availability: They want to be on the team, and their home organization will give them the time.
3. Technological expertise: A positive attitude it great, but the technological expertise that comes with a high level of education and experience is crucial.
4. Credibility: To fit in well with a successful team, each member must have a strong track record and excellent references and credentials.
5. Political connections: It never hurts to have someone on the team who has many contacts and can use them as a resource for information and resources.
6. Ambition, initiative, and energy: These final traits are what give the project team its heart. You can also add desire, and that is something that cannot be taught in schools.

COMMUNICATIONS IN PROJECT MANAGEMENT

The human factors in project management include project sponsorship and leadership, the organization structure and culture, and the project team. What ties them all together? Communications.

As discussed earlier, the project team leader should have excellent communication skills, including clear/concise writing skills (e.g., letters, reports, bulletins, memos); utilize e-mail correspondence; perform well in one-on-one conversations/interviewing; be able to administer effective meetings; be open to "brown-bag" (lunchtime) sessions; fully anticipate questions (think fast); and understand/employ proper formality in written and spoken correspondence.

The importance of communications in project management was discussed in the September 2001 *Incentive*.[21] Studies revealed that companies with open communication policies post higher employee satisfaction rates. Also, the managers employed at companies with open communication channels have a higher satisfaction rate than those who do not, according to a recent study (discussed below) by the Institute of Excellence in Employee-Management Communications, based in New York.

Open Communications

The 2001 Manager's Study entitled "Hey, I've Got an Idea!" was conducted by Perrier Associates, a research consultancy firm. It examined the relationship between managers' sense of belonging to their organizations — measurements were based on company favorability and job satisfaction — and morale. Highlights of the study are summarized below:

- More than 90% of respondents said they are highly satisfied and engaged in their job when they have the ability to offer ideas and to question company *management.*
- Nearly 70% of managers whose organizations do not reported low levels of morale.
- Managers who are better informed and more involved in business planning, goal setting, and other high-level activities exhibit higher job satisfaction.
- A company with effective two-way *communications* produces managers who are less likely to leave their jobs.

Employee retention has obvious economic benefits, including reduced costs associated with hiring and training employees. The benefits listed above promote the belief that the culture in a project team should foster open communications.

The Communication Model

Arlene Alpert[22] offers some excellent suggestions on interpersonal communication that can easily be applied to any project team to enhance communication and teamwork.

Project Teams and Conflict Resolution

Arlene developed a communication model that is very useful to a project manager (or really just about anyone) who finds it necessary to meet with a dissenting individual. As discussed earlier (e.g., *storming*), a project manager's job is not always smooth sailing. From time to time, there will be situations where conflict management skills will come in quite handy. Arlene offers the following techniques to ensure that meetings between individuals with differing points of view have positive team-forming results. Two of these techniques appear below, with a discussion of their relationship to project management.

- Silence: According to an old saying, "God gave us two ears and one mouth, to use in that order." Silence can be a powerful communication technique. A project manager needs to know when to speak and when to listen. Silence combined with acknowledgment — a smile, eye contact, a nod, and/or leaning slightly forward — lets the team member know that he or she has the freedom to be comfortable and open with feelings, and makes it obvious that the project manager is listening. In true listening, "hearing" takes place when nuances are picked up in addition to the sounds the ears hear.
- Be proactive: After hearing the full idea, the response should be clear and concise, stating exactly what you believe to be the proper course of action.

Clear, direct communication is both an art and a science — and a joy and a relief when mastered. Here is a summary of the key suggestions Alpert recommends to project managers:

- Listen
- Empathy is its own reward
- Accept
- Be understanding
- Criticism closes doors
- Speak
- Heartfelt words touch others
- Clarify
- Ask for an explanation
- Assuming, analyzing, and interpreting are roadblocks
- Be open
- Vulnerability and caring count

Meetings

Many companies have begun offering formal training sessions in the art of conducting "effective meetings." FFPM[2] suggests that an effective meeting increases profitability for the company in two ways: (1) the time spent by employees in meetings is reduced to what is needed and wanted, and (2) the time spent between meetings is much more efficient, due to the successful agreements reached during the meetings themselves.

Most workers are very skeptical about meetings. They seem to feel that meetings are a necessary evil that keeps them from getting their work done. Yet, it is almost impossible to have an interagency collaboration without meetings. With technology allowing greater convenience through telephone conference calls and video teleconferencing, meetings are becoming even more frequent, thus increasing the need to ensure they are efficient and effective.

Meetings are held for such purposes as:

- Presenting status on a project
- Determining corrective action
- Decision making and building consensus
- Fostering inclusion
- Moving toward the vision
- Getting things done

Here are some generic hints that may help almost anyone responsible for meetings:

1. Understand the purpose of the meeting in as simple and clear a manner as possible.
2. Be sure to invite only those who truly need to be in attendance.
3. Consider performing a premeeting inquiry. This is especially useful for the first meeting of a team or task force, or when the team is taking on new responsibilities or new challenges. Ask members to suggest several agenda topics. Ask them to indicate what they would like to get out of the discussion and to provide an estimate of how much time it will take. Also ask them to suggest potential meeting agreements and to share concerns or potential problems.
4. Have a clear, concise agenda, and stick to it! The agenda is like a road map in that it is a plan to help the group get to where it wants to go. However, it is rare that a meeting unfolds exactly as prepared. In fact, if it ever did, it would be a miracle. Either that, or the person in charge was one bossy son of a gun. If a premeeting inquiry has been performed, it is an excellent source for helping the meeting planner shape the agenda around what needs to be covered.
5. It is a good idea to send out a copy of the agenda prior to the meeting, as well as any materials with which the attendees need to be familiar.
6. Ensure the meeting is set for a time and place agreed to by all members.
7. The meeting space should be conducive to getting work done.
8. Paying attention to the "little things" like how the meeting room is arranged, the room temperature, or whether or not there is coffee can contribute greatly to the success of a meeting.
9. Set the agenda at the beginning of the meeting, with suggested time limits.
10. Introduce each attendee prior to or at the beginning of the meeting. This is excellent as it enables each member to feel ownership for the meeting, the agenda, and the results. If a premeeting inquiry was performed, share with the team how the inquiry shaped the agenda. ("Three people wanted to discuss this, five wanted that, so those topics are on the agenda." "The following topics were suggested by only one or two people, but we didn't have time on the agenda. We'll try to cover those topics at a future meeting.")
11. The needs of those in attendance should be considered, with an effort toward meeting their related needs.
12. Pay attention to the order in which things are discussed and the amount of time spent on each. Often there is a tendency to spend a lot of time discussing items that are early on the agenda, and then to rush through several items toward the end. This can be avoided by making the group aware of this tendency, putting the most important items at the beginning of the meeting, and by sticking closely to the recommended time allotted to each topic on the agenda.

13. Work to see to it that the format and time allocated for the meeting are a good fit with the purpose of the meeting.
14. Consider changing the agenda as necessary as the meeting progresses.
15. Encourage all members, and give them the opportunity to participate. Do not allow the meeting to be dominated by just a few members.
16. All meetings should include respect and trust and, when appropriate, humor.
17. Remember that conflict and problems are okay, but should be dealt with in an appropriate, safe manner.
18. Strive for a balance between results, team member relationships, and process.
19. Meetings should be conducted primarily for activities that can only happen when the team is together.
20. At the end of each meeting, review decisions and action responsibilities.
21. Also announce the date of, and list tentative agenda items for, the next meeting.
22. Evaluate meetings after the fact along the lines of a "lessons learned" analysis. Ask members to periodically fill out evaluations about meetings to aid in your evaluation. This will help in remembering to keep doing what seems to work and to discontinue what does not.
23. Meeting minutes: Attendees deserve to receive minutes. This is particularly important to document decisions made. It also offers the opportunity to remind team members of the next scheduled meeting. With computers and e-mail, minutes are as easy as adding comments to the earlier published agenda. A push of the button sends the minutes to all attendees.
24. Not all agencies use the same calendar or have the same holidays; it might be a good idea to periodically send out a list of future meeting dates.

Meet at the Right Time

Sometimes, one of the most difficult challenges is just finding a time when every member can attend. For instance, what can be done if there is absolutely no time that every member can meet? While it may be preferred that everyone be there, the meeting can still be scheduled for a date, time, and place that the majority can attend. For those who have conflicts, here are some options:

- They can assign a delegate to attend.
- They can participate via conference call.
- If practical, discussions requiring their participation can be postponed to a future meeting that they can attend.

Once team members are able to get their meeting times in synchronization, it is often easiest to meet at the same time and day of the week or month. However, one critical flaw of meetings is to hold them just because they are scheduled on a weekly or monthly basis.

It is extremely important for meeting leaders to ensure that there truly is a need for a meeting before allowing one to take place. A simple preliminary query to team members may reveal that the next meeting can be canceled. If this is the case, canceling the meeting will most likely come as a very pleasant surprise to the team members. They will certainly view meetings as less of a burden in the future, when they realize that they are held only when a substantive agenda is in place.

Team members should be asked to put the dates on their calendars. Though it sounds obvious, many people still schedule only a week at a time, while periodic meetings can occur weekly and monthly for years into the future. By putting the meeting on the employee's schedule at least 2 months in advance, the chances of scheduling a conflicting meeting are greatly reduced. As the technology behind such devices as Business Organizing and Scheduling Systems, Personal Digital Assistants, Palm Pilots, and Personal Viewers continues to improve and become less costly, people are now able to schedule on-going weekly and monthly meetings very easily.

Meeting at the Right Place

Many companies have rooms that are specifically constructed for meetings. For example, an executive conference room may come equipped with the following:

- Mahogany lectern, sitting on a...
- Podium, equipped with a...
- Microphone or lavaliere mike
- Microphones for all attendees
- Special light with dimmers to make the room conducive to viewing presentations
- Facilities for presenting visual information, including:
  1. Large tablet
  2. Overhead (vu-foil) projector
  3. Slide projector
  4. Computer projection system
  5. Laser pointer

Possible Roles of Attendees and Other Meeting Components

- Neutral facilitator: Takes care of the process of the meeting. A neutral facilitator has no stake in the outcome or content of the meeting. A neutral facilitator can free members to deal with content of the meeting and levels the playing field.
- Facilitating leader: Members are trained in facilitation and take turns facilitating the meetings. They are not completely neutral on the content.
- Chairperson: Often an elected team member who leads meeting.
- Recorder (rarely used): A recorder writes down what members are saying on large pieces of easel paper. Care should be taken to write down the actual words and not to paraphrase. Members are responsible for making sure the recorder has captured the essence of what they said.
- Secretary/notetaker: Often this person will be responsible for preparing and distributing the minutes of the meeting.
- Timekeeper (rarely used): If for some reason the person leading the meeting cannot keep track of the time, the timekeeper is given responsibility for keeping the meeting flowing in line with the agenda's recommended timetable.
- Participants (self-explanatory).
- Observers: If for some reason there are people interested in the content of the meeting, these folks would be allowed to attend, but they better not say anything! (Just kidding. These people may be customers or project sponsors.)
- Set-up crew: Responsible for arranging chairs, setting up the audio/visual equipment.
- Clean-up crew: These people return the room to its original condition (e.g., erase the blackboard).
- Snack providers or chefs: This function, though extremely rare in the corporate world, is also self-explanatory.
- Agenda (self-explanatory).
- Aspirin (self-explanatory).

The Agenda

Having a concise agenda is very important for successful meetings. Linda Shinn[23] calls the agenda "a road map to a predetermined destination." As such, it is a tool to help the project manager, team leaders, and participants achieve the organization's goal.

Shinn suggests that meeting agendas be organized by five key areas to help the team make the best use of its time and to increase the team's sense of accomplishment.

1. Must-do's: The actions that the team has accountability for, such as approving previous minutes or receiving reports from task team leaders.
2. Consent agenda: Contains items the team needs to receive and review but not necessarily discuss. Consent agenda items can be moved to the discussion if so moved.
3. Discussion and decision: Matters that fall under discussion and decision usually include things on which the team must take a position. Examples include standards of practice, codes of ethics, selection of subcontractors, public policy positions, and budgets.
4. Future focus: A good rule of thumb is to have the team spend at least one third of its time at each meeting thinking about and planning for the future. The use of a specific agenda item related to the future is one way for a board to identify trends, consider the implications of a member needs assessment, or brainstorm assumptions about the future from a political, economic, technological, or sociodemographic perspective.
5. Summary and next steps: At the end of each meeting, take a few minutes to review what the project team has accomplished during its time together and be sure that all members know how actions will be followed up, i.e., who will do what and by when. This is also a good time for the team to review what will be said publicly about a particularly difficult or highly charged issue, ensuring that all members carry the same message from the team meeting.

Brainstorming

A valuable part of effective meetings is the use of brainstorming. This is a process that uses more than one person to stimulate the generation of ideas focused toward a particular goal. Brainstorming can be used effectively in a multitude of situations by almost any team (e.g., task force teams, quality circles, natural work teams, and process improvement teams) and can be a great way to use the creativity of the team.

It is imperative that during brainstorming there be no evaluation. Usually very early in a brainstorming session, someone will evaluate an idea. If the "no evaluation" rule is not restated and enforced at that time, the brainstorming will be significantly hampered and participation will quickly cease.

Affinity Diagram

The affinity diagram takes brainstorming one step beyond. It is a team process tool that organizes ideas, created through brainstorming, into natural groupings in a way that stimulates new creative ideas. Without speaking to one another, team members work to generate categories and new ideas. The affinity diagram is also known as the KHJ method.

Virtual Teams/Remote Teams and Communication

The World Wide Web is everywhere. Any organization that is not capitalizing on its ability to shrink the world is missing the boat as far as cost savings are concerned. Teleconferencing had its day, but now it is passé. It was in, but now it is out. Just ask a top-notch project manager if you are in doubt.

It is no longer necessary for team leaders at remote sites to fly to headquarters for status meetings. Effective use of the Internet allows all meeting participants to view the same presentation on their desktop PCs and participate in the meeting via a conference call.

The meeting coordinator is responsible for assembling the agenda and presentation in compatible presentation software (e.g., PowerPoint). The coordinator then makes the presentation available on a company-secured, password-protected web site.

A study performed at Sabre, Inc.[24] described virtual teams as groups of people who work interdependently with shared purpose across space, time, and organization boundaries using technology to communicate and collaborate. Virtual team members may be located across a country or across the world, rarely meet face-to-face, and include members from different cultures.

Many virtual teams are cross-functional and emphasize solving customer problems or generating new work processes. Virtual work allows organizations to combine the best expertise regardless of geographic location.

Advances in communications and information technology create new opportunities for organizations to build and manage virtual teams. Such teams are composed of employees with unique skills, located at a distance from each other, who must collaborate to accomplish important organizational tasks. Based on a comprehensive set of interviews with a subset of team members, team leaders, general managers, and executives on 65 virtual teams at Sabre, Inc. — an innovative organization in the travel industry — we identify 5 challenges that organizations can expect to encounter in establishing, maintaining, and supporting virtual teams, e.g., building trust, cohesion, team identity, and overcoming isolation among virtual team members. Both leaders and members of virtual teams face particular difficulties in selecting team members who have the balance of technical and interpersonal skills and abilities required to work virtually and in evaluating the performance of individuals and teams working in virtual space. Examination of Sabre's strategies for coping with each challenge should be instructive to other organizations using or considering virtual teams.

This study lists the following as the "five challenges to virtual team success:"

■ Challenge 1: Building trust within virtual teams
■ Challenge 2: Maximizing process gains and minimizing process losses on virtual teams
■ Challenge 3: Overcoming feelings of isolation and detachment associated with virtual teamwork
■ Challenge 4: Balancing technical and interpersonal skills among virtual team members
■ Challenge 5: Assessment and recognition of virtual team performance

Groupthink

A note of caution: A major pitfall to avoid in meetings is *Groupthink*. Groupthink has been defined as "a mode of thinking that people engage in when they are deeply involved in a cohesive group, when the members' strivings for unanimity override their motivation to realistically appraise alternative courses of action."

Hawn[25] discusses how psychological concepts such as Groupthink may cause groups of people (such as project teams) to exercise poor judgment.

Just as in junior-high math class, the discomfort of confessing ignorance is heightened in the company of others, particularly peers, says Mardi Horowitz, a professor of psychiatry at the University of California, San Francisco. Indeed, the larger the audience, the more threatening and stultifying the experience — and the more likely a team member is to avoid it. It only takes one brave person to introduce the reality of a situation to break the spell of Groupthink. When that happens, everybody — from the project manager to the administrative assistant — heaves a sigh of relief.

Groupthink arises when a group's desire for agreement somehow overrides its ability to realistically appraise alternative courses of action. On deeper levels, it also accords with the human need to conform, to embrace compatibility rather than its awkward cousin, independence. There is a comforting cohesiveness and belonging in the little word "we," and an absence of both in dissent.

In group situations, many will slip into Groupthink, and it is a special concern in meetings involving project teams. There the ideal is that all alternatives should be considered, as team members bring divergent thinking to the issues confronting them. But project teams are critical to the project and, despite their diversity, are as prone to Groupthink as any other team. The phenomenon of Groupthink was discovered in 1971 by Yale University psychologist Irving Janis, who began tracing the history of major fiascoes in decision making, from Pearl Harbor to the Bay of Pigs Invasion.

Typical Groupthink symptoms are:

■ The illusion of invulnerability: A feeling of power and authority is important to a decision-making group like a project team. The danger is that the level of confidence implicit in their position may be so high that they believe any decision they make will be successful.

■ Rationalization: Explaining away objections to a given decision or plan, often on the basis that what has worked in the past ensures future success.

■ Stereotypes of "out-groups" like media, who might be critical. The result is increased isolation.

■ Self-censorship: Sometimes occurs because some project managers might think they need full concurrence with team members; occurs equally often because they are sublimated to group loyalty or team spirit.

■ Pressure: Direct pressure is applied to those with dissenting views, sometimes with the result that members are conditioned not to believe such views. To do so might put them at odds with the group.

■ Illusion of unanimity: Eventually all the rationalizations and psychological pressures have their effect and a project team coalesces around a decision.

Years later Janis added other conditions conducive to Groupthink: a highly insulated project team with restricted access to outside feedback, a stressful decision-making context such as one brought on by monetary restraints, external pressure, or a history of recent setbacks. Many of these relate directly to project team environments and imply a need for on-going self-monitoring and training, but according to human resources consultant Karen Martyn, many boards are reluctant to do either. "The reason they resist development is that there seems to be an accepted view that…members are all knowing — that they don't need development," she says. "Many think that project managers need to realize that they are as human and as susceptible to error and Groupthink as any other humans."

Martyn believes many executive boards simply do not want to spend time or money on the development they would routinely endorse for management. Groupthink can however be countered by healthy antibodies. The project manager locates the thought-homogenizer and attacks it by creating an atmosphere of openness. Then he or she allows it to be destroyed by diversity, dissent, and vigorous debate, which, ideally, should flourish in this environment.

Sometimes external interventions help and an independent evaluator can be used to examine assumptions. This sometimes helps prevent project teams from becoming isolated. The research draws a distinction between effective teamwork and Groupthink: one cherishes individuality as part of the "we"; the other subordinates it — sometimes at huge cost.

As usual, a poet isolated the essence of both the argument and the challenge long before the advent of managerialism. Lord Byron wrote: "I may stand alone, but would not change my free thoughts for a throne."

The Emperor's New Clothes

Of course, it is not always a brave person who speaks up to enlighten project team members of Groupthink and incorrect thought processes. One only need recall the tale of "The Emperor's New Clothes," which tells the story of a king so obsessed with clothes that he was conned into buying "beautiful magic fabric." Two "very good tailors" told him that, after many years of research, they had invented an extraordinary method to weave a cloth. The resultant material was so light and fine that, as a matter of fact, it was invisible to anyone who was too stupid and incompetent to appreciate its quality. The king himself could not see the fabric, but did not want anyone to know that he was stupid and incompetent. He said, "Wow! This is fantastic!"

News of the beautiful fabric that could not be seen by stupid people quickly spread, and the townspeople urged the emperor to appear before them in his new outfit. Reluctantly, he summoned his carriage and a ceremonial parade was formed.

A group of dignitaries walked at the very front of the procession and anxiously scrutinized the faces of the people in the street. All the people had gathered in the main square, pushing and shoving to get a better look. Applause welcomed the regal procession. Everyone wanted to know how stupid or incompetent his or her neighbor was but, as the Emperor passed, a strange murmur rose from the crowd. Everyone said, loud enough for the others to hear: "Look at the Emperor's new clothes. They're beautiful!"

"What a marvelous train!"

"And the colors! The colors of that beautiful fabric! I have never seen anything like it in my life!"

They all tried to conceal their disappointment at not being able to see the clothes, and since nobody was willing to admit his own stupidity and incompetence, they all behaved as the two scoundrels had predicted.

A child, however, who had no important job and could only see things as his eyes showed them to him, went up to the carriage.

"The Emperor is naked," he said.

"Fool!" his father reprimanded, running after him. "Don't talk nonsense!" He grabbed his child and took him away. But the boy's remark, which had been heard by the bystanders, was repeated over and over again until everyone cried: "The boy is right! The Emperor is naked! It's true!"

The Emperor realized that the people were right but could not admit to that. He thought it better to continue the procession under the illusion that anyone who could not see his clothes was either stupid or incompetent. And he stood stiffly on his carriage, while behind him a page held his imaginary mantle.

SUMMARY OF PROJECT TEAM

It is valuable to understand the roles of project team members and the stages in the life of a project team. The project manager should hand select his or her team to ensure each member has the traits and skills that will contribute to success. Skills related to conflict resolution should also be sharpened.

Much time can be lost in inefficient meeting administration. The first place to start is with an effective agenda. Open communication is important. The Internet has made the world much smaller, and virtual teams are becoming the norm. The effective project manager will make use of today's technology to free up the time of team members. Time is the biggest component of cost for projects, and FFPM aims to reduce the time required to complete projects.

SELF-STUDY/DISCUSSION QUESTIONS

1. When selecting project team members, which attributes do you feel are most important? Why?
2. Have you or someone you know ever been party to the "Groupthink" pitfall? Explain.
3. Is there a relationship between the stock market crash at the turn of the century and Groupthink? Why or why not?
4. What are the advantages of affinity diagrams?
5. Share your experiences with brainstorming. What worked? What did not? What is your overall opinion of brainstorming?
6. What are virtual teams? What is a remote team? What is the difference? What are some of the barriers that must be overcome for team success in both cases?
7. Share some horror stories regarding meetings at your company. Share some successes.

PROJECT MANAGEMENT OFFICE, PORTFOLIO MANAGEMENT, AND PARTNERING

INTRODUCTION

Three project management innovations that have made great strides over the last decade are project management office, portfolio management, and partnering. The former two in particular have had significant impacts in the 21st century alone.

PROJECT MANAGEMENT OFFICE (PMO) STRATEGY, TACTICS, AND OPERATIONS

The *Project Management Journal*[26] declares that the formalization of the implementation of a PMO is one of the most significant developments in recent years. A PMO is also referred to by titles such as project office, project management center of excellence, or directorate of project management. Independent of the operational title, a PMO is the organizational entity with full-time personnel to provide a focal point for the discipline of project management.

As the 21st century began, an increasing number of organizations began establishing a PMO to support and manage their project management efforts. The functions of the PMO support the platform established by financially focused project management (FFPM), in that they cover the quantitative and qualitative areas of project management. Quantitative areas cover creation and utilization of formal tools and procedures in managing scope, cost, quality, schedule, risk, contract, integration, and environmental change. Qualitative areas cover sophistication in managing communications and in managing relationships within the team, with the client, and with vendors.

There can be considerable variation in goals of a PMO. Goals can vary in urgency and sophistication. An enterprise with a forward-looking approach to the performance of enterprise projects would have the goal of establishing industry standards by way of achieving best-in-class results. Other less ambitious objectives might be to improve divisional project management performance or simply — the most common goal — to complete a current project on time and on budget.

Implementing a PMO focuses attention on those areas of the organization's strategic direction that deal with the project management function. Of course, organizational long-range plans should include such items as reduction of project overruns, improving resource allocation procedures, and increasing the delivery speed of projects. The formality and sophistication of the PMO structure and its funding will vary widely depending on the overall goals.

Such goals include improvement of:

- Project-by-project performance
- Divisional project performance
- Organizational project performance
- Organizational project management maturity

According to the editor of *Project Management Journal*, organizational project management maturity is the most enlightened of these goals.

The benefits of the PMO include:

- Attainment of formalized and consistent project management throughout the organization
- Improvements in project performance in the areas of cost, schedule, scope, and people
- Recognition of the project management discipline
- Improvement in organizational profitability

The FFPM system recommends that these potential benefits be weighed against the costs of establishing a PMO (Figure 5.1). Such costs include the following, all of which could be substantial:

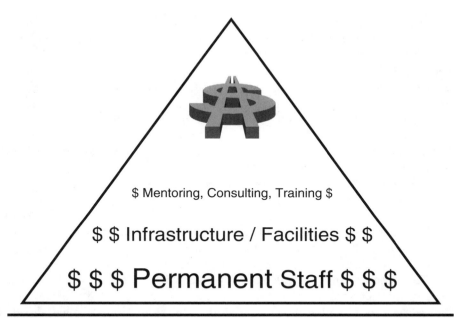

FIGURE 5.1. PMO Costs.

- Cost of a permanent staff for enterprise planning and for customized recordkeeping
- Cost of an appropriate infrastructure for this new organization, including but not limited to the underlying foundation or basic framework, facilities, location, office, computers, and equipment
- Costs associated with mentoring, consulting, and training activities

These costs depend on the size of project management staff, and therefore can be considered operational costs, and not necessarily startup costs.

The advantages of a PMO include development of tools, techniques, and principles to facilitate the implementation of quantitative performance measures for project cost, schedule, and scope.

To be sensitive to the needs and desires of the client, attention is paid to the final values of the triple constraint, in the light of justifiable and nonjustifiable variances in these constraints. Sometimes, with the misplaced hope of achieving expediency, the treatment of the people issues are forgotten or set aside during the intense implementation activities. Therefore, the tools and techniques developed and maintained by the PMO will also provide methods to deal with those seemingly nondescript areas of client satisfaction, team attitude, and team behavior.

The cost of establishing a fully developed PMO can be a major investment if the organization has never consciously paid attention to the needs of projects. On the other hand, organizations that are very sensitive to the success and performance of projects may not have to spend any appreciable additional amount of money in establishing a project office. It is entirely possible that the capabilities discussed above, as those of a PMO, currently do exist in the enterprise either separately or in aggregate; they are just not called a PMO.

Offsetting the cost of the PMO are the advantages. In FFPM, the cost of the PMO should be much more detailed than the discussion above. The cost analysis would be broken into two elements: (1) implementation costs and (2) maintenance/operation costs. The combined costs would be the total costs from implementation through a specific period of time.

The next step is to contrast the cost for establishing and operating the PMO with the savings that would result. These savings start off by calculating the cost of the functions being replaced (e.g., the prior project management system). Since these functions will no longer be performed, their cost is, in fact, a savings.

The second savings are calculated by estimating the impact the PMO will have on project success. The PMO may result in fewer failed projects. The cost/performance relationship is a variation of the relationship that has already been verified for ensuring quality and the cost of nonconformance to quality standards.

Other savings may result as well. Operations may also become more efficient, allowing projects to compress schedules and reduce related costs. The bottom line: If the PMO cannot be expected to save more than it cost, it should not be implemented. However, there is much evidence today to suggest that many companies will benefit from employing this PMO approach to project management.

A PMO's mission and objectives are met by training, consulting, and mentoring the project-related personnel, by augmenting the project teams, and by serving as a clearinghouse for project management best practices. By far, the most exciting functions of the PMO are to instill a project management culture and to facilitate the organizational recognition of the project management profession.

Improving Project Management with PMO

William S. Bates, who has more than 25 years of experience as a project management consultant, is a strong proponent of PMO.[27] Establishing a PMO is usually part of a larger effort to establish effective project management in big organizations. As with most major corporate undertakings, a successful PMO implementation must be led by senior management. Implementation includes:

- Establishing sophisticated technical and professional processes, methods, and procedures for each function of the organization
- Establishing formal project management methods and procedures that are generic to the organization and integrated to fit all of the technical and professional methods and procedures
- Defining and implementing the organization's unique project structures
- Setting up project management automated systems and tools to support the established professional, technical, and project management methods and procedures that are selected and implemented
- Instituting project management and financially focused education, training, and certification

Definitions and Considerations

A PMO should be an organizational focus point in a company for the function of project management. It ensures a consistency of approach to projects and therefore a consistency in results. The PMO is a corporate-level function that provides support, methods, procedures, systems, and policy for project management across the company. While it usually is not directly responsible for the execution of individual projects, it can be.

The organization must consider several questions when establishing a PMO (Figure 5.2):

- What will be the management level of the PMO head and to whom will he or she report?
- Will there be a project review committee? If so, what will be its relationship to the PMO?
- What will be the exact functions of the PMO?

Roles, Responsibilities, and Functions

In most cases, it is recommended that a project review committee (PRC) be established. The PRC is usually composed of senior managers representing those parts of the organization that will be affected by projects either in their execution or through the recipients of its products. The roles of the PRC could be included in another senior management committee if desired. Possible roles of the PRC could include the following:

- Provide an organizational overview of the complete project environment
- Review new project requests and plans and make recommendations
- Recommend priorities between projects
- Review on-going projects periodically

FIGURE 5.2. PMO Questions.

The roles and functions of a PMO depend on the requirements of a specific organization. A PMO could:

- Lead the transition of the organization to an effective project environment
- Manage the organization project environment
- Manage project information
- Provide support to the project environment

Within each of the primary functions listed above are several subfunctions that could be included. For example, the PMO could lead the transition to an effective project environment. In this major role, the PMO manager would establish and lead the project management transition project and manage it to a successful conclusion.

Another major function could be to manage the overall project environment. This normally is required in large organizations when the PMO is to have high visibility and impact. The major subfunctions include:

- Establish and maintain a core of senior project directors or managers who can be assigned to major projects under another part of the organization and provide coaching and consulting services to other project managers.
- Offer instructors for the project management training program.
- Provide risk assessment and post evaluation services for projects as required.

- Provide functional guidance in the career development of project managers and other project management–related staff. This is usually performed in conjunction with the human resources organization.
- Develop and have approved by the corporate executives all project management policy.

The PMO also manages all of the organization's project information. This is one of the earliest of PMO functions, where the PMO provides for the care and use of all the project information. Responsibilities include:

- Information management: Includes maintenance of the corporate project database to which senior managers are provided direct access.
- Secretariat to the PRC responsibilities, when it exists: Includes review of new project plans prior to PRC review and administration of PRC meetings.
- Provide a project archives custodian to collect project information for analysis and historical purposes.

In addition, the PMO serves a project support role, which can encompass two major areas:

1. To provide a source of project staff other than project managers. The PMO could maintain a pool or source list of professional and administrative staff available for projects.
2. To be responsible for the selection, development, and maintenance of project management methodology, procedures, and systems. Processes and systems should be consistent across the organization, and one unit of the organization should have ownership of them. That should be the PMO.

PMO Manager Requirements

The PMO manager is NOT a project manager. For a PMO to be successful, it is essential that the PMO manager have the correct skills. Similar but not identical to the project manager, the selection criteria for a PMO manager should include the following considerations:

- The management experience of the PMO manager should be commensurate with the level of the position to ensure an ability to interact with peers.
- The PMO manager must have significant project management experience. This individual should be seen in the organization as the project management specialist.
- The PMO manager should have excellent people skills, setting the example in leadership. This is an important qualification because it is people who

complete projects. The way all project managers (including PMO managers) handle people is critical to success.

■ As with FFPM, financial management skills and experience are required to provide the PMO manager with an ability to assist the organization with better management of an environment that probably consumes a large portion of the organization's budget.

■ Negotiating skills are required to achieve results with project managers as well as suppliers of goods and services that are necessary to establish and operate the PMO.

Phases of Implementation

The implementation of a PMO is usually part of a larger effort by an organization to bring it to a higher level of project management capability and competency. The following three phases are necessary to implement the PMO requirement (Figure 5.3): (1) assessment, (2) planning, and (3) implementation.

Assessment

The shortest phase is the assessment phase. It is usually completed with a set of interviews and document reviews to determine answers to the following questions as a minimum:

■ Is there active support among executive and senior management to implement the PMO?

■ What are the goals and objectives of the organization?

■ How does the organization want to manage its project environment overall?

■ At what stage of corporate growth is the organization?

■ Are the position and visibility of the PMO likely to increase or decrease over the next 3 to 6 years of the company's development?

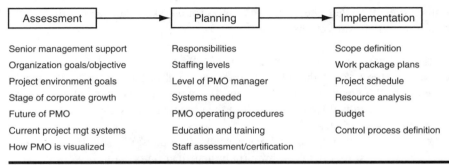

FIGURE 5.3. Phases of PMO Implementation.

- What current project management systems, methodologies, procedures, and processes exist or are planned?
- How does the organization visualize a PMO today? The planning phase has two major elements: the definition of the PMO organization and a project implementation plan for the last phase.

Planning

The PMO planning portion involves defining:

- The responsibilities of the PMO
- PMO staffing positions and levels
- The level of the PMO manager and to whom that person will report
- The systems, methodologies, and procedures needed
- The internal operating procedures required for the PMO
- The project education and training program to be implemented
- The project staff assessment and certification program(s) to be used

Implementation

The project implementation plan should contain:

- Definition of the scope, which includes the project charter and a work breakdown structure with dictionary
- Detailed work package (task) plans that describe the work, as well as identify and estimate resources
- A project schedule with resource analysis completed, which is contained in project management software
- A project budget
- A definition of the control processes to be used for the project

When the project implementation plan has been approved, the implementation phase begins. Depending on the requirements defined, the implementation phase could include the following work:

- Identification of the PMO staff
- Development of the defined PMO internal operating procedures
- Establishment of the corporate project management methodology
- Selection and implementation of project management software tools
- Establishment of the project management education and training program
- Establishment of the project staff assessment and certification program

Processes, Standards, and Methods

This performance domain involves ensuring that generally accepted and effective project management and operational reporting processes and standards are utilized to support execution across projects. It includes selecting, creating, adapting, or maintaining project tools, techniques, systems, and templates to facilitate the performance of project teams.

Professional Development

Staff development functions of a typical PMO include monitoring competency requirements on proposed and approved projects throughout their life cycle in order to ensure human resources with the needed expertise are available at the right time for the required duration. This also can involve implementing education, training, mentoring, or other developmental activities as well as designing performance evaluation and compensation systems.

Knowledge Management

Management of the organization's knowledge involves implementing and maintaining a repository of project and program information including lessons learned that can be easily harvested and result in the effective use of the intellectual capital developed across all projects for the benefit of the organization.

PROJECT PORTFOLIO MANAGEMENT (PPM)

PPM includes evaluating the value and risk to the organization of existing and candidate projects by collecting, analyzing, and maintaining summary project information needed for executive review and decision making. It also involves balancing resources between projects and assessing appropriate project management tools, methods, and processes.

Most frequently and most efficiently, PPM makes use of a sophisticated software package to analyze and maintain summary project information, and assist project managers in their evaluation of the values and risks associated with existing and candidate projects.

Information technology (IT) companies often have many software projects on-going simultaneously. As such, IT profits have benefited greatly from the application of PPM methodologies.

The Importance of Diversification

Melissa Solomon[28] writes that the idea of IT portfolio management has been tossed around academic circles only since the 1980s, and for the most part, it did not start making its way into IT departments until a few years ago.

One of the key functions of PPM is to organize a series of projects into a single portfolio consisting of reports that capture project objectives, costs, timelines, accomplishments, resources, risks, and other critical factors. Executives can then regularly review entire portfolios, spread resources appropriately, and adjust projects to produce the highest departmental returns.

One of the toughest lessons learned from Enron Corp.'s bankruptcy was the importance of diversifying the project undertaken by a company. It is nothing new, though. If you think about it, diversification has been a staple of the financial world for half a century. It is doubtful that a prudent financial advisor would recommend the allocation of 100% of one's savings to just one investment vehicle (e.g., securities, bonds, money markets). Similarly, PPM does not recommend putting "all your eggs in one basket."

Managing Projects as a Portfolio

As its name implies, PPM groups projects, allowing them to be managed as a portfolio, much as an investor would manage his or her stocks, bonds, and mutual funds. In the 1950s, University of Chicago economist Harry Markowitz wrote that a portfolio of diverse investments is more likely than individual investments to reduce risks and produce a higher rate of return. The obvious benefit of PPM is that it gives executives a bird's-eye view of projects so they can spot redundancies, spread resources appropriately, and keep close tabs on progress.

But what is most appealing to many executive managers is the focus on projects as a *portfolio* of investments. Discussions are not only about how much a project will cost, but also about the project's anticipated risks and returns in relation to other projects. This way, entire portfolios can be adjusted to produce the highest returns based on current conditions.

Since the recession began in the late 1990s, companies have been looking at the multimillion-dollar IT investments made during the past decade in an effort to determine what returns, if any, those investments garnered and what can be expected in the future.

Portfolio Project Analysis

Portfolio management helps with this analysis. Lots of details are taken and organized in an easily digestible form. Executives can see where money is spent, why projects are or are not necessary, and what resources are needed.

An increasing number of vendors sell PPM software, which dramatically simplifies the process of building a portfolio. It is recommended, though, that in the first step of portfolio project analysis companies prioritize their business strategies. Portfolios can then be assembled and assessed based on how they meet those strategic needs.

Historically, projects were approved and then managed independently. They were evaluated as a whole at the executive level only when it came time to put together annual reports. This annual evaluation is merely a balance sheet examination of projects and does not involve project potential and risks. In markets that move every day, companies need an on-going overall view so they can keep an eye on projects in real time to make sure that all of them are working together to meet core business goals.

Breaking Down the Portfolio

Once business priorities are established for each project by the company, the portfolios need to be broken down. Solomon gives the following insights into the following three project portfolios:

1. California Public Employees' Retirement System (CalPers)
2. New York–based Verizon Communications
3. Energy Northwest

CalPers includes in its portfolio all projects that last more than 30 days and 100 hours.

Verizon Communications has a series of portfolios. IT teams are assigned to different business units, and each of those teams handles a separate portfolio. So for instance, all of the finance and administrative-support projects make up a portfolio that is maintained by one manager who reports back to the CIO.

The hardest part of portfolio management is developing the metrics used to measure a portfolio's success. Ten milestones were established by Energy Northwest, a Richland, Washington–based public utility. Such milestones include a project plan approval and design work completion. Those milestones are tied to performance indicators and bonuses for project managers. If someone misses a milestone, he or she has to write a trouble evaluation report explaining why.

This reporting mechanism encourages project managers to submit information about incidents that might otherwise not be reported. Energy Northwest uses portfolio management software from Pacific Edge Software, Inc. in Bellevue, Washington.

CalPers uses stoplight reports from Bala Cynwyd, Pennsylvania–based Primavera Systems, Inc. that break metrics down into red, green, or yellow fields. If a project is about to fall behind schedule, for example, or the project team's resources are close to overrunning total budget, the report will fall into the yellow-light category, indicating the need to adjust the portfolio.

Nynex Corporation (predecessor of Verizon) was one of the pioneers of IT portfolio management, starting the process in 1992. Verizon uses a detailed set of metrics developed by its CIO and portfolio managers. Once each month, the managers and CIO review each portfolio's progress on those metrics.

An unexpected bonus of PPM is that it creates a kind of friendly competition between and among the portfolios and their cognizant portfolio managers.

While PPM is not practical for companies with few projects, its merits are considerable for companies administering many major projects simultaneously.

PARTNERING

Partnerships with Suppliers[2]

Many companies have learned that it is not always beneficial to shop around for the lowest price when seeking suppliers. Often, a supplier will bid low to get new business, with the hope of keeping the customer while it recoups its initial loss-leader pricing. When switching to a new supplier, that supplier will most likely experience a learning curve. Often total cost will exceed that of the original supplier, when including the additional effort necessary to break in a new supplier.

Establishing a special partnering relationship with a supplier benefits both parties as follows:

- Suppliers will work extra hard and pull strings (e.g., expedite schedules) for a company that has been its bread and butter in past years.
- Companies can alert suppliers to new trends and requirements in advance, allowing for smooth transitions to new processes.

The longer a supplier and company work together, the more the learning curve allows processes to become finely tuned. Procurement system refinements result in a better bottom line for both companies.

Project Partnering Process

The project partnering process[29] creates a new team-building environment which fosters better communication and problem solving and a mutual trust between the participants. These key elements create a climate in which issues can be raised, openly discussed, and jointly settled, without getting into an adversarial relationship. Through this process of teamwork and problem solving on a project, the goals of project team members and project partners are in the areas of safety, quality, schedule, budget, and disputes. The goals are for the quality of the work to be right the first time, the project to be completed on time, the final cost to be within budget, and disputes/litigation to be minimized. Both the contractor and the subcontractor benefit through the teamwork and pursuit of mutual goals. The use of formal and informal partnering techniques now has widespread use.

Team Building Outside the Company

Companies use a partnering/team-building process to encourage the most productive teamwork from project inception through conclusion. It is based on experience and practical application of transformational quality. By using this structured process, team members create a mutual strategy for communications, commitment, and follow through.

Experience shows that partnering/team building adds value to every project and creates these benefits:

- Expedited projects through open communication
- Improved quality through team commitment to quality measurements
- Increased opportunities for innovative, value-added design changes
- Improved customer satisfaction through team commitment to exceed client expectations
- Increased team camaraderie, improved levels of trust and openness

Factors That Lead to Partnering Success

Professor Paul Patterson[30] stresses the importance of the following factors (Figure 5.4) when considering establishing a partnering relationship:

1. Goodwill trust
2. Communication effectiveness
3. Affective commitment to partner
4. Dependence of partner on us
5. Marketing competencies
6. Contractual trust
7. Perceptions of partner's affective commitment
8. Cultural sensitivity
9. Investment in the partnership
10. Dependence on partner
11. Calculative commitment
12. Competence/trust

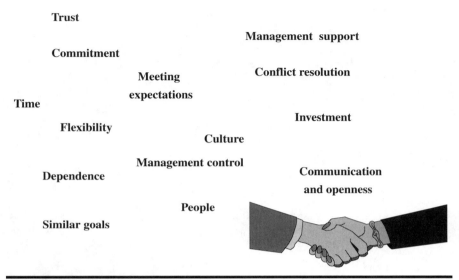

FIGURE 5.4. Factors for Partnering Success.

13. Perceptions of partner's calculative commitment
14. Likeability of partner
15. Reputation of partner

Patterson summarizes the keys to partnering success by building on the layers exhibited in Figure 5.5.

- At the center of the relationship are the partners' competencies. The partners will be looking at each other to analyze their synergistic elements.
- The layer emphasizes the partnering fit and how the competencies become viable contributions for mutual projects.
- Holding it all together are the personal relationships. This is where you find the trust, ethics, reliability, perceptions, and commitment.

Partnering and Mutually Beneficial Negotiations

The goal of partnering is to develop a long-term relationship in which both parties in the partnership prosper. In order for this to happen, negotiations must result in a win/win contract.

An example of the old school approach to negotiations was exhibited in the 1950s television series "Mr. Peepers," which starred Wally Cox as a mild-man-

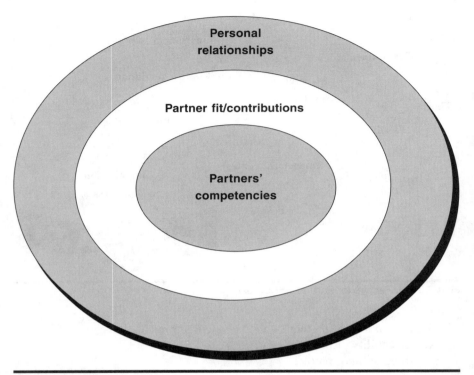

FIGURE 5.5. Partnering Success Layers.

nered schoolteacher. In one episode, Wally Cox's soon-to-be father-in-law comes home after a hard day's work and brags to the family about a real estate deal he had swung earlier that day.

"You know that old swamp way back behind the slaughterhouse?" he smirks. "I just sold it to the country club!" The "Mr. Peepers" show was shot in front of a live audience (like "I Love Lucy"), and the live audience got quite a chuckle out of that one.

But times have changed, and so too has the climate for negotiations.

Win/Win Negotiations[31]

Everyone is involved in negotiations. If someone has a need and must involve someone else in order to satisfy that need, then it is necessary to negotiate. When attempting to influence another person through an exchange of ideas or something of material value, that is negotiating. Negotiations may be involved

TRADITIONAL	WIN/WIN
Identify demands	Identify needs or issues
Present demands and positions	Present and clarify needs or interests
Present facts to support demands	Establish mutual understanding
Present counter-proposals, compromise, horse-trade for agreements	Brainstorm for options without committing to ideas generated
Decide on the basis of power, coercion, and/or threats	Decide on the best options based on objective standards
Settle on the basis of win/lose	Settle on the basis of mutual gain
Attempt to mend broken relationships later	Strengthen relationships based on commitments

FIGURE 5.6. Traditional vs. Win/Win Negotiations.

in an unlimited number of activities — selling an idea, making mutual decisions, purchasing or selling an item, securing or selling a loan, or reaching agreement on a contract. The process used to satisfy needs when someone else controls what is wanted is negotiation.

Win/win negotiations offer an alternative to the traditional adversarial negotiation process that creates winners and losers and oftentimes leaves broken relationships in a wake of mistrust. Traditional bargaining uses power, manipulation, coercion, and intimidation, in addition to a number of additional undesirable tactics to achieve the desired outcome.

Win/win, on the other hand, is a negotiation process that results in meeting the needs of all the parties to the negotiations by applying principles, guidelines, and bargaining steps that are quite different from the tactics used in traditional bargaining. Because win/win negotiations result in agreements that meet the needs of all the parties, relationships are strengthened and maintained (Figure 5.6).

The principles, guidelines, and steps of the win/win negotiation process are not difficult to learn or use. However, the process involves breaking away from the paradigms that most people are accustomed to and use to negotiate.

Trained win/win negotiators always try to conduct themselves according to the behavior appropriate to the win/win process. They are assertive rather than aggressive, creative vs. antagonistic, even if the other person is not willing to cooperate. The skilled win/win negotiator focuses on the issues involved and does not allow personalities to get in the way. If a party to the negotiation resorts to personal attacks or makes outrageous demands, the other party can bring his or her behavior under control by maintaining self-control. The win/win negotiator keeps cool under all circumstances.

The following are a few of the key behaviors essential to the win/win negotiation process:

- Separate the people from the problem: Negotiations take place on two levels — substance and process. Build working relationships; be soft on people but hard on the problems. Proceed independent of trust and do not be influenced by strong wills, manipulation, or power tactics.
- Focus on interests, not positions: Stay flexible, avoid positions, demand fairness. Find out what the other party needs and communicate what you need. Ask "Why?" and "Why not?"
- Invent options for mutual gain: Avoid premature judgment, single answers, or fixed pies to be divided between the bargainers. Separate inventing from deciding, with no commitments expected or required during this creative stage.
- Insist on objective standards: Never yield to pressure, only to principle. Be reasonable and open to reason. Look for shared interests and mutual gains. Use fair standards and procedures. Make their decisions easy.
- Select the best options: After clearly identifying the needs of all the parties, creating, exploring, and evaluating the options based on objective standards, select the options that best address the needs of all the parties to reach an agreement.

Preparing for Negotiations[32]

Partnering does not mean that one should be a pushover in negotiations. On the contrary, the lead estimator and chief price negotiators should do their homework and already have an idea of the other party's position. Here are some basic principles and issues to consider when preparing for negotiations.

Know the Interests at Stake

Negotiators need to understand what their party really wants. Knowledge of how these interests meet underlying values and needs is essential to achieving satisfying results from negotiations, because then negotiators can develop clear priorities on which to fashion flexible positions and strategies.

- Interests are often based on short-, medium-, and long-term objectives. Because you will be relying on instructions from your government or agency, ask for briefings that fill you in on how these negotiations fit into the overarching goals of your government's foreign policy and your state's long-term interests. If it appears that short-term objectives contradict long-term interests, you may want clarification on which to prioritize and which can be more flexible.

■ Develop succinct preparation materials so that you can clearly articulate key points and are thoroughly briefed on the other party's situation. If all members of the delegation team are similarly briefed, coordination will be enhanced and you will be able to work effectively together.

Avoid Taking Inflexible Positions

In many cases, negotiators become trapped by their own uncompromising demands for specific outcomes. These can include demands over select concessions, such as territory or political representation, as well as general political and ideological stances that prohibit open communication. When entering into negotiations, it is important for each side to remember that its positions do not necessarily reflect its true interests.

■ Negotiators should ask themselves why certain positions were taken in the past, and what basic needs those positions were attempting to address. Often demands for territory or political autonomy are actually driven by fundamental needs for security, group identity, or reputation.
■ Positions become entrenched over time and may no longer accurately reflect current conditions.
■ While firm demands may be easy to make, often with the encouragement of home constituencies, they become increasingly problematic over time. Negotiators may be unable to explore more promising solutions at a later date if they have committed themselves to hard positions earlier in negotiations. Successful negotiations often require a great deal of flexibility.
■ Even valid positions often represent only one possible solution to a problem, and may inhibit creative thinking about other ways to address the issues.

Understand Your Best Alternative to a Negotiated Agreement (BATNA)

This is a way to rethink the "bottom line" that has traditionally guided positional negotiations. It involves assessing the relative strengths and weaknesses you and the other party bring to the negotiation table. Often people assume that negotiating power is determined by access to resources and military strength. Yet relative strength in negotiations is often determined by each party's perceptions about viable alternatives to reaching agreement. It is therefore important to remember the reason why you are negotiating and what would be the alternative to a negotiated settlement. If the alternative is good and involves little cost, your party is in a strong position and may better satisfy its interests through a non-negotiated approach. If the alternatives are limited and costly, your position is weak and it will be very important to ensure that the negotiations come to a satisfying conclusion.

- Consider the importance of your relationship with the other party when developing your BATNA. Sometimes developing a mutually satisfying solution through a negotiated process will greatly enhance the long-term working relationship, even if other interests could be realized more easily through a nonnegotiated approach.
- Awareness of your BATNA will keep the negotiations from developing into an independent process, thus avoiding the problem of negotiating for negotiation's sake. This awareness will also keep your party from settling on an agreement for agreement's sake if it does not satisfy your interests. You know that you can always pursue your other alternatives.
- Develop and improve your BATNA. The first step in improving your BATNA is to create a list of actions your government could conceivably take if no satisfactory agreement is reached. Once these fall-back strategies have been identified, steps can be taken to improve some of the more promising plans and prepare a plan for what actions would be needed to implement them. Once you clearly know your BATNA, all other negotiated agreements can be judged against it.

SELF-STUDY/DISCUSSION QUESTIONS

1. What does a PMO do that is not already a part of the traditional project team?
2. What is the difference between a leader of the PMO and the project manager? What are the similarities?
3. What are the phases of PMO implementation? Discuss.
4. What is project portfolio management? What are its advantages?
5. What is involved in portfolio project analysis? How is it performed?
6. What is "partnering"?
7. Explain the project partnering process.
8. What are some of the key factors for partnering success? Why and how are they important?
9. Explain the layers of a strong partnering relationship?
10. What is good about a win/lose negotiation? What is harmful?
11. What are the benefits of a win/win negotiation?

Web
Added
Value™

Free value-added materials available from the
Download Resource Center at www.jrosspub.com.

6

PROPOSALS AND PRICING

INTRODUCTION

When a company makes a commitment to initiate a project, resources need to be allocated. As such, an analysis should be performed to determine if the project would have a favorable impact. This analysis would utilize the financially focused project management (FFPM) tools presented in Chapter 11.

Often a project requires the support of subcontractors. In order to evaluate and establish prices for major subcontracts, a Request for Proposal (RFP) is prepared and sent to potential contractors. An RFP may also be called a Request for Quotation (RFQ).

Every company needs to determine the prices at which it sells its products or services. Many of the procedures that apply to proposing new contracts can also be applied to the process of establishing prices. In either case, there is usually an historical basis to forecast cost associated with the new product or project.

COMMERCIAL CONTRACTING[33]

Perhaps the greatest virtue and challenge of doing business in this country is that the U.S. is a big market — 50 states, each with its own set of laws. But commercial dealings are interstate, crisscrossing the borders. Hence, the Uniform Commercial Code (UCC) has been adopted by most states to assure that companies performing commercial contracting are all playing by the same set of rules.

One of the most significant portions of the UCC is that which has to do with the heart of business: buying and selling. It explains what can and cannot be done, what rights companies have and what risks they run, how to structure transactions, and how to avoid disadvantageous consequences. Indeed, if thoroughly studied and understood — and applied with practical sense — the UCC is a commercial contracting road map by which an enterprise's operations can be advanced and protected.

The UCC explains the following areas that are the foundation of commercial contracting:

- Essential contract elements
  a. Contract offer
  b. Contract acceptance
  c. Lawful purpose
  d. Required definiteness
  e. Capacity of parties
  f. Consideration (no free rides)
  g. Mutual obligations
- Law principles
  a. Absence of UCC
  b. Applicability under UCC
- Types of contracts
  a. Parties involved
  b. Nature of work
  c. Form of payment
  d. Special nature
- Who can do what
  a. The problem of "authority"
  b. Employees
  c. Agents
  d. Independent contractors
  e. Actual authority
  f. Incidental authority
  g. Apparent authority
  h. Authority by ratification
  i. Principal's liability
  j. Agent's liability
  k. Termination of authority

Commercial Contracting and the Homeowner

If a homeowner was planning to build an addition to his or her house, a routine similar to the following might be used:

1. Generate a list of potential contractors. To accomplish this, the home-owner may:
   a. Consult with friends/associates to obtain information about their similar experiences and their referrals.
   b. Check the telephone yellow pages and various advertisements.
   c. Call the Better Business Bureau for recommendations and access its records regarding the list of potential contractors.
2. With the list, begin scheduling appointments, at which time the following will be provided to each contractor:
   a. The specifications (floor plans/blueprints, etc.) of the planned addition.
   b. Desired construction schedule.
   c. Other preferred terms of the contract.
3. At these meetings, the homeowner also should discuss the contractor's performance history (including a review of past jobs, a list of references, etc.).
4. At the end of each appointment, the homeowner should have a feel for the contractor's qualifications and potential employability. As such, a request may be made to the contractor to provide a quote containing the following:
   a. Definition of work to be performed (special materials should be itemized).
   b. Proposed schedule (time frame in which work is to be performed).
   c. The complete cost.
5. Other terms/conditions as specified at the appointment (such as terms of payment, eventual customer selection of accessories, etc.).

By following a routine such as that outlined above, the homeowner would obtain a quote that provides necessary data to narrow the field down and eventually provide a sound basis for selection of a contractor for this job.

The process whereby a contractor prepares a quote is similar to the government contracting process of preparing a proposal, as discussed next.

GOVERNMENT CONTRACTING

Just as commercial contracting has the UCC, so too does government contracting have the Federal Acquisition Regulations (FAR) (Figure 6.1). The FAR was established for the codification and publication of uniform policies and procedures for acquisition by all executive agencies. It consists of rules and regulations governing business with the federal government. These regulations govern all aspects of federal procurement.

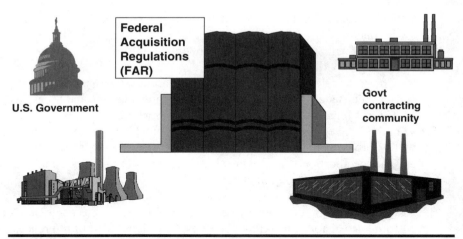

FIGURE 6.1. Federal Acquisition Regulations.

Full-Cycle Corrective Action[34] presents an excellent overview of government contracting and proposal preparation. It points out that for most government procurements, the U.S. customer often is not fortunate enough to have several options when choosing a contractor for many of its projects (e.g., space shuttles). This is because the expertise to develop and manufacture sophisticated equipment is understandably in limited supply. Therefore, in order for the U.S. to maximize and continuously improve on existing technology, there is often one prime contractor in the best position for cost-effective performance. With only one legitimate contractor capable of developing and manufacturing a desired item, the company is designated a sole source. In sole-source contracting, the primary goal of negotiations is a fair price for a safe, reliable product.

There are basically three types of proposals that the contractor uses to pursue government contracts (Figure 6.2):

1. New business, solicited: The government asks the company to develop and manufacture a product with certain specifications. For example, the Navy determines that the U.S. needs an antiballistic missile system with a range and accuracy far superior to any previously built. Desired specifications are generated, the contractor contacted, and via the acquisition process discussed below, a contract eventually results that might call for the development of the system and delivery of 16 such missiles.

2. Follow-on: This second type of contracting calls for the procurement of more of the same product that has already been fully developed and purchased in a previous fiscal year. Using the example above, a follow-on

- Three Types of Proposals

  - Follow-on contracts

  - New business

  - Unsolicited

FIGURE 6.2. Government Contracting.

contract would allow for construction of 16 more of the same antiballistic missiles in the next fiscal year.
3. New business, unsolicited: The contractor asks the government customer if it would be interested in a new product with certain specifications.

A proposal is required for all three of the above procurement types.

The RFP Process

The proposal preparation flow (Figure 6.3) begins when the proposal leader issues a planning document, which performs the following functions: (1) defines the proposal requirements, (2) schedules significant events requiring accomplishment prior to contract award, and (3) contains the concurrences of customer and contractor representatives.

- Requirements
- Meeting:
  - Resp. orgns
  - Contracts
  - Accounting
  - Program office
- Schedule / proposal

Focus on ground rules, premises, and schedule!

FIGURE 6.3. Proposal Preparation Flow.

- Labor (hours)
- Nonlabor (dollars)
- Rates

FIGURE 6.4. Estimated Cost.

When a requirement for a proposal is established, the finance organization prepares and distributes quoting instructions to all involved company organizations including the program office, contracts (legal) organization, finance organization, and operating branches/divisions/departments (the groups that will actually be performing most of the profit-generating effort directly related to delivery of the product).

Raw Resources

The operating branches/divisions/departments are the organizations that prepare the initial estimate of costs (Figure 6.4) at the raw resource (lowest) level. For a manufacturing process, the raw resource is *hours,* to which labor and overhead rates are applied. The nonlabor (e.g., subcontract) raw resource is *dollars*, to which only an overhead rate (e.g., procurement burden) is applied.

Proposal Components

In addition to the estimated cost, the proposal includes the following three sections (Figure 6.5):

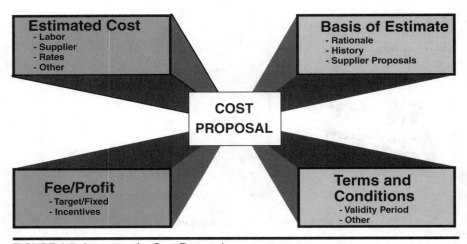

Estimated Cost
- Labor
- Supplier
- Rates
- Other

Basis of Estimate
- Rationale
- History
- Supplier Proposals

COST PROPOSAL

Fee/Profit
- Target/Fixed
- Incentives

Terms and Conditions
- Validity Period
- Other

FIGURE 6.5. Anatomy of a Cost Proposal.

1. Fee (cost reimbursable contract)/profit (fixed price): Incentive/profit components not included in the estimated cost.
2. Terms and conditions: Validity period of proposal, economic price adjustment clauses, warranty, information, deliverables, period of performance, insurance, liability.
3. Basis of estimate: Justification for raw resource requirements, discussed in detail next.

BASIS OF ESTIMATE

The basis of estimate is where the contractor justifies the price quoted for a project. It states in raw resources the lowest level at which costs can be identified. There are primarily four types of basis of estimate, as follows:

1. Engineering estimates: A staff of engineers performs analyses of what steps will be required to accomplish each proposed task.
2. The same as in previous projects: This method is used when quoting a task that has been quoted and/or negotiated previously. For example, the customer may want to order four more cable assemblies. These cable assemblies are identical to some for which a price was established in an earlier procurement. In such an example, a similar unit cost would be quoted. The proposal analyst often factors in a slight deviation in unit cost for reasons such as the following:
   a. Learning curve: The personnel performing this task have become more adept at its performance and, as such, can accomplish it more efficiently.
   b. Rate factor: An increase or decrease in the number of units being procured may sometimes justify a change in cost because of the *economies of scale*. Favorable economies may exist with increasing quantities when assembly line approaches can be utilized, and suppliers offer discounts for ordering greater quantities of components. Conversely, unfavorable economies exist when quantities decrease.
3. Similar to previous projects (with complexity factors/normalizing): For example, the customer may want to order more cable assemblies, but with a different connector. A previous proposal is used as the starting point, from which adjustments are made to tailor the quote to the new requirement.
4. Percentage of effort: Some tasks will relate so closely to other activities that this method will be appropriate. For example, the inspection of certain manufacturing processes historically may be at a level of 60% of the

manufacturing hours (e.g., 10 manufacturing hours requires 6 hours of inspection). Such percentage-of-effort relationships are inspection hours contrasted with total manufacturing hours, tooling hours contrasted with total manufacturing hours, and computer-assisted design and documentation hours contrasted with total design hours.

FFPM, while encouraging *shortcuts* and performing as efficiently as possible, discourages shortcutting in the estimating process, when the potential exists for underestimating. Using a percentage of manufacturing hours for deriving inspection resource requirements does not always consider the potential for failures, which could change inspection requirements without impacting those of manufacturing (e.g., test equipment failures). Similarly, tooling hours will not necessarily remain a constant factor of manufacturing hours. It has been said that he who takes a shortcut sometimes takes twice as long.

Elements of an Historical Basis of Estimate

There are three basic requirements for utilization of an historical basis of estimate:

1. Identify scope of effort and the specific task quoted
2. Identify historical source programs
   a. Develop audit trail
   b. Disclose documents, tapes, etc.
   c. Reflect date of documents
   d. Page numbers
   e. Work order/work authorities
   f. Actual hours
3. Establish relationship of historical programs to new programs
   a. Identify program or contract
   b. Develop complexity factors
   c. Discuss the similarities
   d. Explain why history is applicable
   e. Provide rationale for factors

Engineering Estimates

There are four basic requirements for utilization of engineering estimates to support resource proposals:

1. Disclose similar programs
2. Explain reasons for not using historical data

3. State that the estimate is based on judgment only
4. Break the task down to the lowest practical level of detail

Bid/No Bid Criteria

Obviously, a company should not bid on every RFP that comes its way. To do a creditable job on any RFP, a significant amount of resources must be expended. Therefore prudence must be exercised to ensure such expenditures are made when the likelihood of a contract award actually exists. Bid/no bid criteria refers to the guidelines an enterprise uses to determine if it will respond to an RFP.

Summarized below are some of the key points made by Michael Asner,[35] who presents excellent insight into what needs to be considered when establishing *bid/no bid criteria*.

Saving Time and Money

- Preparing a proposal requires the investment of considerable time and effort — this equates to money.
- Making an early business decision on whether a particular contract is worth chasing can lessen the needless expenditure of valuable resources.
- The bid/no bid decision should be made before one word of the proposal is written and should be done in a systematic manner that takes into account the needs, goals, assets, and limitations of the company.
- Before the first RFP arrives, the decision-making procedures should be in place and functional. Otherwise a company risks squandering resources on proposals that should not be pursued at the expense of proposals that have a much better chance of winning.

Basic Bid/No Bid Concepts

- Bidding on a contract has far-reaching, long-term implications. It is important to reach the right decision, as this decision contributes to the health of the organization.
- If the company decides to "no bid," it may lose an opportunity to make money, enhance its reputation, gain major experience, and cement a relationship with a major new customer.
- If the company decides to "bid," this requires a serious and expensive commitment to create a proposal that will influence the buyer's view of the organization. Additionally, it is a commitment to perform work that could possibly stretch the firm's skills and capabilities and damage its reputation for excellence.

- Bid decision is often based on an informal assessment. A no bid can result from any of the following organizational shortcomings: (1) a senior person being out of town and unable to review the RFP, (2) lack of a project leader to do the analysis, or (3) lack of timely access to marketing or legal staff.
- A company should develop formal decision-making policies to avoid ignoring key factors.
- Projects should be chosen that align with the organization's goals.
- The ability to complete the work and make money must be carefully analyzed. This analysis is sometimes performed too quickly and results in the wrong decision. Caution is required in making this critical decision. An inappropriate or technically deficient proposal can do serious harm to a firm's reputation in the marketplace and its prospects for future business.

The Process

- Organizations that write many proposals often have formal systems (i.e., bid/no bid criteria) for deciding when to bid. These systems usually use a standard form to document the reasoning behind the decision or employ a standard checklist of key considerations.
- Many organizations consider the bid/no bid considerations at several different times during an RFP life cycle: once before the RFP is issued, again when the RFP is received, and a third time after the proposal outline is available.
- The RFP typically goes to a senior person who performs a cursory inspection to see if it even warrants consideration. Unfortunately, major opportunities are lost when this senior person is too busy to review them. An RFP can sit for weeks on the executive's desk awaiting disposition. This inaction invariably leads to a no bid as time runs out.
- The initial review usually takes approximately an hour. The purpose is to determine if the RFP seeks products and services that the firm provides. Selection criteria are also reviewed to determine the basis for the award. Some firms have made large, expensive efforts to differentiate themselves from their competitors. Such firms know they can compete on service, value, price, support, or technical merit and will not bid if their strengths are not reflected in the evaluation criteria.
- The RFP sometimes imposes conditions that a firm is unable to meet. For example, an RFP may require a project manager who has led a similar project. In this instance, the company should either refrain from bidding or consider hiring a person who fits this requirement.

- A brief review of mandatory contractual conditions is also included in the initial review. Some of these conditions may be unacceptable to the firm.
- If the RFP passes preliminary review, much more analysis and consideration is necessary before making a decision to bid. The initial review does not deal with current workload or availability of key personnel. This review specifically concentrates on the business opportunity identified in the RFP.

How to Decide?

- Whether the analysis is an informal discussion among a few key people or a formal procedure, the information required for making a bid/no bid decision is the same. However, formalizing the procedure improves decision-making quality by ensuring that key factors are not ignored.
- One method for analyzing the bid/no bid decision uses a checklist of questions. Such questions are tailored to both the vendor's and buyer's organizations. Some representative questions and concerns include "Is this a strategic opportunity?" and "Is it in line with the business?"
- Proposals for new work should be consistent with the firm's business plan. The nature of the work, product, or service; the type of customer; and the marketing spin-offs should reflect the business the firm wants to be in.

Considerations include:

- Is this opportunity consistent with the business plan?
- Is it a market or a customer that is wanted?
- What are the potential benefits to the company?
- Does this RFP provide an opportunity to expand into new areas or acquire a new type of expertise?
- What are the potential risks?
- What experience will be gained from this contract in the long term?
- Will this contract lead to others? Will this contract provide an advantage in future competitions?

Can the Competition Be Won?

Firms sometimes submit bids as a marketing exercise, to announce their presence in a new area. Most often, though, firms submit proposals to win new business. Winning requires market intelligence, resources, skills, insight into the customer's needs, and knowledge about other potential bidders. Winning also requires skills and knowledge about proposal writing and the related strategies and techniques.

Considerations include:

- Is there enough time and skill to write a winning proposal?
- What skills are required for the project?
- Are the people available?
- Are the resources available?
- Does a relationship already exist with the customer?
- What is the company's reputation within the customer's organization?
- How significant are those requirements that cannot be met?
- Who else will be competing for this work? Who is the incumbent? Is someone already wired into the contract?

Can a Profit Be Made?

Pricing is a key consideration. Few proposals intentionally provide a discounted price to win the award. Most proposals are intended to generate a predefined profit.
Considerations include:

- What is the budget for this work? Is it realistic? Is price a major factor in the evaluation? Can the company compete on price alone?
- Is the investment affordable?
- Are there other approaches or opportunities that would be more profitable at less risk?
- Can the requirements be met now without major hiring or change?

Is the Risk Manageable? Can the Company Do the Job?

If the work represents good business, if the contract can be won, and apparently a profit can be made, can the risks be handled? Have key assumptions been identified and are there ways to mitigate risks?
More specifically:

- Is the proposed solution technically feasible?
- Can the specifications be met? Are they within the company's capabilities (required skills, people, and resources)? Are some requirements new?
- Can the schedule be met? Is there enough time to plan and execute the work?
- What is the probability of overrunning the budget, finishing behind schedule, or not finishing at all?
- Will this new work place other current projects at risk?
- Do the management structure and skills exist to take on this work?

The above narrative can assist a company in establishing its bid/no bid criteria.

Security Guidelines for Cost Proposals

Classified information is data that are not available to the general public. Classifications include sensitive, secret, and top secret. Government contractors have very specific procedures for handling situations in which classified data may be utilized. A general review of such procedures is contained in the following guidelines:

1. Data used in the basis of estimates should be kept unclassified.
2. When classified historical data are essential, such data must be:
   a. Coordinated in advance with high-level management in the contractor's finance organization
   b. Cleared by the appropriate program contracting officer (customer)
3. Stated as "An estimate based upon classified historical information which can be verified through recognized security channels and appropriately cleared Government Contractor Audit Agency personnel."

Audit Checklist for Basis of Estimate

A basis of estimate, which meets the following audit checklist, should comply with Public Law 87-653 and FAR:

1. Verify that the scope of work or task description is accurate in comparison to the work breakdown structure dictionary or to the proposal statement of work.
2. Ensure that the labor justification worksheets conform to accepted formats (should be specified in company procedures).
3. If at all possible, historical data must be utilized. If so, the following should be provided:
   a. Project or document name of historical program(s).
   b. Work order/work authority of historical program(s).
   c. Document number where historical data are located.
   d. Date of document.
   e. Page number of document.
4. If complexity factors or percentages are used:
   a. Factors or percentages must be supported with factual data.
   b. A description of the analysis performed and logic for decision to use the approach.

5. Where engineering judgments are used:
   a. All potential problems should be investigated for similarities.
   b. Explanation must be provided as to why historical data from a similar program were not used as comparative data.
   c. A rationale must be developed that can easily be followed by an auditor.
   d. Estimated raw resources must be related to the program.
   e. Schedule.
   f. Standard bidding conventions must be used.
   g. The task must be described at the lowest practical level.

One of the most important parts of the basis of estimate process is ensuring high quality and accuracy of the data contained therein. For example, if math errors exist, the entire basis of estimate lacks credibility. The customer may award a very high score on a technical proposal, but find the cost proposal deficient because of the lack of rationale for the cost. This deficiency could lower overall proposal scoring and contribute to a loss.

Other Proposals and Negotiations

In contract administration, the project manager needs to be aware of other types of proposals and negotiation activities (see Figure 6.6).

* Termination Proposals
Receive notice of termination — issue stop work notice — termination committee develops cost of termination & terminated cost — submits and negotiates termination proposal.

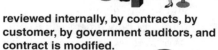

* Variance Proposal
Letter requesting estimate at completion and variance proposal is

reviewed internally, by contracts, by customer, by government auditors, and contract is modified.

* Final Incentive Proposals
Business unit collects data related to cost and incentives, and prepares final incentive proposal.

FIGURE 6.6. Other Proposals and Negotiations.

Termination Proposals

When contract work is terminated for the convenience of the government, the cost of work accomplished prior to the termination plus costs incurred complying with the termination are allowable costs, which are reimbursable. The contractor is also entitled to a fee, in accordance with the FAR.

Variance Proposals

Variance proposals are prepared on cost reimbursable contracts when funding is different from that authorized by contract and needed to complete authorized work. In other words, a variance proposal is prepared when the contract is completed and there has been a cover overrun or a cost underrun. Periodically, during the period of the contract, a report of resources expended to date and an estimate and justification of resources needed to complete the authorized work is prepared. This estimate to complete (ETC) is compared to contract funding to ascertain if additional funding is required to complete the work or if excess funds have been obligated by the contract. That comparison is the basis of any needed variance proposal.

Final Incentive Proposal

Cost, schedule, and/or performance incentive parameters are established and negotiated at the time of prime contract negotiation. During the life of the contract and incentive measurement period, actual performance is monitored to these parameters. Final incentive outcomes are forecast and reported to management and the government customer. An interim incentive fee proposal is submitted to the customer, usually at the end of a measurement period or final delivery, requesting interim incentive funding. A final incentive fee proposal is submitted when all costs are recorded on the contract and all overhead rates are incorporated.

What to Include in an RFP

Community Banker presented a short lesson on what should be included in an RFP from a bank for upgrades or installation of new technology.[36] It is suggested that the technology RFP be quite detailed but it should not request unnecessary information. A typical document may be 5 to 10 pages.

Some items that should be included are listed below:

1. Information about the bank, including mission statement, asset size, market area, customer demographics, number of ATMs and branches, volume at each, etc.
2. Information about current technology use, with specifics about current vendors, business volume, current system in use, etc.

3. The bank's specific technology needs and any timelines or goals that have been set
4. A request for vendor information, including annual reports, financial statements, key staff biographies, etc.
5. A request for complete information about the vendor's products and services that can meet the bank's needs
6. A request for references from current clients
7. The specific evaluation criteria
8. The vendor's costs to implement the solution

In addition, the bank may want to include 5 to 10 key essay questions on the items that are of the most critical importance.

Keys to a Successful RFP Response

Tom Sant[37] offers tips for achieving excellent results when submitting an RFP response, including evaluating an RFP and creating an RFP that stands out among others. He says that many companies feel that responding to an RFP is "a business necessity and sometimes business nightmare." This is because the preparer may feel swamped by the logistics of a complex RFP, and wonder if the message being delivered is effective.

While completing the RFP, the preparer needs to perform the following three tasks:

1. Focus on what matters the most.
2. Respond to the questions and requirements of the RFP, a process sometimes referred to as answering the mail.
3. Develop a persuasive business case that shows why the contracting officer or decision maker should select this offer.

Evaluators looking at RFP responses are trying to find answers to these basic questions:

1. Are we getting what we need?
2. Can the vendor really do it?
3. Is it a good value?

Content that does the following is necessary for an effective proposal:

1. **Presents a clear understanding of the needs, problems, and issues or mission objectives:** It is important not to confuse detailed technical

requirements of an RFP with the organizational needs. The RFP focuses on how the buyer wants something done from a technical perspective, but it does not explain why the buyer needs it. By understanding what is happening in the buyer's organization, this section can explain how the buyer will benefit and what kind of capabilities it will gain.

2. **Recommends a specific solution that addresses the needs and favorably impacts the buyer's operation:** An outstanding proposal will recommend solutions, and not merely describe products or services. "We recommend…" can be "magic words" with a solution that links the specific features of a product or service back to the needs.

3. **Provides evidence that the company presenting the proposal is competent to do the job on time and on budget:** It is not uncommon for government-issued RFPs to specifically request information about corporate capabilities, as well as the resumes of key people and team members. Additionally, data regarding prior experience, management plans, project timelines, references, and other information are also expected.

4. **Uses differentiators to support a compelling value proposition:** One of the most common parts of an RFP response that is left out is the value proposition. This is the section that describes what separates the RFP submitter from the competition. It is needed to show how those differentiators add value to the solution. Buyers in the know look for advantages in total cost of ownership, life cycle cost, return on investment, or other measures of impact. Effective value propositions are quantified and displayed graphically.

Evaluating the RFP

Proposal evaluation should include the following three stages:

- **Stage 1:** The evaluator first checks to see if the RFP complies with the technical standards. Submissions are eliminated if they do not meet the minimum requirements. In most cases, the instructions were not followed precisely.
- **Stage 2:** Next, the proposal is perused in broader terms. The evaluation focuses on usability, reliability, and maintainability. Will the final product meet the specification, doing what is wanted, and can it be implemented easily?
- **Stage 3:** The final stage has the evaluators reviewing the costing in detail, looking at acquisition costs, other cost elements, plus any opportunities to reduce cost by reducing scope (eliminating or reducing quoted activities).

The RFP may limit a persuasive message, but it does not prevent offering one. It is important to focus on the decision maker's key needs in the "executive summary." The "executive summary" is the place where differentiators are emphasized along with the value of the proposing company's solutions and experiences.

Standing Out

Employing the following two suggestions will make a proposal rise above the others being considered:

- The inclusion of a compliance matrix will make an RFP response easier to use and score. This is a table that lists proposal requirements and shows how and where the RFP response has met them. This helps the evaluator, because it helps determine any problems and gives a visual guide to how well the proposal matches the requirements.
- Another advantage can be gained by creating a simple table with four headings:
  1. Question/requirement: The number of the RFQ requirement or question is placed here.
  2. Level of compliance: This column is used to indicate whether the proposal exceeds, fully complies, partially complies, or takes exception to the requirement.
  3. Page number: This column refers the evaluator to the location of the detailed answer.
  4. Comments: This is the place to highlight a strong differentiator and discuss a value-added aspect of the solution. This column could also contain an explanation as to why a requirement is being questioned.

Pricing

As discussed earlier, the primary goal in negotiations in sole-source contracting is to arrive at a fair and equitable price for the contracted effort. The technique of pricing is used to convert raw resources into the total cost price.

The rates applied to raw resources in pricing are known as forward pricing rates. A forward pricing rate agreement is usually negotiated separately with the customer on an annual basis. This saves the costs of negotiating overhead on each individual contract. A partial listing of forward pricing rate possibilities follows:

1. Direct employee labor salary/wage rates
2. Overhead rates

3. G&A rates
4. Allocated direct costs/computer service center costs: These may include such costs as common quality services, common minor material, and computer-related expenses.

TYPES OF CONTRACTS AND CONTRACTING MODES

There are basically two types of contracting modes associated with contracting: fixed price and cost reimbursable contract. The modes of contracting are directly related to the amount of cost risk to the contractor. These modes are outlined below.

Fixed Price (FP)

This type of contracting is far and away the most common type. It implies that there is a set (fixed) price that the customer will pay for contracted effort, except as allowed by clauses in the contract.

FP is the mode often chosen when contracting for routine tasks, such as automobile maintenance or house painting. A profit margin should be included in the quoted price.

The FP mode can be broken down further as either a firm fixed price contract (most common) or as a fixed priced incentive contract.

Firm Fixed Price (FFP)

FFP has the greatest financial risk to the contractor. Under an FFP contract, the company is obligated to perform until completion of the task regardless of cost. Say, for example, that a contractor's quote for $20,000 was accepted and a contract was signed. The contractor may find later that an error was made in the quote, and that the job will cost him more than $20,000. He is contractually obligated to do the job even though he will lose money.

Fixed Price Incentive (FPI)

An FPI contract offers the possibility of the final price paid being higher or lower than the negotiated target cost. This results from prenegotiated incentives.

Incentives can be positive and negative. With a cost incentive, if the company spends more than the negotiated target cost, the customer will pay a portion of the increased cost. On the other hand, if the contractor spends less than the contracted amount, the customer will pay less.

Incentives also may be based on performance to schedule and technical objectives.

Cost Reimbursable Contract (CRC)

CRC provides the most protection and is used most often when there is a maximum technical risk. For example, Motorola Company may contract with Lockheed Martin to design a missile that can launch satellites into orbit for a high-tech communications project. Because the specifications of this type of launch have never been achieved before, Lockheed Martin will most likely not be willing to enter into such a contract in an FFP mode. This is because potential problems could cause the expenses associated with such a project to skyrocket and result in tremendous losses. If Lockheed Martin engineering was having difficulty meeting the contract specifications, a CRC contract would protect it from spending more than it would be paid.

Unlike FFP contracting where all contracted tasks must be performed, CRC performance is only required up to the limitation of cost specified in the contract. This limitation is usually the target cost of the contract.

There are three types of CRC: CPFF, CPIF, and CPAF, as discussed below.

Figure 6.7 displays how the risks are shared in the various contract modes. On a CRC, the customer (government) pays for all allowed costs over the negotiated target price. On the other side of the figure, it is shown that the contractor pays the entire cost of an FFP contract. In the middle are the various negotiated incentives.

The cost reimbursable mode can be broken down further as a cost plus fixed fee, cost plus incentive fee, or a cost plus award fee.

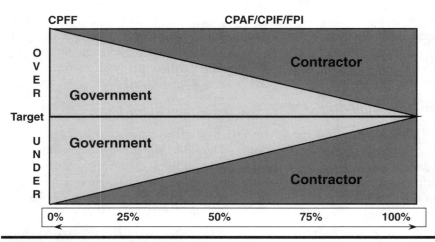

FIGURE 6.7. Negotiable Share Ratios.

- Cost plus fixed fee (CPFF): CPFF ensures the company of a fixed fee, regardless of final cost outcomes.
- Cost plus incentive fee (CPIF): The CPIF mode increases or decreases fees based on cost, schedule, or technical performance.
- Cost plus award fee (CPAF): The CPAF mode increases fees based on a subjective evaluation of the final product performed by the customer's award fee team.

SELF-STUDY/DISCUSSION QUESTIONS

1. What is the UCC? What is the FAR? How are they similar? How do they differ?
2. What is an RFP? What should be included in an RFP? Explain the process.
3. What is a basis of estimate? Why is it needed?
4. Discuss the elements of an histrorical basis of estimate.
5. Why is it important for a company to establish bid/no bid criteria? What risks are involved in establishing such a criteria?
6. What are some of the security guidelines for cost proposals?
7. Who would use an audit checklist for basis of estimate? Why?
8. Explain the concept of "pricing."
9. What is the difference between a fixed price contract and a cost reimbursable contract? Which is the safest for the contractor? Which is safest for the customer?

*Free value-added materials available from the
Download Resource Center at www.jrosspub.com.*

PROJECT PLANNING

INTRODUCTION

The project has a sponsor and the project leader takes the reigns. The next step is confronting the whole matter of project planning. A very big part of project planning is establishing factors and decision points to enable effective risk management (Chapter 8). The key elements of project planning are summarized below.

PROJECT PLANNING STEPS AND THEIR SEQUENCE

- Initial project-related questions to answer
- Determining scope: Establishing project scope, elements, project priorities
- Establishing project plan elements
- Work breakdown structure (WBS) development
- Expansion of the WBS into work packages, action plans, and responsibility charts
- Creating budgets: Cost concepts, cost estimation
- Make vs. buy decisions
- Value engineering
- Estimating project cash flows
- Networks: Work package to network, types and characteristics of networks
- Activity time calculation methods
- Improving time estimations
- Developing schedules: Schedule representations of networks
- Resource planning
- Addressing and planning for project constraints: Types of constraints
- Assigning project work: Responsibility matrix

- Multiproject scheduling and resource allocation
- Optimizing and leveling resource allocation
- Assessing potential risks
- Determining risk factors
- Contingency planning
- Establishing management reserves
- Sharing risk with customers

PROJECT PLANNING — INITIAL QUESTIONS

Important planning decisions[38] are made when answering the following project-related questions:

- How will the project plan be developed?
- Who will develop the project plan, and how involved will the customer be?
- What project management software package will be used, if needed?
- Who on the project team will be responsible for entering the planning information?
- Who will have input on the plan?
- What specifically are the roles and responsibilities of each team member?
- How will team members be informed of decisions?
- Understanding that cost, time, and quality (performance) are all important, what are the priorities?
- What are the deliverables of the project planning process?
- What format is appropriate for each of these deliverables (e.g., milestone charts)
- Who will approve and certify at the completion of each deliverable?
- Who receives each deliverable?

PROJECT PLANNING — SCOPE

The scope of the project (also known as project scope) is simply all the work that is required to satisfy the requirements of the contract. Deliverables are the tangible product or items that will be provided in return for payment. The contract defines the deliverables, and, based on the contract, the contractor needs to establish project scope elements and project priorities.

Contracts vary greatly in the amount of detail they provide in describing deliverables. For example, a contract for a $25,000 landscaping project may be 10 to 20 pages, listing each plant, with many sketches, designs, and detail about such other items as planters, sprinkler systems, decking, lighting, sound systems, and security devices.

On the other hand, a contract to build a $65,000 in-ground swimming pool may consist of only a few pages, with one page of financial terms, a second page with an engineering drawing showing dimensions, and one or two other pages discussing tile, coping, and decking.

The point is that contracts often leave out a lot of the project detail that is necessary to develop a comprehensive project plan. That is why the project manager needs to develop project plan elements, which break the project down into manageable pieces.

MAKE–BUY DECISIONS[39]

Almost any product or service available in the marketplace today involves inputs of one kind or another: raw materials are turned into subcomponents, subcomponents are then assembled to form finished products or are used as an input to some kind of service, and so on. However, few companies have all the resources and expertise required to fulfill all of these functions.

Sooner or later, a firm generally has to rely on other firms to supply at least some of these inputs. The question, though, needs to be asked, "What tasks and functions should be performed in-house, i.e., within the firm, and which ones should be relegated to outside suppliers? For those tasks that it chooses to outsource to other firms, what type of relationship should be developed with the supplying companies? These questions point to a recurring set of issues that are collectively referred to as "make–buy decisions."

A single make–buy decision in and of itself may not seem to be of great consequence to a company. Among the many components and services that a firm uses to generate revenues, relatively few are singularly of critical importance to the firm's immediate survival or success. But the aggregate of these decisions effectively defines the scope of what a company is and is not doing. In other words, the resolution of make–buy questions defines the boundary of the firm.

WBS DEVELOPMENT

As discussed in Chapter 2, WBS development establishes — to the greatest detail practical — the pertinent details of how the company is going to accomplish the goals of the project. Without sound planning activity, the potential for potential problems is greatly increased.

Ted Leemann[10] notes that, almost daily, the media report on dramatic cost overruns in projects from IT systems to small rail systems to the International Space Station. The reason? Organizations are not using cutting-edge project management techniques that could help them focus resources more efficiently. One such technique is the use of the WBS. The discussion on the WBS below is based on information compiled by Mr. Leemann, the executive director for project management with Management Concepts, headquartered in Vienna, Virginia.

The WBS

Project management methodology bridges the gap between company strategy and individual projects, between setting goals and achieving those goals. Its most fundamental tool is the WBS, which breaks a complex, challenging project into levels of manageable components and tasks. The goals of the WBS are to focus and allocate resources more efficiently, facilitate scheduling and budgeting, and keep the project on track. Managing projects using a WBS reduces the confusion people tend to experience when they rush from one task to another without understanding how all the tasks fit together.

It has been said that the WBS is the key tool to relate data structures and reporting structure.[40]

Reports can be shown simply, even though the structures that create the basis for reports could be numerous and complicated. Regardless of the level of computer implementation, any proposed solution must have:

- A developed WBS, in order to identify sources of information and to relate this with information needs
- Skill-area–oriented and –independent data structures, in order to distribute responsibility for data and to maintain data competently
- Identical scope identification for all data structures, in order to be able to summarize different data structures into a base for performance measurement
- Maintenance of scope identification by project managers, in order to control interfaces among data structures
- Maintenance of a communication management plan at the project level, in order to provide communications needs of the stakeholders

Figure 7.1 illustrates a simple WBS for the first stage of constructing a house. The project is broken down into components at the subproject level (foundation, plumbing, framing), each of which is aligned to specific tasks. For example, task one for "foundation" might be grading; task two could be concrete work. Each successively lower, more granular level identifies specific

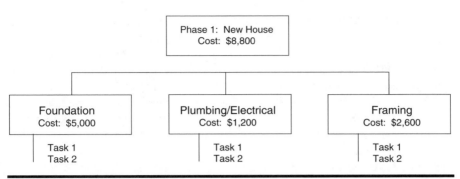

FIGURE 7.1. Construction WBS.

tasks, assigns them to individuals, and allows management to allocate resources to bring them to fruition as appropriate.

Developing a WBS should be fairly simple. One of the most difficult operational challenges is to define what a task is. When is it too big or too small? Where is the line drawn between one task and another? One technique is to view a task as a mini project, with a finite duration and a specific deliverable.

The WBS should be oriented toward what the final product is supposed to be. It specifies precisely what each task should deliver. A key factor is that the sum of all the components of the complete WBS chart should equal the project in its entirety. The tasks at a lower WBS level must describe 100% of the tasks necessary to accomplish the next higher level.

Taking Control

In a WBS, a project's individual segments can be controlled and measured in their contribution to the ultimate completion. Organizations derive substantial benefits in many areas.

Project subtasks can be assigned accounting codes to track actual time spent by component and actual cost associated with the component including manpower, raw materials, and other resources.

At the lowest levels of the WBS is where one could find specific accounting codes (e.g., cost accounts). These are the numbering codes discussed in the previous paragraph. The company should create a budget for every task that is summarized at the cost account level.

For example, if a person is installing a sink in the master bathroom, and it takes 3 hours to accomplish this task, 3 hours would be assigned to that accounting code. When reviewing performance measurement reports, the 3 hours charged to this code could be contrasted against a budgeted amount of 2.5 hours. This would alert program management to the possibility of a cost overrun.

In many companies, separate offices independently track project costs and schedules. The cost accounting organization collects the data that provide management with budget status, not whether the project is on schedule. The project scheduling organization knows whether a project is on schedule, but is unaware of budgetary performance. By the time leadership discovers that 60% of budget has been spent but only 20% of the work accomplished, it is too late to avoid at least a 40% cost overrun. With a WBS, a project manager tracks both costs and schedules to establish the project's "earned value" (see Chapter 9).

Milestones

A WBS assists in establishing the critical path, which is the shortest sequence of project activities. This clarifies the major milestones for completing the project on time and on budget. Without it, management attention can be diverted to an alleged crisis that, since it is not on the critical path, may not actually detract from performance on the project. Such a diversion may waste resources and efforts on a noncritical component while allowing a vital segment to slip unrecognized. The WBS helps management stay focused because it prioritizes tasks and lays the groundwork for computing and managing a critical path. The WBS makes the duration of the project measurable, and performance can be tracked to schedule.

Lack of focus also brings the temptation to add functions and capabilities to a project that are not part of its specification. Employees keep tweaking components and incrementally changing the project without realizing the ripple effect and potentially harmful impact on schedule and budget. The result can be titanium-plated cell phones that can communicate with Mars. Even the software industry, which updates programs on a continuous basis, assigns cut-off dates for the publication of versions. Without change control management or specifications change management, managers can lose sight of the project and it may never be completed.

The WBS and Historical Data

The various tasks performed in different projects are often similar. Use of a WBS for projects accumulates historical data helpful for the estimation of duration, resources, cost, and effort of future projects.

Accurate estimates can also help a company maintain a competitive edge in a marketplace where costs and time to market are critical. Experienced project management organizations use the WBS as a framework for planning and bottom-up cost estimating. Coding their accounts relative to the WBS enables them to compare actual cost data to original estimates, which in turn helps with future cost estimating and forecasting.

Experienced project managers know that a WBS does not limit their options, but instead offers the control they need and helps their employees understand how they fit into the process. It cuts through the confusion of misdirected activities and takes employees beyond cogs in a wheel. They see the big picture and the reasons behind seemingly scattered tasks.

When employees have a clear and focused understanding of their work, they are less likely to miss deadlines. This represents a significant operational advantage. One advantage of this is that employees will often take the time to do it correctly rather than taking the time to do it over. While project management was developed as a discipline separate from the quality movement, it is clear that the two work well together. The smartest people do project management with an eye on quality tools, and the WBS is one that is quite important.

Improves Communication

A WBS identifies all tasks in the project, thus allowing a clearer understanding of the essential information that must be exchanged to stay on track. The WBS is also a valuable communication tool that helps everyone understand how complex the project is and understand the roles of others.

Without that clarity, it is easy to digress and lose focus. Pointless meetings to discuss nonessential elements contribute to a sense of frustration. Without a clear project plan in place, people who are asked to perform a task often wonder what they really are supposed to do.

Controls Workflow

The lowest level of the WBS provides the basis for specifying 100% of the activities and tasks on the schedule. As such, the WBS ensures that 100% of the work is accounted for on the schedule. The WBS provides the structure that facilitates the monitoring of progress on individual tasks. This provides the opportunity to analyze which project components may necessitate corrective action.

Project management is the science that ties products and services to bottom line results. It is adaptable and scalable to any project, from planning a retirement party to building the Hubble Space Telescope. Project management using a WBS improves project performance in terms of communication, accounting, schedules, budgets, and workflow because it clarifies responsibilities and connects all elements of a project.

Developing a WBS

By decomposing a project into manageable parts, managers can shift resources while maintaining a focus on overall business objectives. The steps to developing a WBS are shown below.

- Analyze a specific project to fully understand all of its specifications.
- Brainstorm tasks to be performed, beginning at the top and working down to lower levels of details and tasks. Be sure to capture all deliverables, including implied requirements, in the project statement of work.
- When there are several options for ways to complete tasks, the financially focused project management decision-making process should be employed to make the most cost-effective decision. Break down the major requirements or high-level tasks followed by supporting tasks for each major requirement.
- Group tasks into a logical sequence.
- Assign names to tasks that describe the activity and connote action using active verbs (design, develop, complete, etc.).
- Determine level of detail by complexity, risk factors, and critical nature of tasks.
- Organize tasks in a logical order to facilitate management.
- Establish tracking methods for each task (e.g., Gantt charts, schedules, update meetings).
- Determine criteria for success.

After the WBS has been developed with sequence and duration of activities in place, it is possible to determine the project's critical path. While a WBS itself does not sequence tasks or determine their duration, it forms the basis for developing that information. Once tasks are established, one can begin the process of putting them in order. In some cases the sequence is predetermined; in others, it is a matter of strategic choice. When a project has a tight time frame, for example, performing many activities simultaneously can shorten the total calendar time. However, it may drive up the number of workers needed at any given moment and may increase communication risks.

Every project involves many external and noncritical tasks, which are not on the critical path because time and resources lost by slippage in one can be made up in another. The scheduling of critical path activities, on the other hand, is inflexible. If one takes longer than planned, the entire project will take longer.

Monitoring Progress Against Schedules

One of the best ways to monitor progress is to break the WBS down into levels that are no larger than one reporting period. A middle manager who has a weekly reporting period leverages WBS levels that are 40-hour or 40-FTE (full-time equivalence) increments for given tasks. Senior management tracks performance at a higher level, perhaps quarterly. The idea is to avoid having a weekly meeting with nothing ever being reported as "complete." When many tasks with short duration are budgeted, only three reports are possible: (1) the task has not yet begun, (2) it is in progress, or (3) it is finished.

These reports must match funds expended to time expended in the earned value (Chapter 9) computation. Dealing with measurable increments, it is easy to take timely corrective action if a task cost $500 and took 5 days when it was scheduled to be completed in 3 days and cost only $150.

EXPANSION OF THE WBS INTO A WORK PACKAGE, ACTION PLANS, AND RESPONSIBILITY CHARTS

Responsibility for accomplishing the first-level tasks is usually assigned to various project team members who are asked to develop their own action plans for each task. These plans are usually termed second-level plans. The individual plan components of each second-level action plan can be divided further, sometimes into third-level and even fourth-level plans. The process continues until the lowest level tasks are determined, and they are called "work packages."

Work packages can be monitored on milestone charts with scheduled dates to accomplish each. The milestone chart graphically displays key work package milestones on a linear calendar scaled to the project. Figure 7.2 represents a multiyear project, and displays months across the top. A solid vertical line is drawn to show the current data, while bars are filled in to denote progress. As can be seen in this chart, one work package (PDS Machines Relocation) started early.

Projects of shorter duration may have a time scale of weeks or even days.

Responsibility for completing work packages, as the lowest level of measurable work, is assigned to project team members. These responsibilities can be visually displayed in a responsibility chart.

Figure 7.3 is a simplified linear responsibility chart.[41] This chart shows responsibilities for work packages associated with the planning process. This being a simplified chart, it does not show all the tasks required in the planning process, but it does give a general idea of the purpose and function of the responsibility chart.

The first column lists tasks that need to be accomplished. The subsequent columns list the titles of the individuals with responsibilities relating to the tasks. Responsibility is classified at six levels:

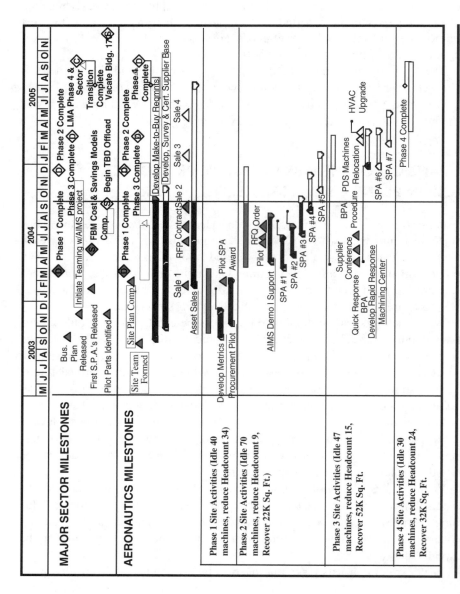

FIGURE 7.2. Milestone Chart.

	Director of Operations	Project Manager	Engineering Manager	Manufacturing Manager	Software Manager	Subprogram I Manager	Subprogram II Manager	Marketing Manager	Resource Manager	Service Manager
Establish project plan	6	1	3	3	3	4	4	4	2	4
Define WBS		1	3	3	3	3	3	3	3	3
Establish engineering specs		2	1	3	4			4		
Establish manufacturing specs		3	4	1	4			4		
Establish marketing plant plan	5	5	4	3	4			1		
Establish time schedules		1	1	1	4	4	4	4	3	4
Establish software specs		3	4	4	1			4		
Prepare labor estimate		3	1	1	1	4	4		2	4

1 Actual responsibility 3 Must be consulted 5 Must be notified
2 General supervision 4 May be consulted 6 Final approval

FIGURE 7.3. Responsibility Chart.

1. Actual responsibility
2. General supervision
3. Must be consulted
4. May be consulted
5. Must be notified
6. Final approval

As would be expected, actual responsibility for cost and schedule estimates lies with the functional managers, while final approval rests with executive management (e.g., director of operations).

Responsibility Matrix (Planning)

Everyone with responsibility for an aspect of the project should also have responsibility for the corresponding budget. The responsibility matrix displays responsibilities.

In a large project, some people may have some role in the creation and approval of project deliverables. At times, this is pretty straightforward, such as one person writing a document and another approving it. In other cases, there may be many people with a hand in the creation, and others that require varying levels of approval.

For complicated scenarios involving many people, it can be helpful to have a responsibility matrix that is tied to deliverables. This helps set expectations and ensures people know what is expected from them. For example, do the members of the steering committee approve the business requirements document? The matrix lays it all out.

Figure 7.4 presents a simple responsibility matrix that is tied to deliverables for effective project management. On the matrix, the different people, or roles, appear as columns, with the specific deliverables listed as rows. Then, the intersecting points are used to describe each person's responsibility for each deliverable. Suggested responsibility categories are A, approves the deliverable; R, reviews the deliverable; and C, creates the deliverable. Usually there is only one person who is responsible for creating a deliverable, although many people may provide input.

In Figure 7.4, the project definition is created by the project manager; approved by the project sponsor, functional manager, and steering committee; and reviewed by the project team. The business requirements are created by the project team, reviewed by the project manager and the functional manager, and approved by the project sponsor and steering committee.

The purpose of the matrix is to gain clarity and agreement on who does what, so you can define the columns with as much detail as makes sense. For instance, in the above example, the project team could have been broken into specific people, or the person responsible for creating the business requirements could have been broken out into a separate column. After the matrix is completed, it should be circulated for approval. If it is done in the planning process, it can be an addendum to the project definition. If it is created as a part of the initial analysis phase, it should be circulated as a separate document. The ability to gain clarity is vital for the matrix to be effective. It must reflect what people's expectations and responsibilities are. For instance, if the sponsor delegated

	Project Sponsor	Functional Manager	Project Manager	Project Team	Steering Committee
Project Definition	A	A	C	R	A
Communication Plan	A	R	C	R	A
Business Requirements	A	R	R	C	A
Status Reports	R	R	C	R	R

FIGURE 7.4. Responsibility Matrix.

the approval of business requirements to a subordinate, then that fact should be represented on the matrix for all to see and approve. On the other hand, if the sponsor agrees that he or she will approve the business requirements, then, in fact, his or her approval is required, not that of a subordinate who was delegated the responsibility.

Examples of responsibility codes are as follows. Your project may define different codes, as long as you explain what they mean so that people know what the expectations are for them.

- A: Approves the deliverable
- R: Reviews the deliverable (and provides feedback)
- C: Responsible for creating the deliverable — could be C (1) for primary, C (2) for backup
- I: Provides input
- N: Notified when a deliverable is complete
- M: Manages the deliverables, such as a librarian or person responsible for the document repository

PROJECT PLANNING — BUDGETS

Budgets are a necessary part of every project and should be established prior to the start of work. If formal project go-ahead has been given (e.g., contract award), budgets are established on an interim basis. Budgets can be formalized and made definitive once a valid agreement is reached with the customer or internal management.

Before funding is allocated to the responsible management to cover the expenses related to the project (e.g., performing organizations, vendors, materials and supplies), such funding restraints as those listed below are considered:

1. Government appropriations and funding fences
2. Management reserve
3. Undistributed budget

Government Appropriations and Funding Fences

Government appropriations are divided into three major categories:

1. Research and development (R&D): R&D appropriations cover many phases of activities ranging from basic research to stopping short of full-scale production.

2. Investment: Investment appropriations are commonly referred to as procurement funds.
3. Operations: Operating funds are open for 1 year while R&D funds are open for 2 years. Investment or procurement funds have different time frames depending on the times being procured.*

The contractor cannot move funds between appropriations, and this limitation is termed a *funding fence*. The term *different color of money* is sometimes used to refer to the different appropriations under which effort is negotiated.

Management Reserve and Undistributed Budget

Before funding is distributed (i.e., made available) for the performance of work, the finance organization, in conjunction with program management, determines the funding to be set aside as either management reserve or undistributed budget.

Management reserve is that portion of the total contract budget that is withheld by the contractor (i.e., not distributed) for management control purposes. Contractors normally withhold management reserve for the following two reasons:

1. To motivate managers to do the job at a lower cost than negotiated: Instead of distributing the entire budget for the contract work authorized, a certain amount may be withheld as management reserve. Management's effectiveness is evaluated in part by its performance to budgets. As a result, management diligently tries to accomplish its tasks within the budgets distributed to it. The withholding of a management reserve in this sense provides an incentive for management to reduce expenditures.
2. To bank a contingency fund: Management reserve also provides budgeting goals for unanticipated program requirements that will impact future effort. Historically, most government contractors can determine for each contract the cost of problems and other program requirements that were unknown at the time of contract award. Using this as a valid history, after each new contract is negotiated, an amount of that contract value may be withheld from distribution. In this sense, a management reserve represents an amount of budget that the contractor feels eventually will be needed before contract completion, but does not know on what it will be spent.

Undistributed budget is budget that is applicable to specific contractual effort, but has not yet been identified to a WBS element at or below the lowest

---

* E. Hearn, Federal Acquisition and Contract Management, Hearn Associates, Los Angeles, California, 1990, p. 5.

level of reporting to the government. For the period of time that this effort remains undefined at a reportable level, it is designated as undistributed budget. Once the effort is defined at a reportable level, budget is distributed to the organizations responsible for its performance.

After management reserve and undistributed budget are set aside, the remaining funds are distributed to the organizations responsible for performance of contract work. This process is often accomplished via a funding allocation plan that is similar to a contract between program management and the organizations responsible for performing the work. Each organization negotiates funding with program management, and eventually a signed agreement is achieved.

PROJECT PLANNING — NETWORKS

The milestone chart is the primary tool for project planning. The milestones shown on the chart can be broken down into extremely small work packages. It is up to the project manager to decide if informational needs can be satisfactorily met with the milestone chart, or if another tool needs to be employed.

Another valuable tool for planning, scheduling, and tracking progress on a project is the project network.[42] The project network is similar to the milestone chart, in that it is based on data in the WBS, and it displays in graphical format the chronological flow of events. The network becomes the skeleton for the system that maintains much of the project's information that will be used by the project manager to stay abreast of project status. As such, it plays a very important role, enabling the project manager to make well-informed decisions regarding schedules, performance, and cost.

Figure 7.5 presents a simplified rollup of network plans into the WBS chart. Networks are built using nodes (squares, rectangles, and boxes) and arrows (e.g., dotted, dashed). The node (rectangle) displays a task or activity, and the arrow shows the dependency and project flow. The task portrays one or more subtasks that require increments of time.

Project Network Construction

Project networks have their own nomenclature, which includes the following terms:

- Activity: A component of the project that requires time to accomplish. Activities almost always consume resources as well (e.g., labor hours, subcontract dollars). Occasionally there will be an activity that does not directly consume funds, such as waiting for government approval for a new drug. However, time spent waiting can also be considered an indirect

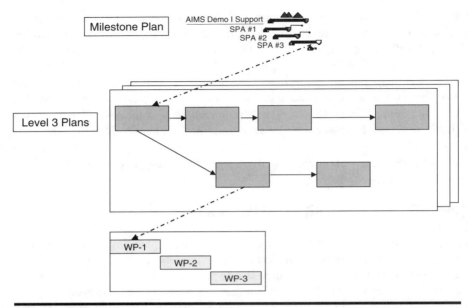

FIGURE 7.5. Network Plan Rollup.

expense, because profitability can be greatly affected by when the product is released for sale.

- Burst activity: An activity that has more than one activity or task following it, and is depicted by a box with more than one dependency arrow flowing from it.
- Critical path: The path (see below) within a network that dictates the fastest time at which the entire plan can run. This path runs from beginning to end such that if any activity on the path is delayed by an amount t, then the entire network function is delayed by time t.
- Destination: This is sink node or stopping point for a timing analysis path.
- End-point: A node that acts as either the driver to begin a path or a destination to end a path.
- Event: Represents a point in time when an activity is started or completed. It does not consume time. This is merely the starting or ending point (destination).
- Merge activity: An activity that has more than one activity immediately preceding it, and is depicted by a box with more than one dependency arrow flowing to it.
- Path: An ordered set of nodes identifying a logic flow pathway through a network. A path may consist of a single net or a grouping of related nets and components.

■ Parallel activities: Activities that can be accomplished simultaneously. This is done to reduce overall project time. It may also be done when a new system is being established to replace an older system. In such a situation, the project manager may schedule both systems to operate in parallel. By so doing, results can be compared to ensure that the new system is functioning properly before shutting down the old system.

■ Task and subtasks: These terms are used as activities in the WBS, and networks are broken down to the lowest level, eventually yielding the lowest measurable work packages.

Project Network Development

The fundamental rules for developing project networks include the following:

■ The typical flow for networks is left to right.
■ An activity cannot begin until all preceding connected activities have been completed.
■ Each activity should have a unique identification number.
■ The numbering system should flow consistently in a logical manner (e.g., an activity identification number is larger than any preceding activity).

There are four main approaches used to develop projected networks:

1. Activity-on-node (AON)
2. Activity-on-arrow (AOA)
3. Activity-in-box (AIB)
4. Gantt charts

All of these methods except for the Gantt chart conform to the previously discussed format for project networks, in that they utilize both nodes and arrows. AON uses a node to depict an activity, while the AOA diagram uses arrows to symbolize activities.

In the 21st century, the AON method has become a widely accepted approach for project network planning.

Activity-on-Node Network

Figure 7.6 presents the activity precedence for AON networking. Arrows show the dependencies among activities between the boxes. The activity in the preceding box must be completed before the activity designated by the following box can begin.

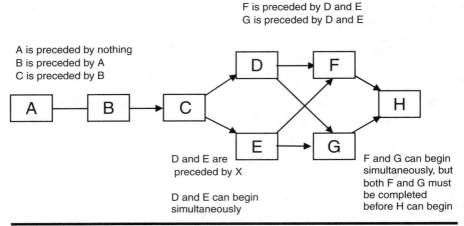

FIGURE 7.6. Activity-on-Node Networking.

Activity-on-Arrow Network

AOA incorporates consideration for time. It displays how long it takes to complete each activity as well as the entire elapsed time for the project. With this approach, the arrow itself symbolizes the activity.

Activity Duration Estimates[43]

One of the big differentiators between the milestone chart and the project-on-node network plan is that the milestone chart offers a date-driven schedule for when the milestones should be completed.

In order to plan such a schedule, it is necessary to determine how long each activity will take, from the time it begins until it is finished. An AOA diagram (Figure 7.7) presents the duration between tasks, the sum total of which equals the time required to complete the project.

Duration time is defined as "the total elapsed time," which includes the time for the work to be done, plus any associated waiting time.

Waiting time is an important consideration. Many activities are dependent on the completion of other events and activities. For example, the "preparation for shipping function" cannot begin until the product is manufactured and completes final inspection, and the exterior of the house cannot be painted until it is constructed.

In the simplified example shown in Figure 7.8, Burt's Bakery is planning to bake a magnificent wedding cake. The AOA network diagram shows the activities, their interdependencies, and the time estimate for each.

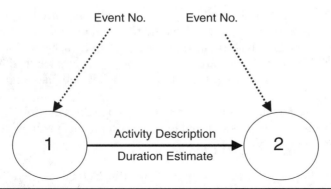

FIGURE 7.7. Activity-on-Arrow Diagram.

Based on the diagram, can you tell the duration time for the entire process, from beginning (mixing the cake) to the end (icing)? The entire duration is 180 minutes, or 3 hours. This time is important for scheduling the availability time for the ovens, mixing equipment, and chefs; 3 hours is NOT, however, a good basis for determining the cost of the cake (see Chapter 6).

Activity-in-Box

The AIB format of network diagrams contains the following information:

■ The activity title appears in the top half of each box.
■ The activity number is shown in the lower left-hand corner of the box. Activity numbers should be unique to each activity in the project and arranged in a consistent and logical manner (e.g., numerical order).
■ The name of the individual performing the activity is listed directly below the activity title. When there is no one performing hands-on labor for an activity, the name of the person who last worked on the project is used, unless the work-in-process has been turned over to the next person

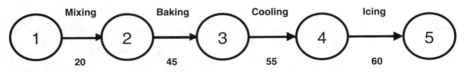

Minutes for each activity to bake a wedding cake

FIGURE 7.8. Activity-on-Arrow Planning for Burt's Bakery.

in the process. For example, one of the activities that needs to be scheduled for a floor-varnishing project is the time it takes for the varnish to dry. This is because the furniture must not be moved back onto the newly varnished floor until the varnish dries. For instances such as this, usage of the centered area below the activity box is discretionary and could even be left blank.

■ The activity duration is shown in the lower right-hand corner of the box. This time component is stated in the lowest practical unit of measurement (e.g., hours, days, weeks).

Again using a simplified example from Burt's Bakery (Figure 7.9), one quickly realizes that Mick is a very important part of the wedding cake project. Not only is Mick responsible for mixing the batter, but Mick also keeps an eye on everything in the oven, with responsibility for removing the cakes when baked and placing them in the cooling area. The cooling area is where Toni picks up the freshly baked cake (after it has cooled). In the final activity, Toni works her magic, icing that cake into a beautiful work of art.

Figure 7.9 can be summarized as follows:

■ Activity 1: Mick mixes batter — 20 minutes
■ Activity 2: Cake bakes — 45 minutes
■ Activity 3: Mick removes cake from oven for cooling — 55 minutes
■ Activity 4: Toni ices cake — 60 minutes

Who Should Do the Estimates?

In most instances, the best person to estimate the time to complete an activity is the person who will be responsible for its completion. This person most likely has the most experience and will have a good idea, based on history, of the time requirements.

Another good reason for having the person responsible make the estimate is that it generates a commitment from that person and avoids any bias that may

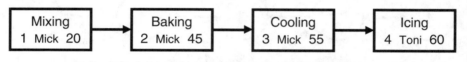

FIGURE 7.9. Activity-in-Box: Burt's Bakery.

be introduced by having one person make the duration estimates for all of the activities.

Major projects such as the Space Station or the Hubble Space Telescope are extremely large and span many years, with thousands of people employed. In such cases, it is not practical for the actual person responsible for different tasks to perform the estimates. The companies that support such major projects have highly trained and skilled staffs of contract estimators.

Teams of estimators support the major organizations (e.g., engineering, manufacturing, inspection, logistics, procurement, remote operations). Each team has access to a dedicated database that houses historical cost and schedule data for all projects completed in the past 20 years.

From these data, it is possible for the estimator to develop fairly accurate cost estimates. The estimator is in frequent contact with management in the area of the estimate and incorporates its input into the final estimates. These estimates, which are approved by executive management, are not only used in the proposals for future contracts but are also utilized to support the various schedules that are used to monitor performance.

GANTT CHARTS[44]

In the late 1910s, Henry L. Gantt, a pioneer in the field of scientific management, developed the Gantt chart. Gantt charts meaningfully display schedule representations of project activities. They are similar to milestone charts in that they use horizontal bars on a calendar-type schedule to show activities and/or resources along with the anticipated dates for start and completion of each task or tasks or usage of the resources. The Gantt chart, however, contains other important data for project management.

The Gantt chart is the standard format for displaying a schedule graphically. It consists of a horizontal bar chart with time as the horizontal axis and either resources, jobs, or orders as the vertical axis. Individual operations are displayed as horizontal bars in the chart, indicating the time at which the job begins and ends. Many variations on the Gantt chart exist to display additional kinds of information.

Before computers, Gantt charts were drawn physically on paper, but in the 21st century, there is abundant computer software that greatly simplifies this detailed task.

Figure 7.10 is a resource Gantt chart that might be used at Burt's Bakery. The vertical axis represents the various resources (e.g., ovens, mixers, refrigerators) that are necessary to bake a wedding cake.

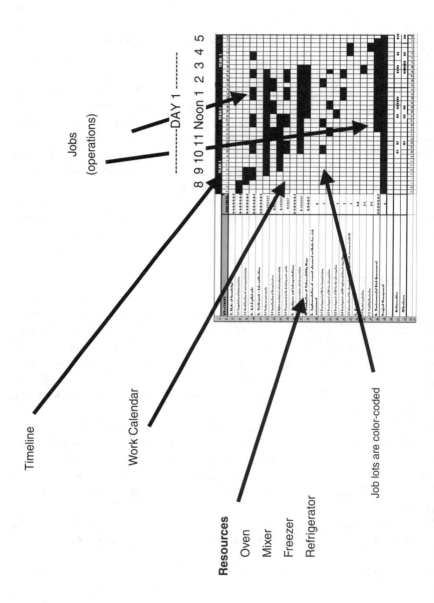

FIGURE 7.10. Burt's Bakery Resource Gantt Chart.

A number of important elements of the Gantt chart are visible in this image:

- **Resources:** Resources are displayed on the left side of the Gantt chart as colored bars marked with their resource codes (Mixer1, Packer1, etc.).
- **Timeline:** At the top of the Gantt chart, you can see the continuous time-line. For Burt's Bakery, the timeline for the project to bake a wedding cake, the timeline is displayed in the lowest practical unit of time, which is the hour. In most cases, the timeline for a Gantt chart displays days, weeks, months, and years, with the days and days of the week marked for clarity.
- **Work calendar:** The gray shaded areas in the Gantt chart represent the time periods in which each resource is available to do work. Unavailable time (e.g., downtime while the oven is cleaned or the mixer is washed) is shown with a plain white background. Bigger projects include such occurrences as vacations, routine calibration and maintenance of equipment, lunch breaks, maintenance breaks, etc.
- **Jobs (operations):** The colored bars in the body of the Gantt chart represent the individual jobs or operations that have been scheduled. From the position of the job on the Gantt chart, you can see which resources the job has been assigned to, when the job is scheduled to start and end, as well as the job's setup time and whether the job will be suspended over any unavailable time periods. The text on the colored bars conveys additional information, such as the job code, the item being produced, and the quantity being produced. For Burt's Bakery, the oven is tied up for 1 hour while the cake is baking. The mixer is scheduled for 0.5 hours to mix the batter.
- **Production lots (orders):** Though not applicable for this Burt's Bakery example, if Burt is working on 20 wedding cakes simultaneously, the chart displays jobs belonging to the same production lot or order.

Features of modern software Gantt charts include:

- Dragging and dropping jobs
- Changing the work calendar from pop-up menus
- Resizing rows and columns with the mouse
- Zooming in and out
- Jumping to other displays and master tables
- Customizing the text displayed
- Customizing color-coding schemes
- Customizing the display order of resources
- Filtering the resources that are displayed
- Displaying tardy jobs in a special way

- Displaying broken constraints in a special way
- Displaying set-up time
- Displaying lines representing precedence constraints between jobs

Gantt charts, when prepared using the software packages of the 21st century, offer the project manager many tools to ease and enhance project management functions.

SELF-STUDY/DISCUSSION QUESTIONS

1. What is project planning and what are the steps?
2. What are some of the initial questions a project manager should ask when starting the planning process?
3. What is the difference between management reserve and undistributed budget?
4. What are activity-on-node, activity-on-arrow, and activity-in-box network planning? How do they differ? Under what circumstance would a project manager utilize each?
5. What options does a project manager have for getting project duration estimates? When might one option be selected over another?
6. What is a Gantt chart? Have you even used or seen a Gantt chart at your place of work? What was the project? What information did it contain?

Free value-added materials available from the
Download Resource Center at <u>www.jrosspub.com</u>.

8

ASSESSING PROJECT RISKS AND POTENTIAL IMPACTS

INTRODUCTION

Risk refers to future conditions or circumstances that exist outside of the control of the project team that will have an adverse impact on the project if they occur. A current problem is an issue that requires attention immediately, while a risk is a potential future problem that has not yet occurred.

Successful projects[45] occur when the team attempts to resolve potential problems before they occur. This is the art of risk management. A reactive project manager tries to resolve issues when they occur. A proactive project manager tries to resolve potential problems before they occur. Not all issues can be seen ahead of time, and some potential problems that seem unlikely to occur may in fact occur.

However, many problems can be seen ahead of time. Risk management is a proactive process that is invoked to attempt to eliminate these potential problems before they occur, and therefore increase the likelihood of success on the project.

There is a concept of opportunity risk or positive risk. In these instances, the project manager or project team may introduce risk, to try to gain much more value later. For instance, the team members may spend time to relocate together because they think the close collaboration will result in productivity savings over the life of the project. This is an example of intelligent risk taking. However, in this step, it is assumed that the risks we are managing are negative risks. They need to be addressed so that the underlying potential problem does not occur.

No project planning process is complete until a very thorough analysis is made of project risks and their potential impacts. Assessing and managing risks is necessary to guard against project catastrophes.

THE BASICS[46]

Effective risk management requires all four of the following steps for assessing and managing risk:

- Identification of potential risks
- Quantification of risks
- Developing a response to risks
- Risk response control

Identifying risk is an on-going activity. The first time to perform an initial risk analysis is prior to bidding on the project. The fact that the project is not in the planning stage assumes that benefits outweighed costs and potential risks in the initial analysis. A more formal risk assessment should take place after the entire project scope has been identified in the detailed plan and before starting the project.

The detailed plan is the starting point for adequately analyzing risk.

Identify Risks

There are many ways to identify risks. The most efficient means to identify risks are to: (1) review the task list and schedule, (2) brainstorm and talk with the experts, and (3) review history and/or lessons learned papers from similar projects.

Review the Task List and Schedule

The critical path on the network plan (discussed above) is an excellent place to anticipate potential problems. The following should be considered:

- Tasks for which the team has little or no expertise: The duration and cost estimates for these tasks are more likely to be inaccurate (possibly understated).
- Duration and cost estimates that are aggressive: Estimators should be asked how confident they are in their estimates, especially for critical path tasks.
- Situations where there is a limited number of resources that can do particular tasks and where those resources are fully allocated, overallocated, or may become unavailable: A human resource can become unavailable when he or she leaves the organization or because of commitments within the organization.

- Tasks with several predecessors: The more dependencies a task has, the greater the likelihood of a delay.
- Tasks with long durations or a lot of resources: The estimates for these tasks are more likely to be inaccurate.

Brainstorm and Talk with the Experts

All of the project risks may not be apparent from analyzing the project plan. It is worth the time to call a brainstorming meeting with key resources on your project. These folks should be asked where they see potential pitfalls and the most risk to the project. What is uncovered can be surprising.

Experienced project managers should be asked to review the plan. Also, people who have expertise in particular areas of the project should be consulted. For example, people who have used outside contractors should be consulted prior to using an outside contractor.

Review History and/or Lessons Learned Papers from Similar Projects

Talking with experts will almost always reveal good information to use in the risk assessment. Unfortunately, experts on every area of the project may not be available. They may have transferred to a new organization or left the company for a new job or retirement.

Fortunately, as part of the "project adjourning process" (see Chapter 4), project teams from prior similar projects may have gathered and maintained data regarding unexpected problems. They should have prepared "lessons learned" papers, which can be very insightful for new projects.

The end of the risk identification process should result in a long list of potential risks, along with historical data that will help with analysis in the next step, quantification of risks.

Quantification of Risks

The task of quantifying risks is a science of its own. There are many options available for quantifying risks. A popular approach is using the risk assessment matrix (Figure 8.1).

The risk assessment matrix begins on the left column where each risk is categorized by severity, as follows: minor, moderate, severe, catastrophic. Each level is given a weight (e.g., 1 through 4).

The next five rows are used for designating the probability or likelihood that the risk will occur. These likelihoods include: frequent, likely, possible, rarely,

		LIKELIHOOD				
Risk Assessment Matrix		Frequent A or 5	Likely B or 4	Possible C or 3	Rarely D or 2	Unlikely E or 1
S E V E R I T Y	Catastrophic 4					
	Severe 3					
	Moderate 2					
	Minor 1					

FIGURE 8.1. Risk Assessment Matrix.

unlikely. These probabilities are assigned an "alpha" weight or a numerical weight. This is the prerogative of the project manager.

Equipped with the list of potential risks, and the risk assessment matrix, the project team begins the process of assessing the risks. Basically, these assessments are either subjective or quantitative in nature. Solid historical data (e.g., failure rates) constitute the type of information necessary to make quantitative assessments.

Figure 8.2[45] presents an example of how subjective assessments can be ranked on an overall level. Subjective assessments are achieved via opinions. Opinions are used to determine the likelihood of different risks. Sources of these subjective opinions range from expert opinion (preferred) to gut-level guess (last resort). The process of assigning likelihood should not be taken lightly, as there can be very serious consequences if an assessment is inaccurate.

When the assessment matrix is employed, a potential risk will receive a score. For example, a risk with a severity of moderate (2) and a likelihood of rarely (D or 4) would receive a weight of 4 (2 × 2) or 2D.

Employing the matrix for all potential risks results in a list arranged in hierarchical order. The risks with the highest weights are the ones to which the project team should devote most of its efforts and resources.

More in-depth quantification of risks can be achieved via the following:

■ Determine tolerance levels: What is an acceptable level of risk? Will an additional project cost of $250,000 or a delay of 2 months put the company at risk? What level of overruns would be acceptable for the project? Hard numbers should be written down. How much cost and delay is acceptable? These are tolerance levels: the bottom line numbers that can be tolerated.

Severity of Risk Impact / Probability of Risk Occurring	Overall Risk Level
High negative impact to project / Highly likely to occur	High
High negative impact to project / Medium likely to occur	High
High negative impact to project / Unlikely to occur	Medium / Low
Medium negative impact to project / Highly likely to occur	Medium
Medium negative impact to project / Medium likely to occur	Medium / Low
Medium negative impact to project / Unlikely to occur	Low
Low negative impact to project / Highly likely to occur	Low
Low negative impact to project / Medium likely to occur	Low
Low negative impact to project / Unlikely to occur	Low

FIGURE 8.2. Overall Risk Level.

- Assign a probability to each risk: Take the risk assessment matrix's "likelihood" ratings of frequent, likely, possible, rarely, and unlikely one critical step further. For example, "frequent" could receive a probability of 95% (preferably this probability is based on historical data); "rarely" could have a probability of 1%.
- Assign a cost to each risk: The cost of a risk can be measured in dollars, lost time, lost quality, or all three. This makes the "severity" ratings more objective, by assigning a dollar amount to the negative cost impact if the risk does materialize and occur. For example, if a critical piece of machinery breaks down, a total cost impact of $22,800 could be calculated to result from the downtime during repair. If the likelihood of the machinery breaking down is 10%, the quantified value of this risk is $2,280.
- Assign a priority to each risk: Based on the tolerance level, the potential cost of the risk, and the probability of it occurring, a priority should be assigned to the risk. For example, if the cost of a risk is beyond the tolerance level and it is very likely to occur, a high priority will be assigned to the risk. These priorities are used to determine which risks to focus efforts on first. This can be done effectively using the risk assessment matrix discussed above.

Plan for Risks

Once risks are identified and quantified, it is time to plan for them. High- or medium-high-priority risks should be addressed first because risk planning can take a lot of time and energy.

Planning entails the following: identifying triggers for each risk and identifying proactive, contingency, or mitigation plans for each risk.

Identifying Triggers

Triggers are important indicators that a risk has occurred or is about to occur. The best triggers will alert project management that a problem is occurring.

To identify triggers, it is important to involve the people who are most likely to cause the risk to occur and those who are most likely to feel its impact. They should be asked how they would know that the problem is occurring, or how they would know that the problem has already occurred. Then they should work the process backward to determine how they would know before the problem actually materialized.

The project manager should consider how the risk would be reflected in the plan. Would the plan show overtime for a specific resource on earlier tasks? Would the plan show delays in specific tasks?

For each risk being addressed, a watch list needs to be created. This list should show the possible triggers, when they are likely to occur, and who should watch for them.

Identifying Plans

Once triggers are identified, action plans need to be created. The risks can be planned for in one of the following three ways.

- The risk can be mitigated by taking action ahead of time, thereby decreasing the likelihood of the problem occurring. For example, if a project is dependent on a single resource with specific expertise, the mitigating action would be to train another resource in that expertise.
- The risk can also be softened by lowering the consequences if the problem does occur, thereby reducing the risk's impact. For example, if a project is dependent on an outside vendor making its delivery dates, the contract with the vendor might be modified to include penalties for late delivery, in order to offset potential losses.
- A contingency plan should be in place, in case the problem does occur. For example, if a task is at risk of being delayed, the contingency plan may be to add additional resources to the task. The plan should include any work that must be done ahead of time to make the contingency successful. For example, the additional resources must be available in case they are needed.

Risk management plans can have unexpected ramifications. These plans should be modeled in a project network plan or with a project management software package to determine the plan's impact on the project. Such modeling will also offer insight into other, new risks that may occur as a result of the plan. These risks too should be analyzed.

Monitor and Manage Risks

With the risk management plan in place, the project manager should ensure that everyone on the project team is aware of it and will act on it. Any necessary actions need to be taken in accordance with these plans. The watch list needs to be monitored to see if triggers are occurring and contingency plans implemented as needed. Risks need to be reassessed regularly. The following suggestions can be used by the project manager when monitoring risks:

- Written and formal presentations of status reports should include a section on risks. Project team leaders should identify any assumptions they are making, as well as any new risks they see.
- At other regular meetings with team members, the risk management plan should be re-evaluated and new risks to the project identified.
- When the project's actual progress varies significantly from the plan, the risks should be reassessed and the risk management plan re-evaluated.

Sharing Risk with Customers

There is one other way that the financial risk of a project can be reduced. This is usually possible when there is a maximum technical risk and the project is also a contracted activity. As discussed in detail in Chapter 6, some customers recognize that risks are substantial when the specifications have never been achieved before. In such situations, the terms of the contract will result in the customer paying a percentage of the costs above a target price. If the contractor is able to deliver the product for LESS than the target price, the customer will SAVE a percentage of the target price.

SELF-STUDY/DISCUSSION QUESTIONS

1. What projects have you worked on that have encountered unusual problems? Were risk mitigation plans in place or contingency plans? What was the effect of having or not having these plans? Can you make any recommendations?

2. How would you quantify the risk of a potential labor strike? What factors would you use to determine a negative cost associated with:
   - Potential training of new staff
   - Possible costs associated with falling behind schedule (e.g., late penalties, not having product to sell)
   - Decrease in morale
   - Loss of expertise
   - Other costs

PROJECT RESOURCE MANAGEMENT AND PERFORMANCE MEASUREMENT[2]

INTRODUCTION

In most instances, the success of a project is measured by its profitability. The probability of a project doing well financially is increased when viable resource management and performance measurement techniques are employed. The concepts include the following:

- Budgeting and cost collection
- Time–cost trade-offs: Impacts on the schedule and total project cost
- Project constraints
- Resource limitations
- Project resource allocation
- Performance measurement and integrated cost/schedule systems
- Scope and change control
- Value engineering
- Estimating cash flows

BUDGETING AND COST COLLECTION

A project *budget* is a plan of estimated expenditures during the project period. This plan is phased in periodic increments (e.g., days, weeks, months, and quarters).

The totals of the increments are stated in dollars, representing the total budget for completing the project. Ideally, the established budget is a lower dollar amount than the offsetting benefits received, and the project manager is usually motivated to complete the project under budget.

The *cost collection system* is the mechanism used to track all costs expended on the project. Such costs include:

- Labor dollars (straight time and overtime)
- Indirect labor dollars (e.g., fringe benefits, the cost of indirect management)
- Materials
- Vendor and subcontractor costs

The tool to record the costs is often a time-recording device such as a time card or on-line device. A comprehensive discussion of project costs appears in Chapter 11.

The budgeting and cost collection processes generally begin after the project has been fairly thoroughly planned. However, from time to time, a project go-ahead may be given prior to finalization of the project scope. In such cases, it is very important that a cost collection system be put in place as soon as costs begin to be incurred. Uncertainty regarding overhead rates used for reporting can be addressed later via modification of rates in the systems reporting tables.

Creating and maintaining a project budget offers the project manager the following capabilities: (1) control project costs by making financial decisions with current project-related information, (2) ensure margin attainment, (3) priority attention on company cash flow requirements, and (4) establish a baseline for project costs to maintain the expected margin.

BUDGET PREPARATION

Depending on the size of the project, budget preparation could involve anywhere from one to many individuals. Usually a project has already gone through a proposal or cost estimate stage. In this case, the proposal or cost estimate is the basis for the budget.

The budget is similar to a proposal in that it is stated in raw resources (e.g., labor), and then rates and factors are used to translate raw resources to dollars. For example, for labor, the raw resource is *hours,* to which labor and overhead rates are applied. The nonlabor (e.g., materials, subcontracts) raw resource is *dollars*, to which only an overhead rate (e.g., procurement burden) is applied.

The rates applied to raw resources in budgeting are known as *reporting rates*. Reporting rates are developed periodically by the finance and/or accounting organizations in the company. A partial listing of reporting rate possibilities follows:

1. Direct employee labor salary/wage
2. Overhead
3. G&A
4. Allocated direct costs/computer service center costs, which could include such costs as common quality services, common minor material, and computer-related expenses

Figure 9.1 presents a simplified budget for the wedding cake project. Burt's Bakery uses *a loaded labor rate* to budget the cost of the chef's time. The loaded labor rate is the hourly labor rate for the employee working on the project, but also includes a factor to cover the employee's benefits (e.g., sick time and vacation time), as well as the other overhead costs (rent, electricity, depreciation of the bakery equipment).

Had the project spanned a significant time period (e.g., several years), the loaded labor rate applied would have been escalated to account for inflation in the later time periods.

Budgeting Considerations

Two budgeting factors that should be considered from the onset of the budgeting process are the concepts of responsible budget vs. performing budget and the importance of load leveling.

Responsible budget refers to the funds allocated to a manager who is responsible for a specific activity within a project. That manager may use the money to pay for all the employees working on the activity, whether or not they are actually

Cost Element	Thursday	Friday	Total
Mixing Hours	0.5		0.5
Icing Hours	1.5		1.5
Final Preparation		0.5	0.5
Total Hours	2.0	0.5	2.5
Bakery Labor Rate per Hour	$45.00	$45.00	$45.00
Total Labor Dollars	**$90.00**	**$22.50**	**$112.50**
Material (e.g., cake ingredients, icing, decorations, box)	$20	$60	$80.00
Total	**$110.00**	**$82.50**	**$192.50**

FIGURE 9.1. Burt's Bakery Budget Plan.

in his or her organization. For example, the manager of an inspection organization may be responsible for a testing function that is performed by a completely different organization. With "responsible budget," the manager would provide the funding for this other organization as well.

Performing budget is the term that designates the funds a manager has to support only the employees who are assigned to his or her organization. This means the manager's budget is usually made up of funds from many different projects. The manager is only cognizant of his or her own employees, and part of the manager's job is to ensure there are enough projects on-going to fund the employees in his or her organization.

Load leveling is the term for the management practice of scheduling tasks so that manpower is utilized the most efficiently. Effective manpower planning has employees and machinery performing productive tasks for as much of their work time as possible. Sometimes contract labor will be used or overtime authorized to ensure that operations flow smoothly. Load leveling is an art and a science. Efficient use of manpower greatly enhances profitability and project success.

TIME–COST TRADE-OFFS: EFFECTS OF SCHEDULE CHANGES

Some of the biggest problems a project manager has to deal with are related to schedules. Frequently, situations arise that result in added time between items situated on the critical path. Without corrective action to keep the project on schedule, the following scenarios may occur:

- Increased cost relating to materials: When a project is behind schedule, one of the following two events will cause material-related costs to increase: (1) material delivered before it is needed results in increased storage and handling costs and (2) if the vendor is told to hold off on delivery of material, there may be an inflationary price increase by the time the materials are actually delivered. This is often because contract terms state that a price is valid through a specific date. If the vendor is asked to deliver the product past this date, the cost could increase.
- Increased costs for subcontractors: Similar to materials, the costs for subcontractors also go up over time. Additionally, most subcontractors have other contracts and schedules by which they must abide. For example, a painting contractor may already have a job scheduled during the weeks for which the project manager would like to slip the schedule. In such cases, overtime may need to be authorized, which often results in at least a 50% increase in costs.
- Increased costs associated with labor (e.g., overtime): One of the options at the disposal of the project manager to keep a project on schedule is

authorizing (or requiring) overtime. In these instances, similar to a sub-contractor working overtime, labor costs increase substantially. Not only does the cost per hour go up, but so do the hours. It is rare that an employee working overtime (more than 8 hours) is as efficient as an employee during the first 8 hours of the shift. This is because exhaustion sets in, leading to slow and sometimes sloppy and careless performance, the result of which is increased costs.

■ Other costs: Employee morale is very important to the success of every project. If employees begin feeling rushed or pressured, attendance may drop (absenteeism due to time off for sickness or vacation). This too has a negative impact on the project and the rest of the staff.

Approaches for Gaining Company Support for Reducing Project Schedules

The project manager needs to be the team captain and inspire the team to support all aspects of the project. When the project is behind schedule, and the best solution is for employees to increase productivity, the following techniques can be employed:

■ When employees work past the usual time they go home for the day, a catered dinner can be brought into the office. Even pizza can be a pleasant surprise to workers starting to get burned out. Employees could be asked what their favorite type of pizza is, and then they are happy when it arrives.

■ Take a short break in the middle of the day or at the end of a status meeting to tell employees how greatly they are appreciated and give them special awards (e.g., certificate of appreciation). A certificate alone may not impress the hardened worker, so the certificate becomes more effective when it is accompanied by something like a pair of movie tickets to be used over the weekend or when the project is complete.

Savings Resulting from Reduced Schedules

There are many benefits to keeping a project on schedule, as well as finishing on schedule, including the following:

■ Cost savings: Project costs decrease (e.g., leased equipment, consultant fees, labor, maintenance, utilities).

■ Goodwill: Customers (internal and external) are all very pleased when projects are completed on time. This greatly enhances the project manager's reputation in the professional community.

- Employee satisfaction: Being on schedule is one of the determinants of a successful project, and all employees want to be part of a successful team.
- The "adjourning party": The celebration that concludes many projects reaches a higher level when the project is deemed a success in all areas, including on-schedule performance.

Contract Schedule Incentives

Contracts for some projects have schedule incentive clauses. Such clauses have negative incentives for projects that finish behind schedule.

An example of a situation where a negative incentive may be practical involves a family moving to a new part of the country. The man of the house is being transferred to Orlando, Florida. He wants to have his new home built so he can move in 1 week before he starts his new job. To ensure the home is constructed by the desired date, a special clause is put into the home construction contract. The clause states that if the home is not completed to the specifications of the contract by the contracted date, the contractor will pay the customer's living expenses at a rate not less than $200 a day until the house is completed. You can be assured that the contractor will be motivated to complete the project on schedule.

Budget Questions

Every organization should have a budget that can be contrasted with all expenditures. Whenever expenditures are not in line with the budget, questions such as the following need to be asked.

When expenditures are higher than budget:

1. What is going on? Why is it costing more than was expected?
2. What are the implications? What else is going wrong or what other problems could arise?

When expenditures are under budget:

1. What is going on? Why is it costing less than was expected? Are we not doing something we are supposed to be doing?
2. How are we doing in relation to schedule? Are we also behind schedule? If so, by how much?

PROJECT CONSTRAINTS

The role of a project manager is very demanding. There are a number of project constraints that must be effectively managed, including the following.

Resource Limitations

1. Project and/or contract requirements
2. Corporate priorities
3. Government restrictions
4. Union restrictions

Imagine a world with unlimited resources, no deadlines, unlimited funding, and all without any risk; imagine. Projects do include deadlines, budgets, assumptions, and resource limitations. They also include technology requirements as well as many unforeseen factors; not everything works out as expected. Documenting and incorporating project constraints and assumptions into the project scope description and project plan are important to help mitigate project problems.

Yet, every project manager dreams of getting a blank check to fund the project. All the hard workers would get raises, there would be special training, and the most current and sophisticated work tools would be acquired. Highly paid consultants would be brought in, and there would be plenty of money to pay for overtime or contract labor if necessary to keep the project on schedule.

Unfortunately, there are no blank checks in project management; there are only resource limitations, including:

- Tight budgets
- Manpower shortages
- Lack of work space
- Shortage of expertise
- Impossible delivery schedule
- Inadequate machinery and equipment
- Inadequate technical support
- And so on...

The project manager often has to be quite the negotiator, working out agreements with other managers in the company for temporary loans and trades of equipment and personnel. Utilizing manpower to the fullest is also instrumental to overcome resource limitations.

Project and/or Contract Requirements

The project or contract itself includes many often difficult constraints, including the following:

■ Project specifications that should not be compromised: This constraint is often compounded by the lack or shortage of expertise. The project manager may attempt to hire consultants, but this can be very expensive.

■ Schedules that should be met: This constraint can be compounded by shortages in manpower and/or equipment and trouble meeting the specifications listed above.

■ Some government requirements may also include the following:
   1. The requirement to subcontract a certain percentage of business to "disadvantaged small businesses (DSBs)." DSBs are businesses that are owned and operated by minorities. Sometimes it may be difficult to identify a DSB that can efficiently assist in satisfying project requirements in a cost-effective manner.
   2. The Federal Acquisition Regulations (FAR) contain volumes and volumes of other requirements. A project manager who manages government projects is wise to become familiar with the FAR.

Corporate Priorities

Project managers often feel helpless when another project being worked in the same company has a higher corporate priority. That project is the one that gets the manpower, the equipment, and the discretionary funds before the project manager's project. The best advice here is to remain cool, calm, and under control. When there is a substantial need for corporate support that otherwise is not forthcoming, the project manager needs to put together a cost/benefits analysis and present it to executive management.

Government Restrictions (Local, City, State, Federal)

Local, city, state, and federal government agencies all have their say in how projects are administered. There are all sorts of regulations that must be followed (e.g., lighting in work areas, ventilation systems). Also, local governments may have restrictions on the hour that construction projects may be worked, which can impact schedules. The project manager needs to be aware of related local, city, state, and federal restrictions.

Union Restrictions

Union bargaining units, working to improve the circumstances for their members, negotiate annual agreements. The agreements often impact more than just wages. In addition to wages and working conditions, these contracts affect holidays, vacations, working hours, and workdays, all of which have the potential to conflict with the project.

Monitoring and Managing Projects with Integrated Cost/Schedule Control

In the 21st century, project managers have at their disposal any number of sophisticated *integrated cost/schedule systems* that provide outstanding visibility into project status.

Suppose the first activity of a project is scheduled to start and end in the month of April. The activity is budgeted to require 100 hours to complete. At the end of the month, you look at your financial report and see that, though 100 hours were budgeted, only 80 hours were expended. Based on this information, do you think the project manager would be happy or sad?

If you said happy, you may be right, but unfortunately not enough information has been given. When an integrated cost/schedule system is in place, the project manager has access to data to fully assess the situation.

Figure 9.2 is a simplified example of an integrated cost/schedule for this scenario. An analysis of the data gives the project manager two reasons to be disappointed, and not happy.

The key concepts to understand include the following:

- Cost: The cost of a project includes all cost elements — labor, overhead, material, subcontract, etc. There are three different budgeted cost categories described below: budgeted cost of work scheduled, budgeted cost of work performed, and actual cost of work performed.
- Schedule: The time-phase schedule of when project deliverables are to be delivered.
- Cost/schedule system: The system (usually on computer) that integrates the time-phased budgeted cost with the actual costs as they occur.
- Budgeted cost of work scheduled (BCWS): The budget as it is put into the system is based on the master schedule. For example, in Figure 9.2, if the first milestone will be started and completed in the month of April, and the budget for the effort is 100 hours, 100 hours will be budgeted for April.

Hours Budgeted and Expended in April

	BCWS	BCWP	ACWP	SV	CV
Activity 1	100	75	80	(25)	(5)

FIGURE 9.2. Integrated Cost/Schedule Control.

- Budgeted cost of work performed (BCWP): Based on the BCWS, but takes into account the *actual* work performed. For example, if the work milestone scheduled for delivery is only 75% complete by the end of April, as in Figure 9.2, the BCWP will only be 75 hours.
- Actual cost of work performed (ACWP): What is actually expended, regardless of how much work was done. For example, in Figure 9.2, if 80 hours were expended in April, the report would show 80 hours.
- Cost variance: The difference between the BCWP and the ACWP. In our example, the cost variance is an unfavorable (negative) 5 hours. This is because only 75 hours worth of work has been accomplished, but 80 hours have been expended. Cost/schedule systems have the capability of further breaking down cost variances into two categories, the sum of which equals the total cost variance. These categories are (1) rate variances, which relate to the labor rates of the workers, and (2) volume variances, which relate to the volume of work they accomplish. Since the simple analysis in Figure 9.2 is stated in the raw resource "hours" only, and does not involve any labor rates, the total cost variance of –5 is entirely a volume variance.
- Schedule variance (SV): The difference between the work that was scheduled to be performed and the work that was actually performed. In our example, the SV is an unfavorable (negative) 25 hours, because the project is 25 hours behind schedule.
- Measured effort: Also termed "earned value," this refers to the process of keeping track of the actual work accomplished as compared to the budgeted schedule.
- Status reports: Cost/schedule systems are capable of generating valuable information, such as that shown in the example above and in the explanation of earned value below.

Now that all the information has been given and explained, the answer to the question posed earlier is that the program manager is disappointed because:

- The project is behind schedule with a schedule variance of –25 hours.
- The project is already over budget with a cost variance of –5 hours.

Earned Value[47]

Earned value is a management technique that relates resource planning to schedules and to technical cost and schedule requirements. All work is planned, budgeted, and scheduled in time-phased "planned value" increments constituting a cost and schedule measurement baseline. There are two major objectives of an earned value system: (1) to encourage project teams to use effective internal cost and schedule management control systems and (2) to provide the project manager, project sponsors, and other interested parties access to timely data produced by those systems for determining project status.

Baseline

The baseline plan in Figure 9.3 shows that six work units (A–F) would be completed at a cost of $100 for the period covered by this report.

Schedule Variance

As work is performed, it is "earned" on the same basis as it was planned, in dollars or other quantifiable units such as labor hours. Planned value compared with earned value measures the dollar volume of work planned vs. the equivalent dollar volume of work accomplished. Any difference is called a schedule variance. In contrast to what was planned, Figure 9.4 shows that work unit D was not completed and work unit F was never started, or $35 of the planned work was not accomplished. As a result, the schedule variance shows that 35% of the work planned for this period was not done.

Cost Variance

Earned value compared with the actual cost incurred (from contractor accounting systems) for the work performed provides an objective measure of planned and actual cost. Any difference is called a cost variance. A negative variance means more money was spent for the work accomplished than was planned. Figure 9.5 shows the calculation of cost variance. The work performed was planned to cost $65 and actually cost $91. The cost variance is 40%.

	A	B	C	D	E	F	Total
Planned value ($)	10	15	10	25	20	20	100

FIGURE 9.3. Baseline Plan Work Units.

	A	B	C	D	E	F	Total
Planned value ($)	10	15	10	25	20	20	100
Earned value ($)	10	15	10	10	20	-	65
Schedule variance	0	0	0	-15	0	-20	-35 = -35%

FIGURE 9.4. Schedule Variance Work Units.

	A	B	C	D	E	F	Total
Earned value ($)	10	15	10	10	20	-	65
Actual cost ($)	9	22	8	30	22	-	91
Cost variance	1	-7	2	-20	-2	0	-26 = -40%

FIGURE 9.5. Cost Variance Work Units.

	A	B	C	D	E	F	Total
Planned spend ($)	10	15	10	25	20	20	100
Actual spend ($)	9	22	8	30	22	-	91
Variance	1	-7	2	-5	-2	20	9 = 9%

FIGURE 9.6. Spend Comparison Approach Work Units.

Spend Comparison

The typical spend comparison approach, whereby project managers report actual expenditures against planned expenditures, is not related to the work that was accomplished. Figure 9.6 shows a simple comparison of planned and actual spending, which is unrelated to work performed and therefore not a useful comparison. The fact that the total amount spent was $9 less than planned for this period is not useful without the comparisons with work accomplished.

Use of Earned Value Data

The benefits to project management of the earned value approach come from the disciplined planning conducted and the availability of metrics that show real variances from plan in order to generate necessary corrective actions.

SELF-STUDY/DISCUSSION QUESTIONS

1. Why is it important to establish budgets for projects? What might happen if there was a project and no budgets were in place?
2. What is a good source for budget information?
3. What is load leveling? How might load leveling be used in a project that involves designing three separate modules for a new software project?
4. Define time–cost trade-offs. What steps can be taken to complete a project ahead of schedule? How do these steps affect costs?

5. What experiences have you or your company had with projects that were behind schedule? Were steps taken to recover the schedule? If so, what were they? If not, why not?
6. What project constraints have affected projects on which you have worked? How were they dealt with?
7. Are you familiar with any public construction projects (e.g., highway modifications) that have been over budget or behind schedule? Were you or other members of the public personally affected?
8. Have you been involved with any projects that have used an integrated cost/schedule system? If so, how was progress measured? Was it effective? Why or why not?

Free value-added materials available from the
Download Resource Center at <u>www.jrosspub.com</u>.

PROJECT AUDIT, TERMINATION, AND CLOSURE

INTRODUCTION

All projects need to be closely monitored to ensure they are progressing as planned. Sometimes troubles surface and it becomes necessary to terminate a project before it is completed. The audit activity is designed to give the project every possible chance to be completed and go to closure.

AUDIT

The term *audit* is synonymous with analysis, checkup, inspection, review, scan, scrutiny, survey, and view. Audits are used throughout the project life cycle as follows:

- Project audit
- Scheduled audits
- Unscheduled audits
- Subcontractor and vendor audits
- Quality audits
- Project safety audits

Project Audit[48]

The main purpose of a project audit is to assist in satisfying the goals of the project in relation to its contribution to the parent organization's goals. All elements of the project are reviewed in an effort to identify and understand strengths and weaknesses.

The project audit thoroughly examines:

- Project management
- Methodologies and procedures
- Records
- Properties
- Budgets and expenditures
- Degree of completion

The result of this audit is a set of recommendations that can help both on-going and future projects to:

- Anticipate and identify potential problems before they get out of hand
- Clarify performance, cost, and time relationships
- Improve project performance
- Locate opportunities for future technological advances
- Evaluate the quality of project management
- Reduce costs
- Speed the achievement of results
- Identify mistakes, remedy them, and avoid them in the future
- Provide information to the client
- Reconfirm the organization's interest in and commitment to the project

Scheduled Audits — The Audit Letter

When an audit is formally scheduled, it often begins with a formal letter sent to representatives of the function or group being audited. The letter describes what is being audited and a general summary of what the audit process will entail. It also includes the date for an introductory meeting.

Unscheduled Audits

With an unscheduled audit, there is no prior announcement. The organization or function being audited will be caught off guard. As such, it is extremely important that all members of the project team are aware of and are following the prescribed procedures.

The Introductory Meeting

The introductory meeting is held at the location of those being audited. The audit team meets with representatives and explains the detail of the audit process. The team covers the who, what, where, when, and how. The why may or may not be discussed.

Process

Over the next several days (or weeks), the audit team follows through on the process discussed at the introductory meeting.

Exit Interview

After the team has audited all the areas targeted for the analysis, the exit interview takes place. It is attended by the same people who attended the introductory meeting. This is an important meeting, as here the audit team reveals its findings. There is a chance that some of the findings will require corrective action.

Audit Report

The formal audit report is completed when the audit has ended. At a minimum, it contains the following points:

1. Current status of the project: In effect, this is a look at the schedule variance discussed in Chapter 9. Does the work accomplished match the schedule of work to be accomplished?
2. Future status: What is the likelihood of significant schedule changes? What is the nature of future changes, if any?
3. Status of critical tasks: What progress has been made on tasks that are on the critical path?
4. Risk assessment: What is the potential for project failure and monetary loss? In order for this point to be adequately addressed, it is essential that those performing the audit receive the proper training in the financially focused mindset.
5. Information pertinent to other projects: This is the "lessons learned" document discussed in Chapters 4 and 8.
6. Limitations of the audit: What assumptions or limitations affect the data in the audit?

OTHER AUDITS

Many companies and corporations have internal audit organizations whose functions include formally investigating different areas of the company to determine areas where improvement is needed. Yet, if all employees act as company auditors while performing their routine tasks (as financially focused project management suggests), the company should experience a much better audit, encompassing the entire corporation every day.

The project team needs to create goals and strategies to meet its business objectives. The team will create an audit improvement process measurable against company goals. Management will also need to continuously assess the competition.

Audit Control

Even the best quality assurance program is vulnerable because of the human factor involved. It should be obvious that a system of checks and balances is necessary. After all, why should litigation regarding a defective product be brought about if the defect could have been detected prior to leaving the factory?

The Travelers Insurance Company's "A Management Guide to Product Quality and Safety"[49] reports that an effective check and balance tool is audit control of all animate and inanimate functions that could contribute to bad products. The type of product, amount of production, and procurement arrangement will dictate the frequency and depth of audit control and the size of the team. The important point is that all audits should be conducted as an additive to routine reviews, inspections, and tests. To be an effective management tool, they should be formally structured with written results.

Effective audit control includes software and hardware audits in the areas of quality assurance programs and procedures, company policies, configuration control prime documents, and secondary control documents.

Vendor Audit

After the vendor has been selected and is supplying components, audits should be conducted to evaluate performance to the previously agreed upon control systems. The audits should evaluate both the system and the product, and they should be conducted at random intervals. Such audits may also be conducted at regular intervals, but there is a lower likelihood of audit findings if the vendor knows in advance exactly when the audit will take place.

Each audit should be performed with adequate preparation. A well-prepared checklist may provide the basis for a thorough supplier evaluation. The following checklist is offered as a sample of the elements that a vendor audit should include:

- Dimensional conformance
- Records of inspection and test with lot traceability
- Written decisions regarding nonconforming material
- Corrective action system (e.g., financially focused quality)
- Evidence of the occurrence of internal audits
- Notification of nonconformances
- Operator job knowledge
- Management knowledge of requirements
- Attitudes of management, staff, and line employees
- Calibration records
- Compliance with product safety guidelines from applicable industry or government standards

After each audit, the results should be discussed with the supplier. During this discussion, corrective action dates should be agreed upon and an audit follow-up date should be established. The purpose of the follow up is of course to ensure that corrective action(s) has been taken and that the supplier is performing within the agreed upon control standards.

Project Safety Audit

Depending on the nature of the project, it may be appropriate to hire a consultant to perform an audit of the activities being performed on the project. The purpose of this audit is to scope out safety hazards, which could lead to employee harm and potential lawsuits.

Product Safety Audit

A manufacturer must establish, document, and implement practices and procedures to ensure both that the product is safe and that it is manufactured safely. It is then critical that these practices and procedures are followed. To ensure compliance, prudent management will initiate an on-going program of safety audits.

Such a program should examine practices and procedures to ensure they are formally documented with job instructions. Job instructions should adequately address the specific requirements of each individual product. Steps are needed to ensure that the actual practice conforms to the documented job instructions.

The program should effectively improve product safety and reduce product liability exposure. The successful product safety audit begins with the preparation phase. Careful preparation is followed by the execution, where the audit is performed. During the third phase — reporting — the auditor presents the audit findings to those who were audited as well as those concerned about the outcome (e.g., management). The last phase — follow up — involves closure to ensure that reported deficiencies have been resolved.

During the preparation phase, the auditor needs to understand the purpose of the audit. With the purpose in mind, the auditor should plan the type of audit to be performed. There are four primary types of product safety audits, each focusing on a different area. These audits encompass the following areas: systems, processes, products, and procedures and methods.

TERMINATION

Hormozi et al.[50] discuss the termination phase of the project life cycle. Termination of a project is inevitable, but how and when it is terminated may have a profound and long-lasting impact on the organization and its employees. The success of future projects may depend not only on the success of past ones, but also on how unsuccessful projects were treated by the organization and its stakeholders. Firms have the option of initiating a variety of entrepreneurial projects with varying degrees of risk. If an organization chooses to accept greater risks, it should avoid penalizing team members of projects that turn out to be unsuccessful. If team members believe they will be penalized for participating in unsuccessful projects, they will be less willing to terminate failed projects and may become risk averse.

Organizing a project's termination process is especially important when it has failed, because of the lasting impact on future projects as well as the organization's image. Including project team members in the termination process will increase their loyalty and commitment, not only to the organization but also to the success of future projects. At the end of a project, a postaudit report will be prepared that summarizes the project and provides recommendations for similar projects in the future. Lastly, as a project is closed down or completed, it is important that senior management recognize the contributions of the project team.

The Termination Phase

Many colorful terms have come into use to describe the abrupt termination of a project. Unsuccessful projects can be *murdered*, commit *projecticide*, or be terminated as a result of a *political assassination*.

Generally speaking, there are three ways to terminate a project:

- Extinction: The project is completed. It may be either successful or unsuccessful, but it is completed.
- Inclusion: The complete project team and its equipment are transferred to a new division. As one might expect, this type of change places

significant additional stress on the day-to-day operations of the organization. Project managers and team members must be sensitive to these stresses until the organization is able to settle into a new and more stable routine.

■ Integration: The project's resources, personnel, and functions are absorbed as a part of the original organization. The major problem associated with this termination process is the ability of the organization to blend technological differences between the project and the organization. Past experience appears to play a key role in successfully integrating terminated projects.

When to Terminate

It is important to be committed to the success of a project. It is equally important to know when and how to pull the plug. During all phases of the project, senior management and the project manager should monitor the success factors discussed above. Significant changes in the project's environment may make the decision to terminate a project relatively clear. Conversely, an accumulation of many minor changes in these factors may make the decision very difficult.

The rate of project failures is accelerating, especially for the information technology (IT) industry. A survey of 500 IT directors by Sequent Computer Systems, Inc. found that 76% had experienced a major project failure at some point in their careers. "Project failures seem to be a cost of being in the IT business."[51] The average cost for an IT development project for a large company is more than $2 million. More than $250 billion is spent in the U.S. each year on approximately 175,000 IT projects, of which only 26% are completed on time and within budget.[52]

Many mathematical models can be used to assist management in determining whether or not to continue a project. Some of the more common rely on financial techniques such as payback or net present value. However, any final decision should take into account other important strategic factors, such as whether the project helps the firm maintain its competitive position or is essential to its survival.

Two common techniques used to monitor projects throughout their life cycle are cybernetic control processes and go/no-go control processes. The cybernetic control method compares the project's actual performance path against the anticipated or scheduled path. This makes the project team aware of schedule deviations so corrective action can be taken. Cybernetic control processes should not be used as a decision model but only as a tool to keep a project on track (in terms of performance, time, and cost) so that it is not terminated prematurely because of poor planning or control.[53] "Go/no-go controls take the form of [periodically] testing to see if some specific precondition has been met."[53] This technique can be used on many facets of the project as the team finds appropriate. In addition, specific weights can be assigned to individual measures to provide a more quantitative dimension to the monitoring process.

How to Terminate

Regardless of whether a successful project is completed by inclusion, integration, or extinction, a plan must be developed to terminate it. An organization that is project oriented may have a "termination manager" whose primary responsibility is to effectively and efficiently end projects. The duties of a termination manager may include the following:[53]

- Ensure the project is complete.
- Ensure delivery and client acceptance.
- Prepare a final report.
- Ensure that all bills have been paid and that the final invoice has been sent to the client.
- Redistribute personnel, materials, equipment, and any other resources.
- Determine what records (manuals, reports, and other paperwork) are to be kept and place them in storage.
- Assign responsibility for product support, if necessary.
- Oversee the closing of the project's books.

It is equally important that team members not be penalized for participating in what may turn out to be an unsuccessful project. If team members are penalized, they will be less willing to end a project or will become risk averse.

Impact of Project Cancellation

A project may be canceled for a variety of reasons including lack of funding, technological obsolescence, changes in consumer trends, mergers and acquisitions, loss of the "champion," and negative cost/benefit relationships. Although the reasons may vary, the impact is frequently the same. Project cancellation can affect employee productivity, the reputation of the firm, and the value of the firm's stock. Although there is little research on the topic of employee productivity and project cancellation, what little there is suggests that a project team's perception of the cancellation may influence its productivity for the next several years. However, there are guidelines to help soften the impact of cancellation on the team. To begin with, it is essential that the project team be included in the cancellation process and be made aware of the rationale behind the cancellation well before the official announcement. Moreover, this rationale should be consistent with the perceptions of the project team.[54]

As might be expected, the output and commitment of team members immediately before a project is canceled, and for 1 or 2 months after the announcement, will be drastically reduced. This loss in productivity and commitment will be exacerbated if the project team perceives the cancellation negatively. Even worse, the individual's commitment to the organization may depend on his or her perception of the cancellation. Employees who view a cancellation in a more positive light will have higher levels of commitment than do those who view it more negatively.[54]

How a project is viewed within the organization is also very important. Because corporate resources can be very limited, projects that are perceived to be draining scarce resources tend to undercut morale. Other project teams envy the resources "squandered" on unproductive or failing projects. This, in turn, leads employees to question the wisdom of senior management[55] and reduces their productivity and level of commitment to the organization.

The impact of canceling a project on the firm's market value can vary. If information on the project was readily available, and Wall Street already viewed the project as a drain on the company's resources, then the announcement will tend to bolster the company's stock.[56,57]

POSTAUDIT REVIEW

The importance of a final report cannot be overemphasized. An objective review of the project's successes and shortcomings can provide senior management with insights into how to improve future projects. The final report is also a valuable tool to help future project managers, since it includes not only what worked but also what did not and recommendations for similar projects in the future.[58]

This report should focus on the following functional areas: project performance, administrative performance, organizational structure, project and administrative teams, and project management techniques.

Keeping a project on target, within budget, and within required specifications entails accurate forecasting and control. A thorough analysis of forecasting, planning, budgeting, scheduling, resource allocation, and control techniques used during the project will help improve future projects.

PROJECT CLOSURE

When a project is physically completed, the sequential steps (Figure 10.1) are followed through to the final disbanding of the project team. The time period can be as short as 1 day for a smaller project (e.g., wedding cake) or as long as

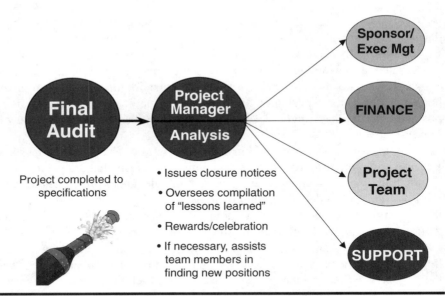

FIGURE 10.1. Project Closure.

5 to 10 years if the project was completed under the terms of a large cost reimbursable contract (CRC). For such activity, finance and the customer review financial cost data to determine allowable costs for CRCs, final overhead rates are incorporated, actual costs are reconciled with billed amounts, and the final fee proposal is prepared. Upon notification of receipt of final payment, all financial documents are formally closed out.

Project closure typically includes the following:

1. The responsible individual(s) for project status, after verifying the project specifications have been met, notifies the project manager that the project is indeed complete.
2. The project manager notifies all involved parties that the project is complete.
   - A formal report is issued to executive management, along with perhaps a formal presentation at an executive board meeting. These reports include all the pertinent data regarding the project, e.g., performance to budget, to schedule, and to specifications and overall summary of the project's success.
   - Notification to the finance organization allows the appropriate people to assess payments to vendors and subcontractors, to ensure all required costs are accounted for and no inappropriate costs are paid. Final accounting on the project may begin.

- The project team members are notified that they are free to return to their original home organizations.
- Individuals from other support organizations and their management are also notified that the project is complete.
- The lessons learned document is compiled via the project manager's oversight and input. This process should be fairly simple, as long as the project team members have been keeping a log of such items throughout the life of the project.
- An enjoyable part of each project is the celebratory get-together that concludes the project. After working closely together for some time on a tough project, the celebration gives team members (and other deserving support personnel) a chance to feel the pleasure of completing a successful task. This activity leaves a very sweet taste in the mouths of team members. As a result, they are more apt to be willing to participate in future projects. The celebration may help eliminate any negative feelings that crept in during project activity.
- The last step in project closure is for the team members to return to their home organizations. Unfortunately, some team members may find that they are no longer needed in their home organizations. In cases such as these, the project manager needs to work diligently to find a place for such individuals. This is critical to the credibility of the project manager, for obvious reasons.

SELF-STUDY/DISCUSSION QUESTIONS

1. Generally speaking, what is the purpose of an audit?
2. Why is an audit conducted during a project? After it is completed?
3. What is the difference between a scheduled and unscheduled audit? What are the advantages of each to the auditor? Which audit would the function being audited prefer? Why?
4. What are the major steps in the project closure process?
5. What groups need to be notified? Why?

Free value-added materials available from the
Download Resource Center at www.jrosspub.com.

11

FINANCIAL ADMINISTRATION AND FINANCIALLY FOCUSED PROJECT MANAGEMENT TRAINING²

INTRODUCTION TO FINANCIALLY FOCUSED PROJECT MANAGEMENT (FFPM)

FFPM aims at getting all members of the project team to think as if they were members of the finance community. By so doing, FFPM enables and empowers every team member to contribute to increased profitability. This is accomplished as follows:

- Educate every team member on the financial information necessary to understand the following:
    1. How the company operates (e.g., how it earns a profit), and how the project team contributes to profitability
    2. What the finance organization is and what it does
    3. How each project team member contributes to the bottom line
    4. How other circumstances (suppliers, customers, other company employees) affect profitability

- Present the FFPM methodology to every employee for analyzing potential changes, purchasing and staffing decisions, process improvements, and corrective actions.
- Stimulate and encourage employees to utilize a "financially focused mindset" when performing daily responsibilities and making decisions.

FINANCIAL TRAINING

In order to utilize financial data, employees need to understand the world of finance. The most common method for gaining such an understanding is to embark on formal classes at institutions of higher education. In increasing numbers, working professionals are enrolling in universities designed specifically for adult higher education.

Accredited in 1978, the University of Phoenix was among the first to recognize the need for degree and continuing education programs for adult professionals. As of February 29, 2000, the university had a total enrollment of 74,421 students, with 12,212 of those students enrolled on-line.[59] It is America's largest private accredited university for working adults. The University of Phoenix is just one of many such institutions. Adults wishing to learn finance principles can take such classes as those listed below:

- Accounting (e.g., cost accounting, financial accounting)
- Cost estimating
- Business administration (e.g., management, marketing)
- Economics (e.g., micro-economics, macro-economics, the economics of state and local finance)
- Quantitative methods for business analysis
- "Finance" (e.g., personal finance, financial management, small business finance, managerial finance, financial theory, international finance, theory of corporate finance)
- Investments (e.g., introduction to investing, portfolio analysis, speculative markets, corporate financial investments)
- Principles of real estate (e.g., income property analysis, residential real estate, site location analysis, mortgage markets)
- Financial institutions (e.g., bank administration, commercial banking)
- Insurance (e.g., life, health, property, and liability insurance, risk management)
- Working capital management (e.g., capital budgeting)
- Business cycles and forecasting
- Money and capital markets

- Commercial bank management
- International financial management

These classes are geared for the adult with a full-time job. The classes can be offered, for example, in five or six weekly 4-hour sessions or in 6- or 8-hour weekend sessions. Such scheduling enables working adults to attend classes without interrupting their full-time jobs. The rapid growth of adult education providers is proof that this approach has been very successful.

The education offered by outside institutions is generic in that it pertains to a wide range of businesses. Much of the classroom information would not be of value to those employees content with their employers and their positions.

A perfect implementation of FFPM has every project team member, and all other employees in the company performing on the team, receiving an education in the financial areas that pertain uniquely to that company. Seldom will an outside institution be approached to supply such education. However, another alternative exists. It is much more affordable and practical for the company to tailor a unique course aimed at the financial issues pertinent to the enterprise. This chapter presents the basic financial education concepts that do apply to almost every company. It is based on the financial concerns of a very large financial operation, but its principles are easily applied to smaller business. Some suggestions for training employees in company-unique financial topics appear at the end of this chapter.

FINANCIAL ACTIVITIES

Figure 11.1 presents an overview of financial activities for a large company.

- *Estimating* refers to the process of establishing prices for products and services. For many businesses, including contractors and service providers, this usually involves preparing, proposing, and negotiating contracts.
- *Budgeting* ties specific performing or responsible business functions to cost targets for accomplishing required tasks. For operations working under contracts, this function usually takes place after contract award, and budgets are established for tracking performance against the negotiated target costs.
- *Reporting* provides management and, when appropriate, the customer with factual detail regarding performance to budgets and schedules, and at the same time offers forecasts and corrective action taken to resolve budgetary problems.
- *General accounting* involves the routine tasks associated with a business (e.g., accounts payable, accounts receivable, etc.).
- *Closure* is the activity that allows the enterprise to book a specific sale. This could be very simple, as with a retail sale where the customer walks

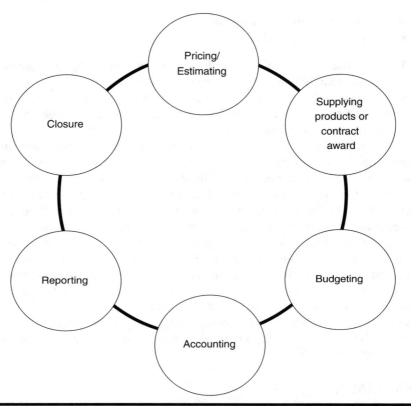

FIGURE 11.1. Cycle of Financial Activities. (Reprinted with permission from Cappels, T.M., *Financially Focused Quality*, CRC Press, 1999. Copyright CRC Press, Boca Raton, Florida.)

away with the product and the receipt. It can also be very cumbersome, as for a very large contracted sale. Often, a contractor will not receive final payment for the work performed until a thorough closure activity is completed. For government contracting, this can involve the finalization of overhead rates and disallowances.

The cycle begins when a product or service has been designed or planned. The finance organization determines the price via a method known as *estimating*.

Once the price has been established, orders are taken and contracts are initiated. For major projects and one-of-a-kind-type services (e.g., construction projects), the company prepares a proposal and submits it to the potential customer. The negotiation process is concluded when both parties sign a contract.

An important element of the contracted terms is the target cost to be paid by the customer to the company for performance of the agreed tasks.

Based on orders and/or negotiated contracts, budgets are established based on a forecast of what is scheduled to be delivered. These budgets are tied to the original estimated cost. Actual costs are tracked periodically (e.g., monthly). Tracking costs makes problem areas visible and enables timely corrective action.

Budgets are established and a tracking system is put in place. The company is operating at full steam. It is essential that the accounting functions be performed smoothly.

The major accounting functions are:

- Payroll accounting
- Supplier accounts payable
- Financial accounting
- Cost accounting
- Accounts receivable
- Property administration

Now it is time for the reporting process to begin. In large companies, quite sophisticated financial systems can be employed to assist management in the tracking of actual performance against cost and schedule criteria.

These activities continue until the last contracted piece of hardware or service is delivered, and then the contract closure process begins.

While the above financial functions are being performed, the company should be actively pursuing new business by investigating new products and services. The actual costs encountered in the process of manufacturing or preparing previous products should be used as a basis for establishing prices for new products and proposing new contracts.

Developing innovative products and preparing new proposals is vital to an on-going business entity because they increase the probability of future business, which enables the cycle to continue.

FINANCIAL CONCEPTS

As with any profession, those in finance have their own unique set of concepts that are necessary to successfully function on the job. Comprehension of the key financial concepts applicable to most businesses will enable employees to better exercise the financially focused mindset. These concepts appear below:

1. Accounting classifications
   - Direct costs vs. indirect costs
   - Labor costs vs. nonlabor costs
   - Direct-direct vs. allocated-direct
   - Work breakdown structure (WBS)

Examples
  * **Accounting systems**
  * **United States**
  * **Library systems**

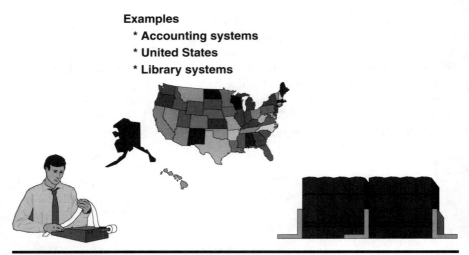

FIGURE 11.2. Examples of Accounting Classifications. (Reprinted with permission from Cappels, T.M., *Financially Focused Quality*, CRC Press, 1999. Copyright CRC Press, Boca Raton, Florida.)

- ■ Cost accumulation structure
- ■ Charge numbers
2. Timekeeping/cost segregation
3. Forecasting personnel

Accounting Classifications (Figure 11.2)

Classifications provide detailed identity to large groups or divisions of information. A reasonable person would not attempt to enter a major public library and begin to search for a specific book without making use of the card file. The U.S. Postal Service now utilizes zip codes to aid in the sorting and delivery of mail. Just as libraries and the Postal Service make use of classification systems, so too does the world of finance. Finance and accounting systems provide detailed identity to large groups of business expenses through classification.

Direct vs. Indirect Costs (Figure 11.3)

Costs may be classified as either *direct* or *indirect*. Direct costs are expenditures directly benefiting and identifiable to projects. Direct costs may also be allocated-direct costs (see below), which provide specifically for the research, design, development, or production needed to accomplish project requirements.

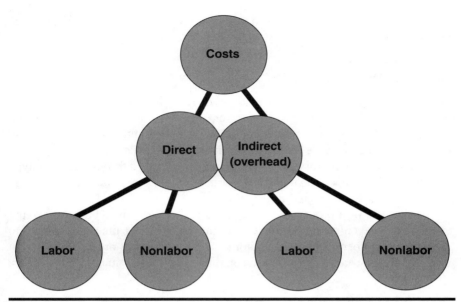

FIGURE 11.3. Accounting Classifications: Direct vs. Indirect. (Reprinted with permission from Cappels, T.M., *Financially Focused Quality*, CRC Press, 1999. Copyright CRC Press, Boca Raton, Florida.)

Indirect costs are those that, under normal requirements for expenditure, do not directly contribute to the accomplishment of project requirements. *Indirect cost* is a term sometimes used synonymously with *overhead*.

In some larger enterprises, it is not uncommon for employees to be referred to as *direct* or *indirect* employees. In this situation, direct employees are those who must account for every minute of their time as benefiting a specific contract charge or an overhead function. Indirect employees are generally required only to account for time spent on uncommon overhead functions (seminars, jury duty, etc.).

Companies that do business with the U.S. government are required to define the detailed makeup of their direct and indirect costs in their company *Disclosure Statements*, which must be approved by government representatives.

Labor vs. Nonlabor Costs

Costs also may be classified as *labor* or *nonlabor*. Labor costs are those paid to company employees. Such costs, at the lowest level, are generally expressed in hours or fractions thereof, to which direct labor rates are applied to get dollar values. Nonlabor costs are those paid to suppliers or subcontractors for purchased parts or services.

Direct-Direct and Allocated-Direct Costs

Direct costs are further classified as direct-direct or allocated-direct. Allocated-direct costs are still direct costs; however, they are not directly assigned to a specific project. They may benefit multiple contracts or multiple projects within a contract, or they may be incurred in a manner that makes identity to specific projects uneconomical; for example, they may be incurred through process-type operations. The terms *allocated prime cost* and *pool work order* have also been used for classifying allocated-direct costs.

An example of a process-type operation is mixing paint. The paint mixing process may take only a few minutes per container, and the paint could be used to support any number of products and/or projects. Such costs are accumulated in pools and are allocated to projects and contracts, on some previously defined basis.

Overhead Costs (Indirect Costs)

Overhead costs also are accumulated in pools. These pools are allocated to contracts on some previously determined basis that may or may not be in proportion to the benefit gained. Similar to the case of allocated-direct costs, certain overhead expenses are not directly related to a specific overhead pool, but are accumulated separately, and then redistributed (allocated) to benefiting pools. Industrial relations, industrial security, office operations, plant services, and material handling organizations might exemplify such costs.

WBS (Figure 11.4)

When contract requirements dictate classification of costs by components of hardware and services or by organization, the customer is provided these costs by use of a WBS, which is a product-oriented, family-tree division of hardware- and services-related effort that breaks the contract work down into ever smaller units. A WBS is used for budgeting the work to be performed.

The highest level of this structure is the total effort to be performed. Similar to the blueprints for a construction project, the WBS represents the major portions of the project for which performance measurement is deemed necessary. The assignment of necessary reporting levels near the top of the structure is most often the responsibility of the government, while the lower levels are established at the option of the company to enable management visibility of expenditures and control of resources.

FIGURE 11.4. Accounting Classifications: Work Breakdown Structure. (Reprinted with permission from Cappels, T.M., *Financially Focused Quality*, CRC Press, 1999. Copyright CRC Press, Boca Raton, Florida.)

Cost Accumulation Structure (Figure 11.5)

Many larger companies, and particularly those that engage in business relations with the U.S. government, use a cost accumulation structure. This structure provides for collection of costs at the lowest level where company effort (resources) is expended. Costs are then summarized through successively higher levels of both the WBS and the organizational (functional) structure.

Charge Numbers

Many enterprises use charge numbers in a time recording system (e.g., time cards) for identifying costs to specific projects or classifications. These charge numbers, sometimes referred to as *work order/work authorities*, are a numbering system that is the basis for summing costs into the accounting (and allocating) structure, the functional organization structure, and the WBS.

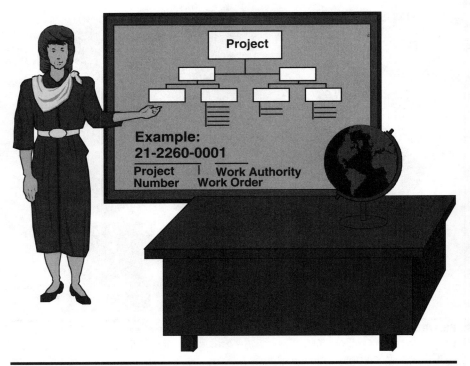

FIGURE 11.5. Accounting Classifications: Cost Accumulation Structure. (Reprinted with permission from Cappels, T.M., *Financially Focused Quality*, CRC Press, 1999. Copyright CRC Press, Boca Raton, Florida.)

Timekeeping, Time Cards, and Cost Segregation

A timekeeping system uses a character coding system to achieve required segregation of costs. This character coding is accomplished through the use of a *charge number* (see above). For direct employees, the charge number for the effort to be performed by the employee is entered on the time card at the time the effort is started on that day. The number of hours worked on that particular job also is entered.

Time cards are the very essence of most employers that require close scrutiny of employee time. They are the official company time records. They are the basis for paying employees and for obtaining reimbursement from the customer.

Figure 11.6 presents an example of a charge number coding structure. In this figure, a 10-character coding system is used. However, a company has no restrictions on the number of digits used in the charge number. Also, the system illustrated here is fairly complex, but a company may devise its coding system as deemed appropriate.

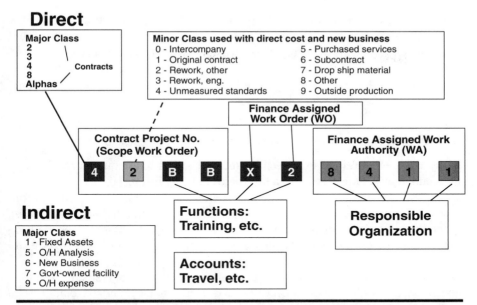

FIGURE 11.6. Example of 10-Character Coding System. (Reprinted with permission from Cappels, T.M., *Financially Focused Quality*, CRC Press, 1999. Copyright CRC Press, Boca Raton, Florida.)

In this example, the charge number is *42-BBX2-8411*. Notice that each character of this number identifies specific costs and reads in two different ways depending on the first digit. The first digit (sometimes referred to as the *major class code*) identifies whether costs are direct or indirect. In the example, the first digit is a *4*, signifying that the charge is direct. Had this digit been a *1, 5, 6, 7,* or *9*, it would mean that the charge is indirect.

The *minor class code* (second digit) identifies type of cost (e.g., intercompany, original contract work, subcontract, etc.) for direct or new business type activity. The number *2* here classifies the effort as *rework, other*. In this example, the minor class code serves no purpose for indirect charges. Therefore, company guidelines might require that a zero be used here for indirect work.

The next four digits may be referred to as the *work order*. For direct effort, this is often where specific contract items are differentiated. In this example, the *BBX2*, when combined with the major class code *4*, means that the effort is supporting item two of a particular contract. For indirect effort, the overhead function is designated here (e.g., training class, jury duty).

The last four digits are referred to here as the *work authority*. For direct effort, this is where the specific tasks might be identified (e.g., receiving inspection, design review). In this example, the work authority is *8411*, where the *84* means the effort is the responsibility of the product assurance organization, and the *11* designates the activity as shipping inspection. For indirect activities, these four digits are used to identify the organization whose overhead budget is funding the indirect activity (e.g., the department of the employee serving on jury duty).

As discussed above, the charge number and its corresponding coding system might be considered the *zip code* of finance.

Virtual and Manual Time Cards and Labor Recording

Many companies utilize PC-based financial systems to account for effort by their employees. Others still use a time card. In many instances, charge numbers are entered into the system. When charge numbers are used, it has been said for government contractors that correctly recording activity is the *most important* function that employees perform. Charge numbers identify labor expended to the proper charge number and, therefore, to the proper contract or overhead account. But why should correct recording of time be most important?

Accurate time card records are necessary to obtain reimbursement from the government, as well as to establish wages and salaries to be paid to the employees.

For any government contractor, misuse of the time card (e.g., knowingly charging to an incorrect charge number) is a serious offense analogous to forging a check and can result in lawsuits and/or loss of government work for the company. The offending employee would be subject to disciplinary action, such as loss of position or employment, and criminal penalties (i.e., jail, fines).

Figure 11.7 illustrates a simplified example of how the timekeeping method discussed above could be applied to record the work provided by a typical direct employee working for a government contractor. On Monday and Tuesday of the week, the employee works 8 hours each day on a specific Air Force contract. The major class code for direct activity is an alpha character, and in this case the *A* designates that this effort is being performed for an Air Force customer. The remainder of the charge number specifies the effort in finer detail. On Wednesday and Thursday, 8 hours each day are worked in support of a Navy contract (identified by a major class code of *N*). On Friday, the employee first spends 4 hours at a medical appointment (major class code *5* for overhead) and wraps up the day working on the same Air Force contract he worked Monday and Tuesday.

Time cards can include other fields for data entry such as overtime and special work hours.

The employee, when signing the time card, is in effect signing a legal document. The employee is saying that he or she has performed the work as defined on the time card, and in return the company will pay the employee for his or her efforts.

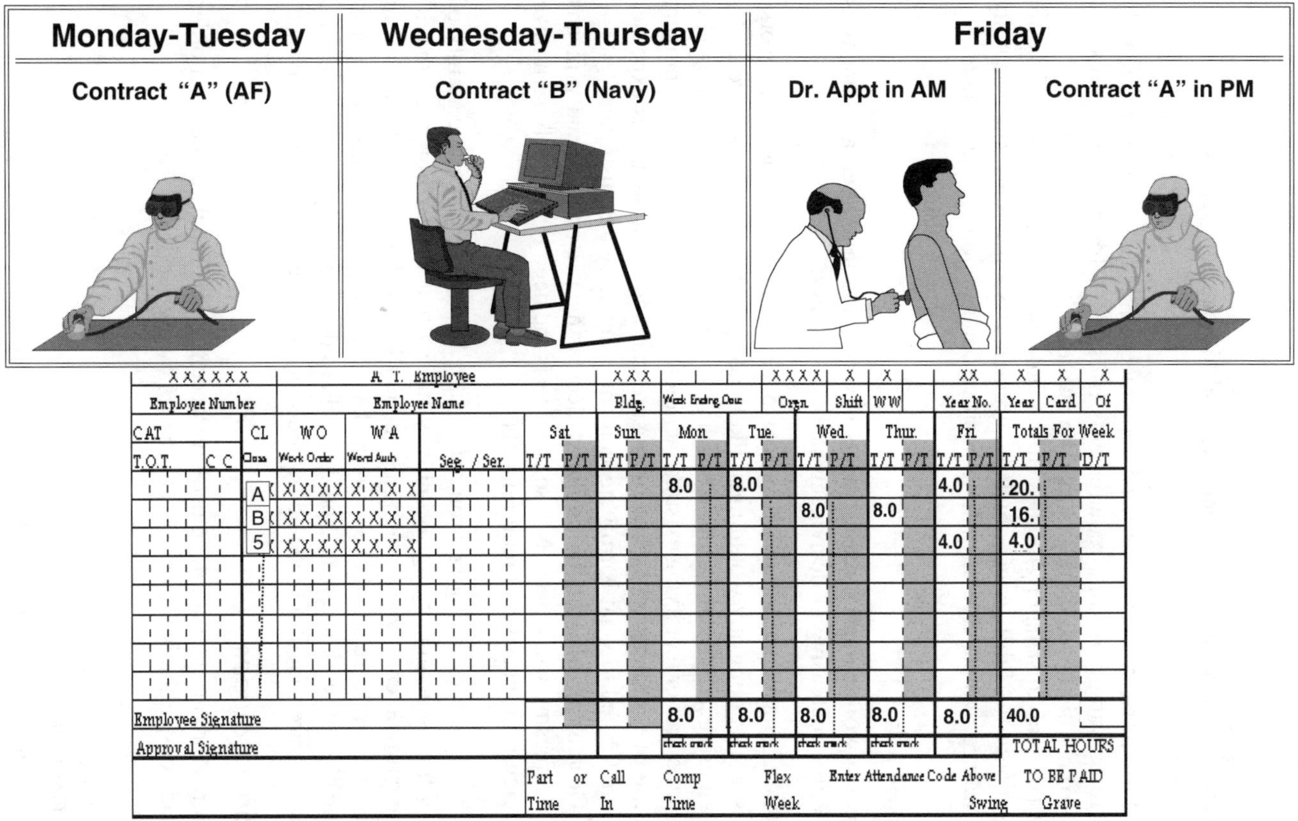

FIGURE 11.7. Time Card/Time Recording. (Reprinted with permission from Cappels, T.M., *Financially Focused Quality*, CRC Press, 1999. Copyright CRC Press, Boca Raton, Florida.)

Forecasting Personnel
Criteria

The accurate forecasting of personnel is vital to financial success, as discussed in the following list of affected areas:

- Proposals: A contractor needs contracts in order to exist. Accurately forecasting personnel requirements is essential for preparing proposals from which such contracts may be awarded.
- Training: Just having bodies in the right place at the right time is not enough to fulfill contractual requirements. Such bodies must be fully trained and capable of making positive contributions to the product.

Facilities

Forecasting working space requirements is very important when a company is facing either increasing or decreasing sales, as follows:

- Increasing personnel: Increasing personnel usually means increasing workspace. A company would most likely accommodate such an increase by entering into leases for more building space or, possibly, by building new structures or modifying existing facilities. It should be obvious that prudent use of resources is essential to ensure that additional facilities expenses are limited to what is truly needed and wanted by the customer.
- Decreasing personnel: Similarly, decreasing personnel usually means decreasing workspace. Not so obvious is the need to routinely scrutinize facility forecasts and requirements.

In the rapidly changing environment of the 21st century, the uncertainty of business trends and changing technology means that most companies should exercise extreme care when examining facility leases. Every time a lease is up for renewal, that lease should be examined as if it were a completely new lease. Consolidation of working areas should be achieved at every opportunity to ensure that each square foot of leased and owned space is necessary and fully utilized.

Human Resources

Human resource organizations must have accurate personnel forecasts in order to provide cost-effective operations of the following services:

- Employment
- Terminations
- Conflict of interest support
- Maintenance of policies and procedures

- Compensation analysis
- Benefits coordination
- Health services (e.g., medical and dental plan coordination)
- Medical services (e.g., in-plant doctors and nurses)
- Equal opportunity programs
- Labor relations
- Security/emergency services (e.g., in-plant fire department, ambulance)
- Government security (e.g., document control, security clearances)
- Other business decision (e.g., mergers/consolidations, etc.)

FORWARD PRICING RATES/OVERHEAD AND G&A

Overhead and G&A costs are often allocated to personnel, and forecasts of future expense for overhead costs are used to develop forward pricing rates.

Forecasting Direct Personnel

The average worker in the U.S. is paid for a 40-hour workweek. This most frequently results from Monday-through-Friday employment of 8 hours each day. Saturday and Sunday are grouped together and termed the *weekend*.

In addition, most companies provide *holiday* compensation of some sort. Most often this takes the form of days off with pay or extra pay for working during holiday periods (e.g., time-and-a-half, double time, triple time, etc.).

The 8 hours that an employee is paid to work each day (excluding holidays) is termed *straight time*. Straight time is the starting point for determining the total time an employee will spend performing productive work.

When forecasting personnel, management first examines the future work requirements in three areas:

- Backlog of work: The activities that are scheduled to satisfy current orders or contractual requirements.
- Forecast or proposed: Effort to support areas where additional orders are anticipated or effort that is in the proposal phase.
- Potential: Activity to support new products that may be designed, or new projects that may be proposed and negotiated, and begun within the time span of the forecast.

The forecasted hours associated with these three groupings are converted to estimated numbers of direct employees, termed *direct head count*. This conversion is achieved by applying a *yield* or *realization* factor.

Statistically "average" direct employee

Criteria

LMMS Yield/Realization	Hours/day
* **Straight time (S/T)**	8.0
* **Vacation/sick leave**	-0.7
* **S/T available for work**	7.3
* **S/T work on overhead**	-0.5
* **S/T available for contracts**	6.8
* **Overtime (OT) at 2%**	0.1
* **S/T+OT available for contracts**	6.9

FIGURE 11.8. Forecasting Personnel: Realization Factor. (Reprinted with permission from Cappels, T.M., *Financially Focused Quality*, CRC Press, 1999. Copyright CRC Press, Boca Raton, Florida.)

Forecasting Personnel: Realization Factor (Figure 11.8)

This factor takes into consideration the effects that vacation/sick leave, work on overhead accounts, and overtime will have on the time that the statistically *average* employee will perform profit-generating work. The calculation is as follows:

■ Straight time (8.0 hours): For this illustration, a 40-hour, 5-day workweek is used, with the average employee working 8-hour days.
■ Vacation/sick leave (–0.7 hours): From the 8 hours straight time, 0.7 hours are removed for vacation and sick leave. For the company in this example, there are 250 working days a year; 250 days times 0.7 hours equals 175 hours that are spent each year by the average employee taking vacation leave and sick leave. That 175 hours equates to just over 4 weeks a year.

After making the vacation and sick leave adjustment, the average employee has 7.3 straight-time hours available for work each day.

■ Overhead accounts (–0.5 hours): The average employee does not spend all of this available time on activities that directly generate profits. He or she occasionally will spend time on overhead activities, such as the following:

1. Engaging in independent research and development studies (the results of which potentially enhance the company's position in technical expertise).
2. Working on bid and proposal activity (efforts to acquire new business).
3. Attending training seminars or classes.
4. Taking care of union business, or other appointments not related to contract work.
5. Participating in work-related professional societies.
6. Performing jury duty or appearing as a court witness.
7. *An act of God* (e.g., a natural disaster like an earthquake) makes it impossible or impractical for the employee to come to work.
8. Taking part in nonwork-related activities felt by the company to provide other benefits (e.g., blood bank, Junior Achievement).

In this example, 0.5 hours a day (125 hours a year) is the adjustment made to the 7.3-hour subtotal. Therefore, the 7.3 straight-time hours available in each 8-hour day is reduced by this 0.5 hours, yielding 6.8 straight-time hours remaining for every 8-hour working day.

Does this mean that, on the average, an individual employed for 8-hour days (5 days a week) will contribute 34 hours (5 × 6.8) for activity that directly generates profit? No, it does not. There is more to consider.

■ Overtime (+0.1 hours): The average employee works a certain amount of overtime. In this example, the average overtime per 8-hour day is 0.1 hours. The *overtime yield factor* is based on the percent of overtime worked by direct employees on contract work.

■ Straight time + overtime available each day (6.9 hours): The result of these computations is that the average employee working an 8-hour day can be expected to contribute 6.9 hours (6.8 hours straight time plus 0.1 hours overtime) per day direct to contracts.

Forecasting Problem

A manager is responsible for delivering 690 direct hours per day on his various contracts. How many employees would he need to employ on these contracts?

One hundred direct employees would work an average of 690 contract direct hours each workday. This is calculated as follows: 6.9 hours × 100 employees = 690 contract direct hours.

Disallowances

The typical employee working for a government contractor flies coach class to Washington, D.C. for company business. The government generally will reimburse the company for the costs of coach-class travel when required. However, do you think the chief executive officer of a major contractor flies coach class to Washington, D.C.? No way! You will find that CEOs almost always fly first class. The company pays these costs, but do you think the government will reimburse the customer for the full cost of the first-class tickets? No again. The government will reimburse only for costs that are deemed necessary, and first-class travel is seldom — if ever — necessary.

As a result, such costs above what is essential are disallowed, which means they will not be reimbursed. The company chooses to fly executive officers first class knowing these costs will be disallowed.

RATES PER DIRECT LABOR HOUR (FIGURE 11.9)

It is not unusual to find a posted *shop rate* when you take your car to the automotive repair shop. Such a rate may be listed as anywhere from $45 to $110 an hour. This does not mean that the mechanic earns this high wage. The mechanic is earning less, and the difference between the posted rate and the rate charged by the repair shop is overhead and profit.

Figure 11.9 illustrates this principle. While an hourly employee may be paid a gross wage of $25.15 each hour, the company is charging the customer much more. An example of the components of the direct labor rate follows:

Direct Labor Rate per Hour

$25.15	Employee direct wage
10.52	Fringe benefits
10.34	Indirect labor
4.54	Indirect fringes
10.80	Occupancy
4.96	New business
11.54	Other
77.85	Total Cost
8.00	Fee or profit (10% est)
85.85	Total Cost per Hour

Management	Customer	Employee
$85.85	$85.85	$25.15

FIGURE 11.9. Rates per Direct Labor Hour.

- The employee earns a gross wage (before taxes) of $25.15 per hour.
- The average employee in this company also receives fringe benefits, such as vacation leave, sick pay, or a retirement plan, which equate to approximately another $10.52 an hour.
- Overhead must be included as well. A portion of the overhead pays for indirect labor (e.g., managers, vice presidents); $10.34 is added to the labor rate for indirect labor.
- The indirect employees also have fringe benefits, so another $4.54 is added.
- Costs associated with the company facilities are included. Such costs include depreciation and maintenance. The costs associated with supplying each employee with a computer may also be included here; $10.80 is added.
- An on-going business concern is always performing special projects in an effort to generate new business. A certain amount of these costs are anticipated; $4.96 is added in this example.
- Other costs might include insurance, corporate management allocations, supplies, equipment rental, professional outside services, and indirect travel; here $11.54 is used.
- An on-going business concern should be making a profit for the stockholders, and finally a profit component can be tacked onto each direct labor hour. Here, the total direct labor amount is $85.85 per hour.

TEACHING FFPM AND FINANCIAL CONCEPTS

FFPM requires that all employees maintain a financial focus throughout their workday. This is best facilitated by offering employees financial training. Reading this text is an excellent manner to grasp fundamental concepts and learn about FFPM tools, discussed in this chapter and in Chapter 12. The next step in implementing FFPM is project team and organization-wide education. In smaller companies, the mere reading of this text with interactive discussions can create the financially focused mindset that fosters significant savings. Larger companies have taken this further by making formalized training available to all employees.

It is of utmost importance when considering formalized FFPM training to use resources only for what is needed and wanted. In the early days of total quality management (TQM), the executive boards of many companies would give a blank check to their training organizations to develop TQM courses. The result: hundreds of millions of dollars in time and resources expended to teach vast concepts, many of which were never used.

For example a corporate executive was asked why his company had recently spent $500,000 to send 100 staff members to a TQM off-site training seminar.

He responded: "We wanted to let the employees know that we are quite serious about this TQM." Unfortunately, attendees gave very little favorable feedback regarding the event, and nothing changed.

In the instance just mentioned, management had not previously utilized FFPM tools and did not perform a cost analysis (see Chapter 10) before deciding to schedule the seminar. If they had, the company could have saved half a million dollars.

An Effective FFPM Training Guideline

FFPM would not allow an indiscriminant approach to training like the one mentioned above. A formal FFPM training program should have the following qualities:

1. FFPM training is available to all employees.
2. Company employees attend one session, which is 2 to 4 hours in duration, with two or three 10-minute breaks.
3. Each session should be taught as a seminar, allowing interactive discussion about topics covered.
4. The seminar should be attended by no more than 80 students at a time, and these students should be from a similar discipline within the company. This ensures that seminar discussion and questions are relevant to all in attendance.
5. The class is formatted in four modules as follows:
   a. Module 1 (30 to 60 minutes), *Introduction to Finance:* This is a tailored introduction to the company's financial health and organization structure, in the following format:
      i. Key financial data unique to the enterprise are presented (e.g., sales, earnings before interest and taxes, earnings per share, backlog).
      ii. The next part of the introduction is a description of how the company obtains and uses funds to generate a profit.
      iii. Module I concludes with a summary of the financial organization, with the names of managers and employees to call with questions.
   b. Module II (15 to 30 minutes), *FFPM Overview:*
      i. The basic FFPM tools are presented.
      ii. Case studies and examples of FFPM success stories are used to illustrate the application of FFPM tools. It is best if the case studies are drawn or developed from the sponsoring company's own FFPM experience. Examples from this text can also be used.

  c. Module III (30 to 60 minutes), *Financial Concepts:* Not all the concepts presented in this text are applicable to every company. Therefore, only relevant financial concepts should be included in the module.

  d. Module IV (15 to 60 minutes), *Implementation:* The course concludes with a summary of recent company programs relevant to the attendees. This may include project management or product liability issues pertinent to the enterprise. Current projects or initiatives can be used to stimulate much discussion. The facilitator of this seminar should take every opportunity to encourage the attendees to be financially focused. Employees should feel challenged to examine old and new work processes with a financially focused mindset, asking such questions as:

    i. Do I really need to be doing this?

    ii. Is there a way I can accomplish this more quickly and effectively (using the latest technology or using plain old common sense)?

    iii. Is there an activity that another employee or group is performing to support me that I really do not need or that could be made easier?

    iv. Is there anything anywhere in this company that I feel could be improved?

Getting an accurate answer to the above questions will be possible after the employee has completed the earlier three modules. If the answer to any of the above questions is yes, the appropriate FFPM tool should be initiated (e.g., process change recommendation).

Examples of Financially Focused Training Materials

Some of the figures contained in this text were developed from presentations and handouts used for financially focused training classes that have been taught to literally thousands of Lockheed Martin Missiles and Space employees.

These classes have been taught to groups encompassing all disciplines. They have been tailored using unclassified Lockheed Martin financial data that are found in financial statements available to the public (e.g., annual reports to stockholders).

Classes average 1 to 4 hours. There have been classes designed specifically to teach financially focused concepts to such program-specific areas as fleet ballistic missile and government customers, at remote sites across the U.S., as well as the employee population at large.

As a result of this financially focused training, millions of dollars in documented savings have been achieved, and savings continue to accrue.

Self-Paced Training

Another method for teaching FFPM concepts is self-paced training. Technology has made this a very simple process, using already developed formalized training materials. Classroom charts can be formatted and saved onto CDs that any employee can access inexpensively on a desktop computer. Mainframe-based self-paced training is also a viable option.

Each company is encouraged to a find a combination of such training techniques when implementing its own FFPM program.

SUMMARY

Understanding basic financial terminology and concepts is critical for obtaining the financially focused mindset. As the employee receives training in company-unique financial aspects, the tools of FFPM will offer the prospect of greater profitability.

SELF-STUDY/DISCUSSION QUESTIONS

1. If you were to design a company-unique financially focused training program for your company, what topics would you include?
2. How does your company make a profit?
3. How does your company account for time?
4. Assuming a 6.9-hour-per-day yield factor, how many employees working for 1 week would be necessary to deliver 1,725 hours?
5. What is the difference between direct and indirect costs?
6. What is the difference between labor and nonlabor costs?
7. Explain the process used for forecasting personnel.
8. Why might the realization factor be lower in summer months than winter months?
9. What is a "disallowance"? What is the purpose of having disallowances?

Free value-added materials available from the
Download Resource Center at www.jrosspub.com.

12

FINANCIALLY FOCUSED PROJECT MANAGEMENT PERFORMERS AND COMPONENTS

INTRODUCTION

The performers and components necessary for operating a large-scale financially focused project management (FFPM) system are presented in the next two chapters. This chapter presents an FFPM overview, and then focuses on the first phase of the process improvement activity: determining areas for improvement.

FFPM enters the scene when a decision needs to be made regarding investment of resources. Such investments may involve analyzing the opportunity for a new project or when some sort of failure occurs. Therefore, all processes, procedures, products, or product components that are targeted for improvement or corrective action are appropriate FFPM subjects. The following is a sampling of the types of situations to which FFPM has been successfully applied:

1. Process improvement for streamlining the process of obtaining quotes from vendors in the advertising field.
2. Projects to improve operation of hotel courtesy car service to airport.
3. Project to manufacture an innovative new product called Penguin-in-a-Helmet.
4. Training employees in the operation of a new MRP2 system.
5. Projects aimed at identifying ideal level of test console repair and maintenance support.

6. Job instructions for handling returned retail merchandise.
7. Improvements in after-market support for manufacturer warranty service.
8. Domestic applications have ranged from child rearing to improvements in landscaping and interior design.

The use of FFPM is particularly encouraged when considering such projects to implement process improvement programs as continuous quality improvement, process management, employee suggestion systems, cost reduction or avoidance programs, total quality management, total quality service, and value engineering.

Imagine the effect a structured FFPM approach could have on the salaries/pensions/benefits of corporate executives and government appointees. FFPM applications exist for manufactured products that have resulted in injury to users, and the administration of *nonprofit* and *charitable* organizations. The list of potential FFPM applications is seemingly endless.

FFPM OVERVIEW

As shown in Figure 12.1, there are 11 basic FFPM components. Few FFPM applications would require the simultaneous involvement of all ingredients. Figure 12.1 illustrates each component and its relationship to the others.

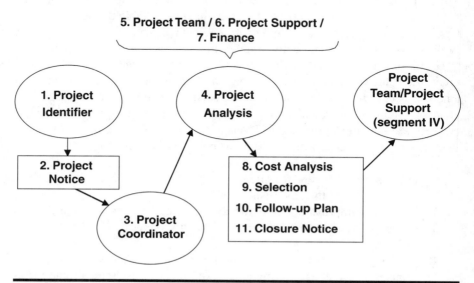

FIGURE 12.1. FFPM Overview.

The *project identifier* (#1) begins the FFPM process by identifying a potential project or noting a failure of some sort. The identifier completes some form of official documentation describing the project. The *project notice* (#2) is the formal document that begins the project or project activity. The *project coordinator* (#3) becomes involved on receipt of the project notice. If this is a totally new project, the project manager is the project coordinator. For all other projects (e.g., process improvements, failures), the project coordinator is often a designated member of the project team.

The project coordinator might be the technical expert in the area involving the failure notice, or the project team leader for the team involved in the process improvement recommendation. The project notice is received and logged in. The coordinator then works with others to generate a listing of the appropriate project team members, support members, and/or finance team members to participate in *project analysis* (#4). This step is necessary before resources are expended. Project analysis is one of the most important components of the FFPM process. This is where the mathematical calculations are made that determine activities to be performed. As a result, it is very important that the appropriate individuals be invited to participate.

The project analysis meeting is held so that the experts can determine what actions need to be taken. If the coordinator has not had FFPM training, a properly schooled representative from the finance organization should also attend.

The *project team* (#5) and *project support* (#6) individuals participate in the project analysis and are divided into two groups:

1. Potential project or failure analysts: Potential project analysts are those individuals with even the slightest chance of being able to provide technical or administrative expertise in evaluating and/or resolving the reported situation. Included in this category are the product support organizations whose activities may influence the situation noted on the notification document.
2. Primary project or failure analysts: The primary analysts are individuals who are determined to have the greatest likelihood of positively influencing the process improvement or corrective action process. Again, the category may include the product support group influencing the noted situation. Primary analysts are invited to the project analysis meeting.

Finance (#7) is preferably represented by a coordinator who has received basic financial training via FFPM. As such, finance is actively involved in the determination and evaluation of potential projects. This includes the selection of the activities involved in the project, development of the project follow-up plan, and sign-off on the project closure notice.

A *cost analysis* (#8) is generated for each potential activity.

In *selection* (#9), the most cost-effective project activity or activities are selected and implemented. Finance tracks expenditures and ensures that costs associated with the selected activities are in line with cost analysis. This is particularly important when there are several options under consideration for the same goal. Comparing the costs analyses for the options offers the project team objective data for decision making.

The *follow-up plan* (#10) is developed to ensure that the activity is successful. Finance provides prompts to ensure adherence to the follow-up plan. The selected activity is forwarded to the project team and/or product support organizations that will be performing the project activity.

The *closure notice* (#11) is forwarded to product support when required. Finance ensures costs are in line with final instructions of the closure notice. All peripheral activities related to the implemented process improvement (e.g., tracking unique costs) cease. This step ensures that activities that require increased expenditures (e.g., tightened inspection specifications) are discontinued when no longer merited.

Each of the above basic components may have numerous subcomponents, as discussed below.

Project Identifier

The application of FFPM begins with the identification of a project or failure or other opportunity for correction or improvement. For example, the project identifier could be the customer and the company project identifier an employee in the warranty service organization. The project coordinator resides in the quality engineering department.

1. The customer returns the failed product (e.g., television) to the warranty service department.
2. The warranty service department originates the project notice and forwards it with the failed product to the project coordinator in quality engineering.
3. The project coordinator works with the product support organizations (e.g., shipping, manufacturing, etc.) and corrects the cause of the failure.
4. The product is repaired.
5. The product is returned to the warranty service department.
6. The warranty service department returns the product to the customer.

Cost Analysis

As discussed earlier, the cost analysis is essential for determining whether or not to undertake a project or implement a process improvement recommendation or for determining corrective action(s) related to a failure. This analysis may be used by anyone considering alternatives. However, because the research and computations required for accurate analyses can sometimes be quite time consuming, its judicious use is encouraged.

All projects, process improvements, and recommended procedural changes have financial implications that can be measured either directly or indirectly. For example, a corrective action or process improvement that results in savings of 10 minutes per test in the inspection process has savings that can be quantified as follows:

1. Hourly direct labor rate of inspector: $18 per hour.
2. Time saved per test equals 10 minutes.
3. Ten minutes equals one sixth of an hour saved per test by the inspector.
4. One sixth of an inspector's hour equals one sixth of $18 saved for each test.
5. One sixth of $18 (inspector's wage per hour) equals $3 saved for each test.
6. Assuming there are 100 tests each month, the process improvement yields gross savings of $300 each month.
7. The costs associated with implementation should be subtracted from the gross savings, because certain one-time costs may be unavoidable (e.g., rewriting procedures or purchase of new equipment).
8. When appropriate, further computations may be performed to account for savings related to any elements of overhead involved in the cost.

The cost analysis processing procedure is outlined below:

A. The cost analysis is completed for process improvement #1 as described below:
   1. The top data block is completed with the following information:
      a. Name of individual completing the analysis (e.g., the project coordinator)
      b. Analysis number
      c. Date
      d. Organization and phone extension
   2. The block entitled *recommended project* is completed with:
      a. A description of the project activity
      b. The estimated labor costs associated with the new procedures
      c. The estimated nonlabor costs associated with the new procedures
      d. Any one-time implementation (set-up) costs that might be necessary
      e. These costs are totaled to yield *total costs of project*. These costs can be expressed in any number of ways, including annual costs, monthly costs, costs per manufactured item, etc. What is important,

however, is that all cost analyses be consistent in the manner the costs are estimated.

3. In a similar fashion, the costs of superseded functions are calculated and totaled.
4. The fourth step is computing the difference in costs between the new procedure and that superseded. This could show the following:
   a. The new method will cost $5,000 more each month.
   b. In the case of a recommended change to improve a process, it could be documented that the new procedure results in less cost than the old; in other words, savings will result from implementation.

B. Another cost analysis is completed for each project and/or process improvement. Process improvement #2 could show that an additional cost of $8,000 is estimated.
C. A comparison is made between the estimated costs for each potential process improvement, and the most cost-effective action is selected for implementation.
D. The copy of the analysis for the selected process improvement is forwarded to the finance administration organization.
E. The analyses related to the project notice are attached and filed for future reference.

Follow-Up Plan

A follow-up plan is necessary to continue with the financial focus. The purpose of the follow-up plan is to increase profitability in three ways:

1. If the project did not fully achieve its goal (e.g., product did not meet certain specifications or cause of failure was not resolved), follow-up action in a timely manner can lead to the generation of alternate procedures.
2. If a project has proven to be successful, follow-up can alert the project team quality engineer and/or other project team members that this may be useful in other applications.
3. By following up, it can be learned that newly added project activities are no longer required. (For example, 100% inspection may have been implemented when parts coming from suppliers were generally poorly produced. The supplier may have implemented process improvements and corrected component problems. Receiving inspection may revert from 100% to cost-effective sample inspection.)

The follow-up plan contains narrative explaining exactly what tests or procedures are necessary to ensure the implemented process improvement has been successful. The recommended duration between subsequent follow-ups is also provided.

The follow-up plan contains the following blocks:

1. Name of supervisor responsible for follow-up
2. Process improvement number
3. Date
4. Organization
5. Phone extension
6. Multiple follow-ups may be desired, and the form contains a separate area for each follow-up as follows:
   a. Date of follow-up
   b. Name of individual performing follow-up
   c. Phone extension
   d. Outcome of follow-up:
      i. The follow-up was successful, so move on to next follow-up procedure.
      ii. The follow-up found anomalies; recommend revising corrective action.
      iii. The final follow-up activity has been completed successfully. (In this case, the project closure notice should be issued.)

Closure Notice

When it has been clearly determined that a project or corrective action has been successful, i.e., that the cause of the failure has been corrected, the project coordinator issues a project activity closure notice. And it does just that! The closure notice completes the project activity cycle by closing the activity initiated by the project notice.

Copies of the closure notice are forwarded to the project team members, project support, and financial administration organization to alert everyone of the final procedural changes (if any). The data are also entered into the database for referral by all who have access.

The data contained on the closure notice follow:

1. Name
2. Process improvement number
3. Date
4. Organization
5. Phone extension
6. Narrative explaining events performed closing the action, e.g., modifying procedures

The action is closed. It is no longer a process improvement or a corrective action, but becomes that standard operating procedure. Reference to the failure notice may also be made in this narrative portion.

FINANCIAL ADMINISTRATION

The financial administration plays a vital role in FFPM. The traditional functions of finance affected by FFPM procedures are (1) propose/negotiate new prices and contracts and (2) track company performance to proposed/negotiated prices and funding. These activities are almost always reactive in nature.

Within FFPM, the responsibilities of finance are dramatically increased. Preferably, the financial role listed below is performed by the project coordinator, who has had specific FFPM training. The financially focused mindset of the coordinator or a member of the finance community is needed to perform the following:

1. Receive the cost analysis: Often, finance will be involved in preparation of the cost analysis. Upon its receipt, finance performs the following functions:
   a. Validate the data (e.g., labor rates, computer costs).
   b. Incorporate these increased costs into prices, in-process proposals, and budgets.
   c. Monitor the actual expenses incurred by organizations performing the process improvement procedures to verify that costs are being incurred as projected. Identifying anomalies here may lead to the realization that the designated process improvement procedures are not being followed properly.
2. Receive the follow-up plan: Referred to occasionally as a tickler file, reminding finance to occasionally prompt the process improvement coordinator to ensure that follow-up actions are being taken.
3. Receive the closure notice: Upon receipt, further justification is available for supporting negotiations of new contracts or recommending new pricing policies. Also, this alerts finance that the changes to procedures have been formally approved and that any further changes noted while monitoring and tracking actual costs could signal other deviations.

The financial administration organization's involvement in the process improvement cycle provides executive management as well as its customers with an immediate source of critical cost data. Prior to FFPM, these data were not available until many months or sometimes years after significant changes had taken place.

When pricing, proposing, or negotiating new products or contracts, finance relies very heavily on historical data. It is advantageous to alert finance to the cost impact of new process improvements. Finance can immediately update prices or quotes to ensure that any additional effort is included.

Finance is also in the ideal position to prompt process improvement coordinators (e.g., quality engineering management) when expenditures are not in line with the process improvement cost analysis. Perhaps the performing organization has misunderstood the process improvement and is not performing properly. Finance, in reviewing cost data, can identify this situation and also work with the coordinator in determining the cost effectiveness of the corrective action.

Finally, finance should ensure that the coordinator is adhering to the process improvement follow-up plan, issuing alternative corrective actions and closure notices as required and in a timely manner.

PRODUCT SUPPORT ORGANIZATIONS

The product support organizations are those with either direct or indirect contact with the product. They often identify failures, cause failures, and correct failures. The project team and project support organizations are involved in FFPM as follows:

1. Project team and project support performance is tracked by finance.
2. When significant variances exist between actual costs and expected costs, the finance organization seeks justification from product support organizations.
3. When product support identifies failures, the failure notice is completed and forwarded to the process improvement coordinator.
4. Product support implements process improvements and corrective actions as assigned by the process improvement coordinator. If failures continue, product support originates and forwards more failure notices.
5. Product support formalizes/modifies/discontinues process improvements and corrective actions upon receipt of the process improvement closure notice.
6. Product support responds to inquiries from finance.

Anyone can be a project, failure, or opportunity identifier. For example, a dissatisfied customer, if able to explain the discontent, is a project identifier. A person who realizes that a different tool would help expedite the work is a project identifier. Within the context of FFPM, the individual who initiates the FFPM cycle by completing the project notice is the project identifier. In a company, that person should be the first person to identify a situation for potential improvement. Such conditions are likely to be determined by people in the following environments:

1. Routine failure reporting mechanisms within business concerns, including:
   a. Any/all employees with customer contact, such as the customer service department, warranty service organization, contract negotiators, or program office
   b. Quality assurance inspection/test
   c. Employees responsible for reporting on performance to budget quality and schedule criteria
2. Informal failure reporting mechanisms within business concerns
3. Basically, any observations made by employees in the line of work, such as:
   a. Manufacturing employees experiencing difficulty in performance of assigned tasks
   b. Accountants who feel *there must be a better way* to deal with certain reporting requirements
   c. Supervision and management receiving comments from employees

Everyday citizens can identify failures and opportunities and utilize FFPM tools and techniques to enhance decision making and problem solving in such areas as follows:

- Family disagreements involving a major purchase (e.g., car, home, appliance)
- Major personal decisions (e.g., high school graduate considering college choices)

Process Improvement Begins with Opportunity Identification

From the listings in the previous section, one can conclude that it is plausible that every company employee could be a project identifier. However, the identifier designation is earned only when that person completes the project notice. Many employees may know of a specific area where there is the likelihood for improvement, but only that employee taking FFPM action is recognized.

In most companies, the individuals or groups with primary responsibility for reporting failures will be obvious: customer service and inspection personnel. However, since all employees are potential project identifiers, management needs to ensure that proper motivation exists. This section looks specifically at motivating employees to maintain a financially focused mindset and participate in the project identification process.

Methods for Project Identification

There are many ways to identify a project opportunity or failure, including the utilization of sophisticated inspection and test equipment. There is also the less sophisticated but often very effective use of the human senses, including:

- Sight: For measuring and seeing that something does not conform to specifications or observing activities and process. Also, the eyes are used to read about new methods, better procedures, and/or state-of-the-art equipment, which could improve productivity.
- Sound: By using the ears, one can hear an unusual sound coming from machinery, listen to a customer complaint, or hear a lecture, presentation, or discussion on new methods, better procedures, and/or state-of-the-art equipment, which could improve productivity.
- Smell: The nose can detect an unusual odor or the presence of smoke.
- Taste: Can be used to determine, for example, if something is too sweet or too sour.
- Touch: Can alert someone to a slippery floor or a shock from a frayed electric cord.

Anyone recognizing a situation for potential improvement uses at least one of the five senses to make this identification.

The Failure and Opportunity Identification Process

A listing and discussion of project identifiers follow:

1. Shipping inspection employee observes a dent in product
2. Consumer
3. Mail courier who notices a truck with excess emissions while delivering mail
4. Failures that are not product failures

Anyone who thinks a situation exists that might be improved could be an opportunity or failure identifier (FI). The word *thinks* is emphasized in this context, because for any number of reasons (as listed below) a perceived failure/discrepancy/opportunity for improvement may not, in reality, exist. Listed below are five situations in which a failure may be reported, when in reality the product (while in the factory) met requirements.

1. The test equipment used to test a unit was not working properly. The unit met specifications, but faulty test equipment caused rejection.
2. The FI (e.g., a customer) was not fully aware of the contracted specifications of the product.
3. The FI (e.g., an inspector in the manufacturing process) misunderstood inspection criteria and rejected an acceptable unit.
4. The product was damaged in shipment from the factory.
5. The FI (a customer) was not operating the product properly because either the customer (with the education level of the target consumer for the product) read the instructions but was not able to understand them or

214 Financially Focused Project Management

the instructions were clearly written and easily accessible within the product packaging but the customer did not bother to read them.

The company should recognize, though, that there was a failure of some sort in all but one of the above situations. The failures are not in the design of the product, but as follows:

1. The test equipment failed.
2. The customer had false expectations, and there was a failure to clearly communicate details about the product.
3. The inspector misunderstood manufacturing criteria. Management failed to train the inspector properly.
4. There was a failure to properly package and/or ship the product, which was damaged in transit.
5. The average customer is unable to comprehend instructions. The writer of the instructions failed to prepare clear operating instructions, or the customer failed to read the instructions.

The last failure mentioned is the only one for which the company would not need to consider a process improvement. In this case, the customer should have at least tried to read the instructions.

When a sales contract is prepared or a sale is made, an intellect level slightly below average must be assumed for the prospective customers. However, analysis may reveal that certain limits must be placed on the extent to which a company goes when packaging and selling its product. For example, a company that manufacturers small model toys is aware that an infant could potentially choke on a toy. Therefore, the following steps could be taken to reduce the chances of such an event occurring:

1. The package is clearly marked with the statement *"Not recommended for children under the age of 4."*
2. Instructions included with the toy state: *"Caution: Toy should be kept out of reach of infants, and should not be placed in mouth."*
3. A mechanism is rigged inside the toy package to play a taped message that says in a loud booming voice: *"Caution! Toy should be kept out of reach of infants, and should not be placed in mouths."*
4. The company stations security officers at the sales registers everywhere the toy is sold. Before a sale is allowed, the officer explains the hazards of the product, and the customer must sign a declaration that he or she understands the risks.

In determining how far a company should go to ensure clear communications with the customer, one must consider what is reasonable. For the sake of this text, a failure is defined as a discrepancy or defect that is determined by a reasonable person. This definition is used regardless of the FI, and it must be assumed that the identifier has, at best, intelligence that is slightly below average, and that this person is also reasonable.

Customers

There is no doubt that, after a product is manufactured or a service provided, the customer is the most common FI. Customers can be broken down into subsets: (1) the general public (purchasers of high-price items/services and/or purchasers of low-price items/services) and (2) government customers.

Government Failure Identification

Government customers differ greatly from the general public. Whereas a manufacturer of inexpensive headphone radios may eventually get feedback on 1 of 100 failures in the field, most government contractors receive an amazing 100% notification.

This 100% really is not so amazing, when you realize that many of the individuals (e.g., military) inspecting for discrepancies have but one reason for employment by the government, i.e., they are being paid a salary (and often provided room and board) for finding flaws. This is different from the manner in which feedback is gained for products sold to the general public. The public is not paid directly for inspecting the products they purchase. It is, however, to their benefit to have certain problems corrected.

Only with government contractors like the military do you have the ultimate form of inspection by the end user.

Warranty Service Organization

Employees in the warranty service organization routinely come in contact with failures. These employees are usually employed by the retailer, distributor, or manufacturer. Failures can be revealed to them by way of telephone calls, over-the-counter returns, or mail.

Often their perception of the failure may be quite different from that of the customer. Often, the stated problem is actually only a symptom of a root problem with much wider implications.

Failure Identifiers in the Factory

Inspectors

Obvious FIs include those whose title is *inspector*, individuals employed in a manufacturing concern whose job instructions specify actions to ensure consistent quality.

Manufacturing Employees

Although it is not generally in their charter, manufacturing employees in the shop are in an ideal situation to identify areas for potential improvement. It might very well have been a manufacturing employee who, while sitting around watching an inspector, thought to himself, "Hey, I can do that!" With that thought transferred to an FFPM document (process improvement recommendataion), he becomes an opportunity identifier, and tremendous savings can result (see Chapter 13).

All Other Company Employees

Many companies and corporations have internal audit organizations whose functions include formally investigating different areas of the company to determine areas where improvement is needed. Yet, with all employees acting as company auditors while performing their routine tasks (as FFPM suggests), the company should experience a much better audit, encompassing the entire corporation every day.

Failure and Opportunity Identifier Summary

Any human being can be a failure or opportunity identifier. So too can a machine or computer when designed and/or programmed to identify anomalies (defined as areas for potential improvement). In the FFPM context, the goal is to (1) utilize every conceivable source for failure and opportunity identification, and (2) enter these data into a financially focused process improvement activity.

FFPM is initiated via processing a project notice. The project notice is used to formally cite, for example, the existence of a problem or defect.

Failure During Manufacturing

For a failure occurring during the manufacturing process, the project notice contains fields in which the following key elements are contained:

1. Project notice form number
2. Date of failure
3. FI information, including the name, organization, and telephone extension of the identifier
4. Failed hardware information, including the nomenclature of the failed hardware and serial number and lot number of failed hardware, if applicable
5. Narrative regarding the failure, such as measured specifications, required specifications, conditions of test/inspection, unusual circumstances, and any other information felt to be relevant; for example, the FI also is encouraged to list preliminary potential failure analysts
6. The project closure notice block, to be checked off when the closure notice has been issued

Failure: Customer Return

For the failure of a manufactured item returned to the manufacturer by a customer, the form includes the following data:

1. Project notice form number
2. Date of failure
3. Company FI information, including the name, organization, and telephone extension
4. Customer FI information, including the customer's name, address, area code, and phone number
5. Failed hardware (product) information, including the nomenclature, serial number, and lot number of failed hardware, if applicable
6. Narrative regarding the failure, such as what the customer says happened, conditions of customer use, the results of any tests performed by the company project identifier (customer service representative) on receipt of the defective unit, unusual circumstances, and other information felt to be relevant
7. Steps taken by the customer service representative (dependent on the warranty policy of the company)
8. The closure notice field, to be checked off as required

Failure: Hotel Industry

For failures related to the hotel industry, the notice contains blocks for the following information:

1. Failure notice form number
2. Date of failure

3. FI information, most likely supplied by a maid, desk clerk, PBX operator, cashier, or reservation agent and including the name, organization, and supervisor
4. Failure information, such as location of failure (e.g., room number), narrative regarding the failure, such as:
   a. Television is not functioning properly
   b. Wake-up call buzzer will not shut off
   c. Room heater/air conditioning will not operate
   d. Geckos (lizards) are running around in guest rooms
   e. Other problems noted by guests
   f. Any other information felt to be relevant; for example, the FI is also encouraged to list preliminary potential failure analysts
5. The closure notice field, to be checked off when the situation has been corrected

Generic Failure

The generic failure notice can be summarized as having the following five key elements:

1. Project notice number
2. Company identifier data
3. Customer identifier data
4. Nature of problem
5. The closure notice fields, to be checked off when the failure has been corrected

The project notice may also be used to identify opportunities for process improvements.

PROCESS IMPROVEMENT RECOMMENDATIONS (PIR)

The PIR form is similar to forms utilized in many employee suggestion systems. The recommendation form is a valuable tool for facilitating and motivating employee participation in FFPM. FFPM makes it easy for every employee to participate in process improvement activity by offering tools and techniques that are effective with minimal implementation cost. A major advantage to the PIR is its ease and simplicity of use.

The PIR contains the following data elements:

1. The name of the employee appears on the top of the form.
2. A unique PIR number is preprinted on each form.
3. The date of the submission is important because, in the case of similar offerings, the PIR with the earliest date takes ownership of the recommendation. This does not mean, however, that those submitting similar ideas are not able to participate in the recommendation development process. Individuals with similar thoughts should be brought together, if appropriate, for the synergistic exchange of ideas.
4. The organization of the submitter appears along with the name.
5. The phone extension also appears on the form.
6. Two blocks are used for classifying the recommendation as either a *concern* or a *project*.
   a. Concern: When an employee observes a situation for which there could be potential improvement, the *concern* block is checked, and the idea is written in a simple paragraph or two. There is no further work required on his or her part. That is it. It could not get much simpler. Yet, by performing this simple task, management may learn of some key information, which could save millions of dollars for the company.
   b. Project: Occasionally, an employee is fortunate enough to have the ability to implement his or her own recommendation. When this is the case, the employee can undertake the project and document related efforts with a PIR. Similar to the *concern* process, the block labeled *project* is checked. The submitter proceeds to write one or two paragraphs about the project being undertaken, explaining what will be done and how the project will benefit the company. Again, what could be easier?
7. Finally, the PIR contains two blocks on the bottom, one of which will be marked at a later date. These blocks are described as follows:
   a. Process improvement closure notice attached: As discussed later in this chapter, the closure notice formalizes procedural changes and closes activity associated with the PIR.
   b. Process improvement completed: This block is marked with a check mark when the recommendation discussed on the PIR has been completed, and no further explanation is required.

PIR Success Factors

The three key reasons why the PIR is such a successful FFPM tool are discussed below.

Ease of Processing

Unlike many suggestion systems or cost-savings programs, there is no requirement to perform extensive analysis or calculations before the recommendation
is submitted. It takes only a few minutes to complete the form. Also, because the
form is submitted to one's own manager, the following benefits should occur:

1. The person receiving the form will be familiar with the terminology used
   by the submitter.
2. The person receiving the form will not reject it because it was not filled
   out perfectly. Many coordinators of traditional programs take pride in
   having forms filled out properly, and much time is wasted in administrative
   detail. A manager is motivated to use time effectively. Already having a
   full-time job managing the organization, time most likely will not be
   wasted on meaningless details.

The ease with which the required FFPM paperwork is processed is a true
motivator for participation.

Low Implementation/Administration Costs

The group responsible for such programs in many companies often is comprised
of full-time employees, with designated part-time representatives in organizations
throughout the company. These individuals meet periodically (e.g., monthly) to
review activities during the previous time period.

Such meetings may turn into social affairs, where coffee and doughnuts are
served, while attendees determine, among other things, which participating
employees should be recognized for outstanding achievements. Such recognition, as mentioned earlier, is usually through the awarding of prizes and money.
Tremendous amounts of corporate budgets fund this type of program.

Let's examine the costs involved in administering the PIR. Each manager
(whose time can be quite expensive) must read a one- or two-paragraph statement from an employee. This is time well spent for the following reasons:

1. The employee achieves visibility with management — a motivator.
2. The manager gets to know the employee better, which can lead to better
   utilization of manpower.
3. And to top it off, the employee actually may have a beneficial idea,
   which could lead to significant savings for the company.

The mandatory management involvement is the only cost-significant factor,
and this involvement reaps rewards not found in tradition programs. More than

offsetting the cost of management time is the elimination of the following customary costs:

1. Full-time program administrators and staff for administration of the prior program
2. Part-time participation of organizational program support
3. Associated nonlabor costs include publication and presentation costs; refreshments at meeting/luncheons, etc.; prizes, awards, and cash; and travel expenses related to training for program staff

The bottom line: The FFPM program outlined above is much less costly to administer.

Mandatory Management Involvement

The traditional quality and productivity improvement program (e.g., quality management, continuous improvement) announces the premise that *management support is necessary*. However, FFPM goes that crucial step further, by expounding the principle that *management participation is mandatory*, by procedurally requiring that the manager interact with involved employees. This is another way FFPM cuts costs but increases effectiveness in suggestion programs.

It is not practical to involve an individual actually assigned to a finance organization in *every* conceivable corrective action and process improvement activity. For those corrective action activities with potentially wide-ranging financial implications, FFPM undeniably requires that a well-versed representative of finance be involved. However, for recommendations involving low cost levels, a manager who has received the fundamental FFPM financial training should be able to represent financial interests and determine cost effectiveness.

As discussed earlier, most corporate suggestion systems and cost improvement programs require costly administration, often involving individuals dedicated to administering the program. In addition, these programs have large budgets for promoting such concepts as *continuous improvement* and offer significant awards (e.g., prizes, money) to those participating in the program.

An important drawback of the above-mentioned legacy programs is that ideas are initially submitted to the individuals administering the program. In most cases, management only gets involved in these traditional programs after the fact, after the improvement has been achieved. When the contribution is approved, the employee is recognized openly among peers in a management-conducted ceremony.

The individuals running the program are not as motivated to assist the employee submitting the suggestion as that employee's manager would be. Traditional programs required that detailed forms be submitted to *higher authorities*, which is a major problem because the individuals are not, in reality, higher authorities. One's manager truly fits this definition.

FFPM procedures require that a PIR be submitted to the employee's manager. It is the responsibility of the employee's manager to pass judgment or coordinate review of the recommendation.

When the recommendation has been written as a concern, the manager will log it into a master file. The next step is to make contact with management in the affected areas and discuss the potential of the recommendation. If a good probability exists for an improvement, the manager can seek additional information from his or her employee and/or organize appropriate contacts to continue the investigation.

For productivity improvement recommendation projects, the manager will log the recommendation into the master file and discuss the advantages and disadvantages of the project with the employee. If deemed worthwhile, the employee begins the activity, and management periodically checks on progress. It may be concluded that perhaps the project is not cost effective. In this case, 2 minutes are spent completing a process improvement closure notice, the *process improvement closure notice attached* block on the PIR is checked, and the closure notice is filed with the PIR.

Last and by all means most important, the manager is directly responsible for the primary benefits an individual receives from employment. The manager offers promotions, raises, bonuses, training opportunities, and other benefits that traditional quality programs do not. The manager should include FFPM participation in the employee review process (see next section). With the final ingredient of mandatory management involvement, the recommendation becomes a vital tool for most business entities.

PIR Motivation

A.H. Maslow theorized that employee motivation results from five broad classes of needs. These needs are arranged in hierarchical levels of prepotency so that when one level is satisfied, the next level is activated. The five levels are (1) physiological needs; (2) security or safety needs; (3) social, belonging, or membership needs; (4) esteem needs, including esteem of others and self-esteem; and (5) self-actualization or self-fulfillment needs.

The fact that the manager is reviewing the recommendation provides a means by which all five levels can potentially be satisfied. Employees feel that they have much more control over their environments when they can easily submit suggested changes to management. The synergistic paradox suggests that the more control an employee has over his or her work environment, the more self-esteem he or she will hold.

Of course, Maslow's final need, that of self-actualization or self-fulfillment, depends on many factors that may be out of management's control. Yet, effective management has opportunities to positively influence the lives of its employees.

Another method of motivation worth mentioning here is almost in contradiction to one of Deming's 14 points listed in his theory of management (see Chapter 13). Deming states that companies should eliminate management by numbers and numerical goals. Yet FFPM offers a reminder that there can be positive benefits associated with setting numerical goals.

Take a pole-vaulter, for example. The pole-vaulter loves his sport. It is almost impossible to express the powerful feeling of the pole-vaulter as he stands on the runway, grasping his pole tightly and eyeing that bar high up in the sky. A deep breath is taken, which is slowly exhaled. The pole-vaulter looks down with determination and begins the first steps down the path to the pit. He is picking up speed, going faster and faster. It is poetry in motion as the pole is planted, and the vaulter gracefully rises up in the air, sailing like a picturesque seagull. Up, up, and finally over the bar, landing — exhausted — on the foam rubber padding in the pit. The pole-vaulter's eyes are closed. He felt his foot touch the bar as he went over. Did it fall? He is afraid to open his eyes. He hears the fans in the stands cheering loudly. He opens his eyes, and *the bar is still there*! He did it. The jubilant pole-vaulter stands and jabs his fist triumphantly into the air.

Nice story, yes. But wouldn't you agree that a significant amount of the story's impact would have been lost if, prior to the vault, a track meet official had removed the bar? Don't you also feel that the pole-vaulter would lose much of his motivation without the bar — without a goal?

The financial focus encourages management to offer goals to employees — goals tied to PIR submittal. Such goals can be established for individuals or entire groups of employees as follows:

- Groups of employees: A work group would strive to submit a certain number of valid recommendations by a certain date, or to submit more recommendations than another group. The prize for achieving the goal number, or for submitting more than the other group, could be a group picnic. Such an approach would provide such benefits as encouraging teamwork and fostering a healthy competition between working groups.
- Individual employees: Employees would be informed that the number of PIR submittals will be a factor in the performance review process, and could have both positive and negative effects. On the positive side, employees who normally would not participate in such an activity will feel more compelled so do so. However, there may be some employees that feel pressured and object, saying, "It isn't my job!" Management is

encouraged to explain and respond to such employees with something like, "You are right. It is not your job to cut costs and work more efficiently. In fact, it is *my* job. But your job is to help me do my job, and I'd really appreciate your help trying your best to improve our company's cost effectiveness. You can show me that you are trying to help by looking for and submitting some recommendations. You can do it!"

PIR Examples

Recommendations can have extremely beneficial impacts on a business concern. Below is a sampling of simple recommendations that resulted in significant savings. Each recommendation first appeared in the one- or two-paragraph narrative form.

1. Add "was" and "is" columns to existing report to ease identification of changes.
2. Take advantage of state-of-the-art technology to improve communications.
3. Centralize financial control of low-value activities.
4. Utilize a 12-month moving average for forward pricing rates, instead of formal forward pricing rate negotiations.
5. Generate contract-unique estimate-to-complete rates.
6. Budget and track common minor material expenditures.
7. Publish annual supplements instead of annually republishing an entire text.
8. Automate course presentation to eliminate requirement of teaching assistant.
9. Consolidate impact studies into one large report instead of preparing and distributing 35 small reports.
10. Discontinue maintenance of unnecessary documents.
11. Discontinue performance of unnecessary tasks.
12. Generate equivalent rates for estimates-to-complete.
13. Create a model 204 computer program for generation of reports previously performed manually.
14. Implement numerous word processing applications.
15. Computerize exception report analysis.
16. Discontinue preparing and including unnecessary data in certain reports.
17. Consolidate variance reporting.
18. Include rate-volume analyses on existing reports.
19. Directly transfer data files from one system to another.
20. Utilize badge entry units for access to buildings with special security requirements.
21. Take advantage of bar-code technology for many inventory functions.

PIR Illustration

To illustrate the ease of processing a PIR, the following case is presented. In this organization, the manager has explained the PIR process to employees and requested that each employee submit at least one PIR each quarter. An employee responsible for performing a series of monthly reports learns of an accounting change that will cause her to make several procedural changes. Traditionally, the employee would make the changes in report formats and procedures as time permitted. Because in most business environments there is a tendency to reject change, the employee may avoid taking corrective action until the last minute, and even then implement such changes reluctantly. In this case, the employee learns of the coming accounting change and performs the following steps:

1. Takes a PIR form from the desk
2. Fills out the heading information
3. Puts a check mark in the *project* block
4. Writes the following: A consolidation of overhead pools will be effective month-end August. I will no longer need to report two sets of data. Therefore, the following steps should be taken:
   a. Modify the overhead report accordingly
   b. Modify accordingly my job instructions and procedures
5. The completed PIR is copied, with the original going to the organization manager and the employee retaining the copy for reference
6. The manager receives the PIR and performs the following:
   a. Reviews the PIR
   b. Interacts with the submitter
   c. Coordinates meetings and research toward the goal of improving company cost effectiveness
   d. Ensures the PIR is eventually closed either with a process improvement closure notice or with a check mark in the *CA completed* block
   e. Utilizes records regarding employee FFPM involvement in the periodic performance appraisal process

In the above procedure, the following benefits are easily achieved:

1. The employee creates an *action item* and thus has defined a goal.
2. The manager is aware of employee activities, providing management with the opportunity to better evaluate employee performance.
3. With management attention, the employee has an incentive to perform the task in a thoroughly competent fashion.

As a result of the above points, the task will most likely be given a high priority by the employee and accomplished in a timely manner.

Note that, in this model, the savings are not easily quantified. This situation is quite acceptable within the realm of FFPM. Anytime corrective action or process improvement costs are less than the benefits derived, the process improvement activity has been successful.

SUMMARY

This chapter has discussed the many methods for identifying failures and ensuring that the other areas for potential improvement are targeted as well. Once the appropriate FFPM documentation has been generated, the cycle continues with the coordination and eventual selection of cost-effective project activities.

FFPM should be applied when an enterprise is considering implementing a new project or taking any other significant steps to improve profitability. On the surface, it may often appear that certain activities will yield improvements in operations and cost savings. The effective utilization of FFPM has revealed in many instances that costs will outweigh the benefits, and often alternate more advantageous improvements have been implemented. The key is understanding all financial ramifications.

SELF-STUDY/DISCUSSION QUESTIONS

1. Select a recent improvement implemented at your company. Make assumptions and attempt to calculate one-time implementation cost, on-going cost of new processes, and the costs associated with superceded activities. Summarize your findings.
2. Offer suggestions for calculating increased training costs associated with head count reductions. What sort of cost impact could you associate with a reduction in quality?
3. If your boss encouraged you to make recommendations, how would you feel? Do you think he or she would take your recommendations seriously? Or would you think, "Well, here's another one of those suggestion programs"? What would it take to really motivate you to participate?
4. Have you previously participated in a suggestion program? Share your experience.
5. For what business process improvements have you personally been responsible? How were you rewarded for your efforts?

Free value-added materials available from the
Download Resource Center at www.jrosspub.com.

13

THE ROLE OF QUALITY IN PROJECT MANAGEMENT

INTRODUCTION

In addition to having a financially focused mindset, the effective project manager should also have a command of the tools available from the science of quality. Quality began with applications to manufacturing processes and initially was intended to reduce failure rates and improve reliability of products. This chapter presents basic quality terms and concepts. In no way does it attempt to address every lesson involved in the science of quality. In fact, no document could achieve such a goal because pages are being added to this knowledge bank every day.

DR. W. EDWARDS DEMING

Dr. W. Edwards Deming has been credited with providing much of the foundation for the evolving science of quality management. Deming's *A Theory for Management* offers 14 points to success in the workplace, as follows:

1. Create constancy of purpose toward improvement of product and service, with the aim to become competitive and to stay in business and to provide jobs.
2. Adopt the new philosophy. We are in a new economic age. Western management must awaken to the challenge, must learn its responsibilities, and take on leadership for change.

3. Cease dependence on inspection to achieve quality. Eliminate the need for inspection on a mass basis by building quality into the product in the first place.
4. End the practice of awarding business on the basis of price tag. Instead, minimize total cost. Move toward a single supplier for any one item, on a long-term relationship of loyalty and trust.
5. Improve constantly and forever the system of production and service, to improve quality and productivity, and thus constantly decrease costs.
6. Institute training on the job.
7. Institute leadership (see point 12). The aim of leadership should be to help people and machines and gadgets to do a better job. Leadership of management is in need of overhaul, as well as leadership of production workers.
8. Drive out fear, so that everyone may work effectively for the company.
9. Break down barriers between departments. People in research, design, sales, and production must work as a team, to foresee problems in production and in use that may be encountered with the product or service.
10. Eliminate slogans, exhortations, and targets for the workforce asking for zero defects and new levels of productivity.
11. Eliminate:
    a. Work standards (quotas) on the factory floor. Substitute leadership.
    b. Management by objective and management by numbers or numerical goals. Substitute leadership.
12. Remove:
    a. Barriers that rob the hourly worker of his right to pride of workmanship. The responsibility of supervisors must be changed from sheer numbers to quality.
    b. Barriers that rob people in management and in engineering of their right to pride of workmanship. This means abolishment of the annual or merit rating and of management by objective and management by the numbers.
13. Institute a vigorous program of education and self-improvement.
14. Put everybody in the company to work to accomplish the transformation. The transformation is everybody's job.

Deming is also considered to be the father of statistical process control, which is discussed below.

PROCESS QUALITY CONTROL AND STATISTICAL ANALYSIS

Quality control goes far beyond simple inspection and test. The science of quality is sophisticated and ever-expanding. Complex sampling techniques and statistical analyses offer advantages as follows:

1. Reduction in the cost of inspection
2. Reduction in the cost of rejections
3. Maximization of the benefits from quantity production
4. Attainment of uniform quality even though inspection test is destructive
5. Reduction in tolerance limits

Process quality control and statistical process control aid in achieving high levels of quality. The text *Process Quality Control*[60] addresses this area in terms of the following three key aspects:

1. Process control: Maintaining the process on target with respect to centering and spread
2. Process capability: Determining the inherent spread of a controlled process for establishing realistic specifications, use for comparative purposes, and so forth
3. Process change: Implementing process modifications as a part of process improvement and troubleshooting

DIMINISHING RETURNS OF QUALITY CONTROL MEASURES

Advantages such as those listed above impact a company's profitability. However, while one would expect such an impact to always be positive, financially focused project management (FFPM) recognizes that a point of diminishing returns exists. A "financially focused mindset" must be instilled in those responsible for administering the science of quality.

Businesspeople recognize that it is often beneficial to implement quality measures. As more money is spent on such prevention costs (training assemblers, tightening inspection criteria), there will generally be less money spent on failures. This is in line with the old adage: "An ounce of prevention is worth a pound of cure." The philosophy goes a step further, with formulaic expressions showing that eventually, as prevention costs go up, a point will be reached where failure costs do not decrease at a greater proportion than prevention costs increase. Eventually a point of diminishing returns is reached.

Figure 13.1 shows that as prevention costs increase, failure costs decrease. The x-axis has six points, showing an increasing level of expenditures for preventative costs. When $0 is spent on preventative costs, there is $100 of failure costs, yielding a total cost of $100.

When $25 is spent on preventative costs, failure costs drop to only $50, and total costs are $75. The point of diminishing returns is hit when $50 is spent on prevention. Failure costs are only $10, and total cost is $60. When $75 is spent on prevention, failure costs are only $5, but total cost is $80.

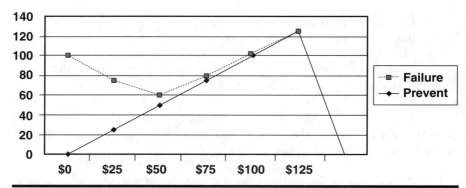

FIGURE 13.1. Diminishing Returns of Quality Control Measures. (Reprinted with permission from Cappels, T.M., *Financially Focused Quality*, CRC Press, 1999. Copyright CRC Press, Boca Raton, Florida.)

A good analogy can be drawn with the value of an automobile tune-up. Most mechanics concur that is it wise to periodically tune the engine. It is probably better to get a tune-up every 50,000 miles than to wait and have it done every 100,000. And it is probably better still to get a tune-up every 30,000 miles than every 50,000. But eventually you will reach a point of diminishing returns. Is it practical to tune a car every 5 miles?

Aside from minimizing costs and increasing profitability, the goal of FFPM is superior quality control. When considering the statement "Quality is a thought that resides in every executive's mind," one must examine the precepts of FFPM to understand the financial impacts of perceived quality improvements.

QUALITY CONTROL DEFINITION AND GOALS

The *Handbook of Industrial Engineering and Management*[61] broadly defines quality control as "those activities which ensure that quality creation is performed in such a manner that the resulting product will in fact perform the intended function." In this sense, quality assurance strives to achieve several goals.

The first is to ensure that the product characteristics selected will achieve the intended result. A second goal of this function is to ensure that the items produced will be manufactured to the desired quality level.

In some organizations, quality assurance responsibilities have been expanded to include evaluation of the safety performance in the original design. Thus, a third goal of quality assurance is for customer verification of safe performance.

QUALITY ASSURANCE AND THE PRODUCT LIFE CYCLE

The responsibilities of the quality assurance organization throughout the product life cycle are discussed below.

Research and Development (R&D) Phase

During the R&D phase, the need for a new product is identified, and potential methods for satisfying this need are examined.

Design Phase

The product is completely defined in the design phase. Then the design is tested to ensure proper operation. The role of quality assurance is critical in this phase. Ideally, quality assurance test engineers can identify all design anomalies prior to the beginning of formal production.

Testing is extended to include proper operation of the product in the various environments (e.g., life, temperature, salt spray, humidity, vibration, shock, sand, dust, rain, sunshine, etc.) in which the product is expected to operate. The design phase concludes when the product has been completely identified and qualified by test for each environment.

Production Phase

It is in the production phase that the role of quality control is perhaps best understood. The production phase requires a complete quality assurance check of the drawings and inspection of hardware to ensure complete compatibility. Any changes in the design should once again undergo full qualification testing and the product definition should be continuous so that each configuration always can be included in the active drawings and technical data package. The definition and hardware must always match with all nonconformances controlled.

Operation Phase

As the product enters the operation phase, it becomes available to the customer. The user must be trained adequately for proper operation. Both the manufacturer and user must work together in developing a maintenance plan and operational system to ensure that the product is utilized properly.

Disposal Phase

This phase begins when a decision has been made that useful life of the product has ended. Quality assurance tests are used to make this determination.

Nuclear systems have made the public more aware of the disposal phase. Nuclear waste cannot be stored in junkyards like old automobiles.

The product life cycle summarized above is followed for appliances, aircraft, boats, farm equipment, consumer products, trains, ships, and nuclear installations. To be effective, each phase must be scheduled and completed in the proper sequence.

The quality assurance organization interacts with virtually every group involved with the product. Quality assurance begins with program control functions in *product planning and development*. The next step is developing test criteria and design control as the product enters *design engineering*. Quality assurance material control functions play a major role as *material requirements* are addressed. With *production*, quality assurance performs inspection, test, and process control. *Field service* is supported by maintainability control activities.

QUALITY ASSURANCE FUNCTIONS

An overview of quality assurance functions and definitions is provided below.

- Receiving inspection: Receiving inspection of components to be used in the manufacturing process is usually performed on receiving docks and receiving areas throughout the company. Such inspection includes simple identification and inspection for damage during shipment. An inspection technique known as *sampling* is used when many items are received at the same time. The size of the sample lot to be inspected varies. As more parts are found to be out of spec (not compliant with required specifications), the quantity in the sample size increases.
- In-process inspection: As the manufacturing process progresses, inspectors are there to ensure the product is coming together as designed. In government contracting, the government generally wants the inspector to perform no manufacturing and the manufacturer to perform no inspection. This is to ensure a system of checks and balances in the process. However, this can be very costly. Often, the inspector will wait for the manufacturing worker to perform a function, and then the manufacturer waits while the inspector uses tools to inspect the work. Some government contractors have significantly reduced costs by developing a *production partnership*. This partnership involves, among other things, training manufacturers in the skill of inspection, thus allowing a manufacturing employee to inspect his or her own work.

- Shipping inspection and/or final inspection: The examination and testing of products prior to shipment to customers to determine whether they conform to specifications. Any final tests are also performed at this stage to make sure the customer is getting what is wanted.
- Accelerated test: Testing at abnormally high stress or environmental levels in order to induce earlier failures. Extrapolation is used to convert short life under severe conditions into expected life under normal conditions.
- Configuration management: A discipline applying technical and administrative direction and surveillance to identify and document the functional and physical characteristics of a configuration item, control changes to these characteristics, and record and report change processing and implementation status.
- Destructive testing: Testing that may impair subsequent usefulness of a product.
- Electrical in-process inspection: Performed during the manufacturing or repair cycle in an effort to prevent defects from occurring and to inspect the characteristics and attributes that are not capable of being inspected at final inspection.
- Engineering evaluation test: Performed to prove that items meet function environmental design limits.
- Fabrication and assembly inspection and test: Performed during the manufacturing or repair cycle in an effort to prevent defects from occurring and to inspect the characteristics and attributes that are not capable of being inspected at final inspection.
- Failure analysis: Series of actions performed on a verified failure to separate the problem into parts or elements for examination and determination of specific cause of failure and corrective action required.
- Failure diagnosis: A planned physical examination to determine cause of failure. Failure diagnosis is a portion of failure analysis.
- Failure verification: Series of actions to determine whether or not the hardware is discrepant or if a problem is traceable to operator error, test equipment, or procedural problems.
- First article compatibility test: Testing of the first unit produced in the first production run to confirm that the item meets drawing requirements.
- Material review board: A formal contractor–government board established for the purpose of reviewing, evaluating, and disposing of specific nonconforming supplies or services and for ensuring the initiation and accomplishment of corrective action to preclude recurrence.
- Mechanical in-process inspection: Performed during the manufacturing or repair cycle in an effort to prevent defects from occurring. It is also performed to inspect the characteristics and attributes that are not capable of being inspected at final inspection.

■ Metrology audits: The systematic review and evaluation by technical specialists to determine the adequacy of the contractor's system for calibration and measurements.
■ Parts application review: An engineering analysis of the effects of electrical, environmental, operational, and packaging stresses on part reliability.
■ Product evaluation test: Evaluates factory screening and design margins.
■ Quality assessment: A critical appraisal including qualitative judgments about an item (e.g., importance of analysis results, design criticality, and failure effect).
■ Quality audit: An independent review conducted to compare some aspect of quality performance with a standard for that performance.
■ Receiving inspection and test: The examination and testing of purchased materials to determine whether they conform to specifications.
■ Source acceptance: The validation of supplier acceptance of hardware in accordance with acceptance criteria, performed at the supplier's facility.
■ Source verification inspection: Verification at the supplier's facility of conformance to specified process, inspection, and test requirements.
■ Statistical process control: Program for ensuring that the product of a manufacturing or inspection process meets the requirements of the engineering specification.
■ Value engineering: An organized effort directed at identifying the functions of a product, either hardware or software, in order to achieve the required functions at the lowest overall cost consistent with the requirements of performance, reliability, quality, and maintainability.

Quality Assurance Functions Summary

These functions are a sampling of those performed in manufacturing enterprises. It would not be practical to list all of the quality assurance functions, but such functions could conceivably exist in support of most activities required to deliver products to the customer.

TRADITIONAL FINANCE INVOLVEMENT IN THE CYCLE OF QUALITY ACTIVITIES

Finance traditionally participates as an outsider, reacting to cost and schedule data involving many events. Sales to customer, and returns from customers, result in debits and credits to the income ledger. Product development and planning activities cause accounts payable to process checks for market research consultants and the administration of and miscellaneous costs associated with questionnaires, surveys, focus groups, R&D, and bid and proposal for new products. Other costs for which there must be accounting and payment include:

1. Test and analysis of engineering designs
2. Subcontractor review and audit
3. Inspection and analysis of materials used in the manufacturing process
4. Inspection and test of in-process assemblies and subassemblies
5. Final test and checkout of product before shipment
6. Review and on-going analysis of the shipping process

Field support activity requires finance to administer costs associated with:

1. Verifying that the product is installed properly
2. Ensuring instructions for use and care are clearly presented
3. Providing warranty service as required

The finance organization is the first to receive reports of such cost data and reacts to the data by performing many functions, including:

1. Summarizing
2. Preparing financial reports to management
3. Preparing financial reports for federal, state, city, and local taxing authorities
4. Preparing reports for customers
5. Preparing reports for stockholders
6. Preparing reports for public record
7. Administering accounts receivable
8. Administering accounts payable

The tasks described in this section are critical to the successful financial operation of a company. Yet, FFPM provides a means whereby *increased* financial success can be obtained.

COMPLETING THE CYCLE OF QUALITY ACTIVITIES: FINANCE

The finance organization is no longer on the outside looking in — merely reacting to the cycle of quality activities. Finance becomes the hub for all business operations, a predominant mechanism of the product delivery wheel around which the other product delivery systems revolve.

SELF-STUDY/DISCUSSION QUESTIONS

1. How are the quality assurance measures used in a manufacturing concern similar to those in a service organization? How do they differ?
2. How often do you have your car tuned or your oil changed? How do you determine the frequency?
3. How important is it in your company that its products be 100% error free? What quality control measures are in place? Are more needed? Are there too many? How does your company determine the right balance? Is statistical process control used in your company? What statistical process control processes might be applicable?

Free value-added materials available from the
Download Resource Center at <u>www.jrosspub.com</u>.

14

PROJECT MANAGEMENT IN THE 21st CENTURY

INTRODUCTION

The science and art of project management continues to evolve at an amazing pace. Today's trends of project management office (PMO) and project portfolio management (PPM) are already giving way to much more comprehensive and financially sound principles as financially focused project management (FFPM). And thanks to continued advances in technology, the world is getting smaller, greatly changing the way projects will be managed in the future. Project management professionals of the future must master the management of cross-cultural differences as international projects become the norm.

CROSSING CULTURES WITH PROJECT MANAGEMENT[62]

Differences in approaches, values, and expectations between customers, suppliers, and team members with different cultural backgrounds have resulted in many project failures. By understanding the impact of cross-cultural differences, engineers can increase the probability of an international venture's success — from setting up a new plant abroad to selling advanced equipment, products, or services to international clients.

Engineers are trained to focus on technical data, scientific evidence, and hard facts. Because the laws of physics are universal, they tend to expect that nationality and cultural differences will not play a significant role in the practice of engineering. After all, a car is a car and it performs the same transportation function the world over.

Yet car designs differ significantly from country to country. For example, the models sold by General Motors and Ford in Europe are quite different from their North American counterparts. Few people mistake cars designed by such Italian manufacturers as Ferrari and Lamborghini with cars designed by such Swedish manufacturers as Volvo and Saab. The unique characteristics of these car models are the result of differences in the approaches, values, and preferences of both engineers and consumers. In fact, cross-cultural differences have a significant impact on the engineering profession as a whole, which goes well beyond the design, development, and manufacturing of products.

Communication

Miscommunication across cultural lines is usually the most important cause of cross-cultural problems in multinational projects. Miscommunication can have several sources, including:

- Differences in body language or gestures: The same gesture can have different meanings in different parts of the world. For example, Bulgarians shake their heads up and down to mean no. In addition, the way people count on their fingers is not universal — the Chinese count from one to ten on one hand, and eight is displayed by extending the thumb and index finger. The same gesture is interpreted as meaning two in France and as pointing a gun in North America.
- Different meanings for the same word: Like gestures, words can have different meanings or connotations in different parts of the world. The French word "char" means Army tank in France and car in Quebec. The word "exciting" has different connotations in British English and in North American English. While North American executives talk about "exciting" challenges repeatedly, British executives use this word to describe only children's activities (children do exciting things in England, not executives).
- Different assumptions made in the same situation: The same event can be interpreted many different ways depending on where one comes from. For example, seeing a black cat is considered to be lucky in Britain, but it is considered to be unlucky in many other countries. Dragons are viewed positively in China, but negatively in Europe and North America.

Examples such as these illustrate dissimilarities between cultures that are both large and simple in the sense that they focus on a single cultural aspect that keeps the same meaning regardless of context. As a result, such variations in communication will often be identified on the spot. By contrast, subtle or complex differences are often identified much later in the communication process, when corrective action requires considerable effort and money. Sometimes, this realization takes place so late that there is not enough time to address it, resulting in a missed deadline.

In extreme cases, miscommunication can lead to casualties. As a case in point, a few years ago, a plane crash in the northeastern U.S. was caused — at least in part — by miscommunication between the pilot and air traffic controller. The plane was running short on fuel, but somehow the pilot did not manage to communicate the urgency of the situation to the air traffic controller, who put the plane on a holding pattern because of airport congestion. The plane eventually crashed when it ran out of fuel.

Standards

Different countries use different standards and measurement systems. These differences are well known in the case of measurements for temperature (Fahrenheit vs. Celsius) and pressure (pounds per square inch vs. Pascal). Other variations in the use of standards are not as well known and can result in significant difficulties. For example, differences in power frequency have led European users of high-tech American equipment to purchase dedicated power generators that deliver the right voltage frequency for the equipment, i.e., 60 Hz vs. 50 Hz.

In another case, a British pulp and paper mill sent back a set of right-handed motors to a U.S. manufacturer, even though they were the correct ones for the intended use. The British engineers were expecting a set of left-handed motors, and therefore rejected the motors without opening the crates. Eventually, the British and American engineers working on this project realized that the reference directions for the motors are the exact opposite in the British and American pulp and paper industries, thereby creating the problem.

Approaches to Problem Solving

The approaches used by engineers of different cultural backgrounds to tackle the same technical problem are likely to have significant differences. The approach used to solve engineering problems is often a reflection of what is emphasized in educational curricula leading to engineering degrees in various countries. In France and Greece, for example, engineers tend to emphasize theoretical or mathematical approaches over experimental or numerical ones. Other countries, such as Canada and the U.S., tend to favor experimental or numerical approaches.

Although there is no absolute "right way" to approach technical problems, issues are likely to arise when engineers with different inclinations work together to solve them. A French engineer is likely to approach a new problem by writing down all of the relevant differential equations and then trying to simplify them to obtain an analytical solution. Meanwhile, a Canadian engineer is likely to start from the simplest expression of the problem and build a model (either physical or numerical) of it. When French and Canadian engineers work together, they are both likely to feel that the other is wasting time by approaching the problem from the wrong angle.

On a practical basis, the approaches used by engineers in different countries can also depend on the types of resources available. For example, high labor costs and the availability of skilled workers make process automation and the use of heavy equipment valuable in developed countries, while using large numbers of unskilled workers may be a preferred approach in some developing countries.

Cross-Cultural Differences and Engineering Firms

Cross-cultural issues also arise at the organizational level, because companies in different countries organize their daily business differently. Some of the most noticeable differences are described below.

Relative Hierarchy of Departments

The relative power of the various departments within a corporation is often a function of the country where the corporation has its headquarters. For example, the manufacturing departments of German-based companies have influence over their marketing and sales counterparts that many Canadian and American manufacturing departments can only dream of. German manufacturing departments are often able to limit the number of products offered to a few options, thereby optimizing production and improving the quality of the products offered. By contrast, Canadian and American manufacturing departments tend to follow the lead of marketing and sales departments, which tend to favor a larger number of product options since this increases the probability of attracting a broader group of customers.

These differences in the way products are manufactured and marketed create the need for different approaches to selling products and services. The same type of argument cannot be used to win customers in North America and Germany — whether through sales presentations or general marketing efforts. While North American customers look for flexibility and response speed in the products and services they purchase, German customers want durability, reliability, and quality.

Way Information Is Shared and Distributed

The way information moves within a company varies significantly from country to country. For example, in Germany, the flow of information tends to be fairly compartmentalized. Information flows within departments along hierarchical lines and does not flow easily within a given hierarchical level or from department to department. In addition, Germans tend to share information with only those people they believe need to know the information. In Canadian companies, information tends to move within departments and to cross departmental boundaries more freely. It also tends to flow along the lines of communication networks used by individual employees.

As a result, when working with German engineers as suppliers, partners, or customers, Canadian engineers are likely to receive less information than they would generally expect. A Canadian engineer supplying products or services to a German company may not receive all of the information he or she believes is necessary to fulfill orders or complete projects on time, resulting in either missed deadlines or incomplete orders.

Hiring Process

Cross-cultural differences are fairly significant in this area. For example, people interviewed for positions in France will be asked personal questions that are considered illegal in Canada, such as their age, marital status, and number of children, while German interviewers routinely ask candidates for the profession of their parents.

More importantly, there are significant differences in the types of skills that companies in different countries look for in candidates. In France, for example, large corporations expect their engineers to work for them throughout much of their careers. They therefore tend to hire graduate engineers who appear to have long-term potential and create jobs for these engineers. As a result, large French companies tend to emphasize specific technical knowledge less and soft skills more than Canadian companies.

For their part, Canadian companies tend to look for engineers who have the technical skills required to fill an existing vacant position. They also do not expect their engineer employees to remain with the company throughout their careers.

These differences in the hiring process for engineers can lead to frustration. When Canadian engineers interact with French engineers who are fresh out of school, they are likely to feel that these engineers do not have the same level of knowledge as Canadian engineers with a similar level of seniority. This impression is often justified. However, it is best to keep in mind that these engineers were not hired for their specific technical knowledge and that allowances will have to be made to keep a project running smoothly.

Avoiding Cross-Cultural Pitfalls

Engineers working with foreign clients, suppliers, or peers can prevent many cross-cultural issues from turning into problems by paying an unusual amount of attention to proper communication. Here are a few tips that will help avoid miscommunication:

- Clarify: When in doubt, ask; when not, ask anyway. It is important to ensure that your foreign colleagues have understood everything you meant to say and nothing else. Ask them to give you feedback about what you have told them in their own words. This will help you discover and address any major misunderstandings.
- Get into the details: Although it is often tempting to agree on general principles and leave details to further discussions for brevity's sake, this can create major problems at later stages. Indeed, an agreement on general principles may turn out to be empty, if it is not tested through negotiation on the finer details.
- Summarize: The time taken to summarize the decisions made during a meeting and to issue minutes to all participants is often a good investment. It helps to prevent future challenges of decisions reached at meetings and to ensure that action items agreed to at meetings are actually implemented.
- Simplify: Use simple words that are easily understood and be consistent. Using synonyms can confuse your counterparts unnecessarily, particularly if they are not native English speakers. For similar reasons, technical jargon should be avoided where possible and explained clearly when it must be used.

Breaking into Foreign Markets

Strategies that engineering firms can use to avoid cross-cultural problems while breaking into foreign markets include hiring foreign engineers, which can be very effective when a company has decided that a given country or countries will play a major role in its future. In this case, hiring engineers with the right technical background who have lived and worked in the targeted country or region, and therefore understand the culture, can be a tremendous asset to a company. Indeed, these people have the knowledge and experience needed to understand how to handle delicate cross-cultural situations and avoid faux pas.

This solution has some possible limitations, however. Important business transactions are often handled at high levels within the company. Although it is relatively easy to locate and hire entry-level engineers from a given country or region, finding engineers with many years of experience in a given field can be quite challenging. In addition, depending on the circumstances, people who have the appropriate cultural experience may not be able to share their knowledge with others in the organization, thereby reducing the speed of organizational learning.

Cross-cultural training organizations can also shorten the learning curve by delivering training to companies in a timely and targeted fashion. The necessary cross-cultural information should be shared with all employees involved in international ventures, rather than being limited to those who have already had experience with them. Cross-cultural training organizations are experts in the area of cross-cultural relationships and can provide training on many topics, including how to:

- Do business in a given country or region
- Make presentations in a given country of region
- Select the right people for international assignments
- Prepare employees for expatriate assignments
- Improve the productivity of multinational teams

Finding Local Partners

Setting up agreements with local partners, in the form of joint ventures or licenses, or purchasing a local company can be effective ways of combining strengths. This approach can be very effective when your firm is trying to break into a new market quickly, since it will enable your company to benefit from the knowledge and experience of its partners. In many cases, this approach works best when combined with one or more of the strategies mentioned above, since finding and working with the right partners often requires knowledge about the targeted country and its culture.

Patent Protection

To achieve the desired level of protection for their intellectual property, engineering firms need to be aware of the differences in patent systems that exist around the world. For example, the U.S. has a "first-to-invent" policy, while the Japanese and the Europeans have a "first-to-file" policy.

The "first-to-file" patent system does not require the company that files the patent to be the original inventor of the technology for which the patent is being sought. As a result, a company can receive a patent for an invention that was made in another country but is not protected by patent in the country where the company is located. This situation occurred in the case of the invention of high-temperature superconducting materials. Although the initial discovery was made in the U.S., the Japanese patent is held by two Japanese researchers who obtained enough information about this invention to file a patent application in Japan.

Taking Advantage of Cultural Diversity

When managed effectively, the diversity of approaches that exist around the world can lead to significant improvements in both work processes and outputs. One way to take advantage of cross-cultural differences was devised by a captain in the French Foreign Legion. When faced with significant problems, he would pair someone from a northern European country (like Germany) with someone from a southern European country (like France or Italy). The southern European individual would take the lead during the brainstorming part of the problem-solving process, when potential solutions are generated and compared. The northern European person would then take the lead during the implementation phase. This strategy enabled the captain to take advantage of both the "theoretical" bent of French and Italians and the attention to detail and execution typically shown by Germans.

ELEMENTS AFFECTING INTERNATIONAL PROJECT TEAMWORK[63]

The members of international project teams are very different, depending on their background. Figure 14.1 presents just a few of the elements that may cause dissension on a project team.

- **Cultural Differences**
  - **Apparent and Not So Apparent**
  - **"Culture Shock" when experiencing a different culture**
  - **Religious Beliefs/Habits**
  - **Political, Social and Economic Influences**
  - **Language Barriers**

FIGURE 14.1. Impacts to International Project Teamwork.

Apparent and Not So Apparent

Some things that are obvious to certain people may be not so obvious to others. This is because different cultures emphasize different areas and different items are looked upon in a different manner. Much of it has a lot to do with culture.

Culture Shock

When international project teams are formed, by their very nature, some people are geographically moved to new countries, with different cultures. Culture shock is the reaction one faces when confronted with a new cultural environment. By the time one begins to orient oneself, one could be experiencing the first signs of culture shock.

There are four stages of culture shock:

- Euphoria: This is the first stage of culture shock, which tends to blend in with the highs of planning a trip and starting off on an adventure. Like a new love, some tend to overlook some of the host country's shortcomings and delight in all the new pleasures of being abroad. A quaint 3-hour walk to the closest market and source of food is an interesting representation of how to enjoy the simple things of life. This initial stage should be enjoyed, but one should prepare for a comedown.
- Anxiety: A growing amount of anxiety can develop during which the project team member may feel helpless. The difficulties of living abroad, such as language barriers, absence of social cues, and familiar geographic references, can come to the surface. This can develop into frustration, anger, and sleeplessness. Not knowing where and when to cross the street or even how to find one's way to the market can result in a physical discomfort.
- Rejection of the new culture: This is when that once quaint 3-hour walk becomes an unbearable nuisance. Things now seem to be "wrong" or "backwards." Commonly, project team members in this stage start to withdraw themselves from the local community, preferring to surround themselves with other foreigners. One should beware of the 3 a.m. impulse to suddenly call a family member or friend back home.
- Adjustment: With a lot of luck and advance preparation, one enters the adjusted stage. At this point, the project team member recognizes some of the perceived shortcomings of the host culture without rejecting everything. The 3-hour walk becomes just that — a necessary inconvenience.

Religious Beliefs/Habits

The project team member should be aware that different geographic locations may have different cultures, which could also have different religious beliefs and habits. As long as one expects this sort of difference, it should not be overwhelming.

Political, Social, and Economic Influences

Political barriers cannot be crossed until they are recognized. Some barriers can be neither crossed nor breached even when identified. These must be recognized for what they are and a way around them found that is not a disguised way back. Turning these insurmountable barriers into barricades usually gains nothing and potentially wastes much productive effort.

Language Barriers

Language is the last great divide for international project management. A project manager is very fortunate if all members of his or her international team speak the same language. Interpreters may be required, and the project plan definitely must be translated so all team members are on the same page.

PROJECT MANAGEMENT — WHAT THE FUTURE HOLDS[64]

Having crossed over into a new millennium, "project management" reaches the half-century mark. Despite the promise inherent in the concept of project management, there can be no doubt that there has only been a partial fulfillment. This does not imply that things might have been better if the project approach had not been devised, but rather that "project management" does not come with a guarantee that, once installed, all objectives will be fulfilled to everyone's satisfaction.

Historically, the discipline has evolved, like every other, through a series of methodologies and theories that have become fashionable for a time but, in one way or another, have been found wanting. To be fair, those methods have had their successes, and each has laid a foundation on which more suitable and sophisticated approaches have been built (e.g., PMO, PPM). The newer methods may have broadened in scope, but with their increasing sophistication and differing emphases they do not always live happily together; furthermore, they do not address all the issues.

FIGURE 14.2. New Project Management Model.

New Model

One thing is very clear from this brief history: Viewing the role of the project manager as simply delivering the project in terms of cost, time, and performance is too narrow a view. The external world has a part to play in the whole process, and the higher the profile of the project or the more advanced the technology involved, the more significant will be the process of managing the external dimensions. Figure 14.2 shows a new model for the issues that project management must handle successfully.

Four new items have been added, as follows:

- Technology: The technology itself and the opportunities it creates.
- Expectations: The expectations that are not only the reasons for starting the project but the rising level of expectation in society as a whole.
- Risks: The risks that exist with all new ventures.
- Profitability: The fourth element is not really new, it is *old*, but it is being looked at in a *new* way via the financial focus of FFPM. After all, profitability is what it is all about. By ensuring costs are kept to a minimum without sacrificing quality or schedules, the project will be successful and allow the opportunity for further projects and increasing profits.

For the most part, the risks are that the expectations will not be fulfilled. None of these factors is so simply dealt with as time, cost, and performance, and they cannot be easily reduced to a computer algorithm. Effective project managers must learn to be aware of all of them and adjust the project strategy to ensure that none of these factors brings the whole project down.

The new model can be seen as a general statement of the project management problem, but it does not contain the elements of an answer. Perhaps the answer will come with the advent of an overall philosophy and a methodological framework (general theory) that will unite all the diverse strands.

Bodies of Knowledge

Professionally, the discipline has come of age through the formation of national associations for project management and the formation of a body with worldwide recognition: the International Association of Project Management. Looking to such associations may lead to a unifying philosophy, but here one may still be disappointed. Although they have made great strides to bring together all the strands that make up "project management," it is significant that they have chosen to call their combined efforts "the body of knowledge."

Project manager education has become more and more sophisticated, including interactive cases for students, and with the best project managers receiving certifications and credentials, e.g., project management professional (PMP). Project management is a collection of techniques and theories but lacks an accepted unifying philosophy other than that contained in the idea of an expedient or pragmatic route to an end goal. Is that unifying philosophy profitability and the financial focus? Many have been jumping on the financially focused bandwagon, but will it last?

The body of knowledge has produced FFPM, which is a near-term philosophy, but a thrust in its development is still needed to provide the following results:

- Ensure all parties to a project are financially trained to the point of being financially focused enough to understand the total financial ramifications of the venture
- Categorize and classify all project management knowledge
- Produce a set of project management practices
- Be a basis for qualifying project managers

Not Scientific

We might, therefore, ask ourselves if any philosophy or general theory is likely to emerge that will tie together all the strands of the subject into a unified whole that will relate each aspect in a way that is unambiguous and completely compatible. Clearly, we would like a philosophy that will tell us how to use all the tools and techniques in a way that makes each supportive of the others.

Project management was born in the context of "scientific management" with its inherent ideas of objectivity and certainty. Where disorder and uncertainty existed in the old system, these unfortunate properties would be displaced in the new discipline. But the process of management is not susceptible to the scientific treatment.

For the most part, science has advanced through the process of "reductionism," i.e., the act of reducing each phenomenon to progressively lower and more fundamental elements where, at the most fundamental level, completely unifying theories can be developed. This approach has had its most spectacular successes in the field of physics, and all branches of natural science have structured their activities around this model. With the humanities-based sciences, this approach has not worked as well, as physical laws are replaced by "influences" and "relationships" whose behavior cannot be described in increasingly precise terms.

Management, in general, and project management, in particular, have even more problems when it comes to the scientific approach as it deals with that even less definable quantity — the future. For project management is nothing if it is not the very process of turning future expectations into present realities. Science deals with repeatable phenomena; the principle that past observations can be replicated exactly is fundamental to the scientific process, but management processes can never be repeated exactly because they represent reactions to a surrounding world that is constantly changing without repetition.

Attempts have been made to produce an overall philosophy or general theory for project management, but the results look unconvincing so far, if only because they tend to be extremely general and contain too little detail to be of much practical use.

A purely scientific approach is unlikely to produce an overall philosophy for the reasons already explained, but the more pragmatic attitude adopted by engineers might be more appropriate; at least they will see it as an adaptive process rather than a phenomenon explainable in theoretical terms.

Can It Survive?

Project management, as it stands at the moment, is no more than an expedient set of tools and techniques that can be used in certain common industrial situations. The addition of a financial focus gives it tremendous credibility, but can it survive in the longer term as a separate discipline or is it in danger of being subsumed into the overall process of general management?

The fact that practicing project managers are already debating this point must indicate a danger is perceived. This danger may actually be exacerbated by the current trend to change the emphasis of the process to one of "management by projects."

This change of emphasis contains the hidden implication that the project approach is a new methodology that can be applied to the process of general management. In other words, all management actions can be constructed along the project model. That, of course, is a mistake as there are many management tasks that do not easily fit that model.

However, even without an overall philosophy, and in the wake of both successes and failures, project management does provide a current solution to a particular type of industrial problem that is quite distinct from those industrial activities that are "processes" and distinct again from the activities of "commerce" or "finance." FFPM does an outstanding job of incorporating the finance activity, but where is the commerce component? And does it need to be included?

Technology

How to ensure the success of a unique endeavor is a problem that is not going to go away, and the project management approach looks likely to be the only one that will provide answers in the near term. The demands of the approach are becoming ever more deeply embedded in software tools that are increasingly seen as essential elements of the process.

These software tools are becoming easier to use at an individual level, but the inter-relationship between them is becoming more complex as the process grows in sophistication. It may well be that for many of the smaller projects, the full rigors of the procedure will be seen as inappropriately complex or expensive, which in turn will lead to a recourse to earlier methods or an abandonment of the "project" approach.

"Gone Mad?"

Some firms have shown signs of "project management gone mad,"[64] with every activity and initiative labeled a "project" with somebody, often in far too low a position, given the title "project manager" however inappropriate to his or her real status or effectiveness. This only cheapens the project approach and hastens its demise, as ineffective project managers will surely discredit the process more quickly than anything else will.

Most Effective

If project management is to survive without being lost in some new management gospel, it will have to remain as a discipline apart, and it can only do that if it sets out to deal in the areas where it can be most effective. Its complex evolution has ensured that project management is no simple subject, and to master it in theory and practice requires both intellect and application on the part of its practitioners.

"Project manager" is not a title to be handed out lightly, yet many advocates of the project management technique see it as something that can be used on every occasion from running a major construction project to organizing the office Christmas party, and, by definition, every "project" needs a manager.

Given the strict definition of a "project" as a one-off undertaking, a project-managed approach is applicable in both instances, but there is a huge difference of degree. It is that difference of degree that will need to be maintained when the title project manager is handed out if we are not to see its eventual disappearance.

The professional bodies probably provide the best assurance for the future of project management as a distinct discipline if only for the reason that as long as they exist they will emphasize its distinctiveness.

Project management has come a long way in its 50 years. It is now the subject of serious study at postgraduate level. It is in the process of education that the greatest opportunity lies. The more people that know and understand what project management is all about and know how and when to use it wisely, the more likely it is to remain distinct and be recognized for its worth.

The institutions have made a start with the certification process but this has tended to be an inward-looking approach of confirming the already converted; the danger in this is that it could be seen as creating a clique open only to the initiated and not relevant to those outside.

A better long-term strategy lies in a more outward vision that raises awareness and understanding and includes a structured program. This would be a program of learning that will encourage people from outside to come into the profession in the knowledge that they can be guided through its many mysteries and conclude with a meaningful qualification. That will not, of course, ensure that they will all be good project managers, but at least they will not be ignorant ones.

Getting Harder

Project management is a complex and many-faceted process that is certainly not becoming easier to practice as the subject is constantly evolving and the demands on project managers are undoubtedly growing. The constraints placed on managers are becoming increasingly restrictive at a time when expectations continue to rise.

This has never been clearer than in the area of project cost. It is probably true to say that until the 1960s, the general approach to starting projects was "do what we can do," but now it is evolving into "do what we can afford to do"; hence the gospel for some of the latest advanced technology projects is "affordability." This may generate a new realism about the prospects for a project at its outset, but if realism is not there, it may turn into an even heavier cross to bear and lead to further disillusionment.

However, it is in the field of complex and multifaceted undertakings with tight constraints that the project management approach can be most effective. Although it contains no guarantee of success, it brings with it the discipline of thought and the assortment of techniques that are needed to address complex issues and also guidance as to the types of solution that might be applicable.

BELIEF IN THE FUTURE

So the future ultimately lies with the project managers themselves; in particular, how much effort they devote to refining the process and educating people at all levels in industry as to the contribution it can make and where it is best applied.

The omens look good at the moment with new education initiatives, and qualifications such as the PMP. FFPM, PMO, and PPM are also steps in the right direction. But one should always remember that a movement will only remain a force with which to be reckoned as long as both its members and those outside who stand to benefit from it believe in it. That will only happen as long as the process it promotes continues to live up to the expectations placed upon it.

May the project you manage be delivered to contract specifications, ahead of schedule, under budget, and with a financial focus. Good luck!

SELF-STUDY/DISCUSSION QUESTIONS

1. What are some cross-cultural differences that could impact a project?
2. What are some techniques for avoiding cross-cultural pitfalls?
3. What are some strategies for breaking into foreign markets?
4. Suggest some ways to take advantage of cultural diversity.
5. Describe the four states of culture shock.
6. What are some of your thoughts on the "new model"? On its application to project management?

Free value-added materials available from the
Download Resource Center at www.jrosspub.com.

CASE STUDIES[2]

CASE STUDY A: OUTSOURCING PROJECT — MACHINING OUTSOURCING INITIATIVE

INTRODUCTION

On August 30, 1994, Lockheed Corporation and Martin Marietta jointly announced that their respective boards of directors had unanimously agreed to merge the two corporations through an exchange of common stock valued in excess of $10 billion.

There were millions of dollars in merger-related expenses, and the new company — Lockheed Martin — expected to be reimbursed by its government customers for such costs. To justify the merger-related expenses, Lockheed Martin had to prove that the consolidation would result in tremendous savings. For example, there would no longer be the need for each company to have its own board of directors. An entire set of executive management could be eliminated.

The merger team identified other areas of savings as well, and several "centers of excellence" (COE) were established. Each COE was an area where the economies of scale could be fully utilized, and related operations would be centralized. This chapter focuses on the Machining Outsourcing COE, and how the application of financially focused project management (FFPM) at Lockheed Martin Missiles and Space (LMMS) in Sunnyvale, California substantially increased profitability.

MACHINING OUTSOURCING INITIATIVE (MOI)

The MOI is the end product of the Machining COE study. This study concluded that even if all machining for the entire Space and Strategic Missiles Sector of Lockheed Martin were centralized, it would still be less expensive to outsource production-machining activity.

Therefore, the MOI was chartered to provide high-quality, machined hardware at optimized cost and schedule using the best industry resources available. With these resources, sector hardware requirements from product development through final production phases would be met via a network of internal manufacturing centers and key outside suppliers.

MOI Mission Statement

Accordingly, the MOI project team's mission was expressed as follows:

To satisfy Space and Strategic Missiles Sector requirements for machined mechanical components with the best value to customers through:

- A fully implemented Sector Make-or-Buy Policy
- A standardized outsourcing process (Sector Purchasing Agreements)
- Strategic partnerships with "Best-In-Class" suppliers
- Consolidation of in-house resources to provide a lean and agile development/modification capability

FFPM

FFPM is a proven management system designed for maximum project quality at minimum cost. Marshall Kyger (director of LMMS Programs, Planning, and Analysis) says that FFPM "takes the philosophy of total quality management one important step further by including the financial community in the process from the beginning, and integrating recognition of cost at each step of the process. This happy marriage of the finance and quality communities offers the prospect of improving the translation of better quality to the bottom line."[65]

FFPM focuses on developing the "full-cycle mindset," which gives primary consideration to financial implications of every function involved in project performance. Figure A.1 summarizes those FFPM components incorporated into the MOI activity in three stages: (1) identification of the need for FFPM; (2) coordination, analysis, and selection of the process or corrective action; and (3) follow-up and closure of the need identified in (1).

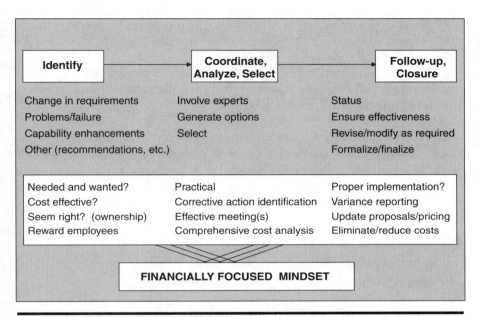

FIGURE A.1. Outsourcing Project with FFPM. (Reprinted with permission from Cappels, T.M., *Financially Focused Quality*, CRC Press, 1999. Copyright CRC Press, Boca Raton, Florida.)

Identification of Need

FFPM begins with identification of any situation for which there is the potential for improvement (e.g., change in customer requirements, failures). Note that all employees/customers are encouraged to initiate the FFPM cycle. FFPM tools and techniques assist by ensuring a financial perspective is applied to the options that arise at this stage of the cycle:

a. Is the need identified needed and/or wanted?
b. Is the current process or that proposed cost effective?
c. Do employees feel all their activities contribute favorably to the product/process?

Coordinate/Analyze/Select Process/Corrective Action

FFPM requires that someone perform FFPM coordination with a true financial perspective. It is not always practical to include a member of the financial community, so often a member of management coordinates these activities and ensures that the appropriate employees have a general understanding of pertinent financial considerations. An effective tool for providing such information is the ASQ Quality Press publication *Full-Cycle Corrective Action: Managing for Quality and Profits.*[34]

As part of the routine coordination process, experts are consulted as options are generated, and eventually a revised process or corrective action is selected.

The FFPM approach ensures the following:

    a. The practicality of pursuing the need identified in the first stage.
    b. An appropriate amount of resources is expended to understand the process with effective meetings and management involvement.
    c. Generation of comprehensive cost analyses for options with merit.
    d. Cost is given appropriate weight when selecting options.

Follow-Up and Closure

The FFPM process ensures effectiveness, calling for revision, modification, and formalization of procedures to enhance profitability:

    a. Ensures proper implementation of selected options.
    b. Reporting mechanism allows cost tracking.
    c. Cost data can be used for proposal and pricing updates.
    d. Selected options are re-examined after the fact for elimination or reduction in scope to ensure every activity yields full benefit.

MOI AND FFPM

LMMS has saved millions of dollars by applying the financial principles of FFPM to its manufacturing and TQM processes.[34] For the MOI, the decision was made to create a full-time position of "business deputy," to serve on the project team, with the following responsibilities:

1. Propose/negotiate resources.
2. Establish budgets.
3. Direct the tracking of weekly labor and nonlabor expenses.
4. Summarize and report actuals vs. budgets and analyze variances.
5. Design/implement program-unique cost models for forecasting and reporting MOI savings.
6. Establish/oversee MOI parts forecasting and tracking system.
7. Oversee MOI performance schedules/milestone tracking system.
8. Maintain the "full-cycle mindset," ensuring that recognition of cost is integrated at each step of the process.

The individual selected for this position had a broad, well-founded financial background and several years of direct experience working with the FFPM management system.

Cost Modeling

FFPM concepts first were utilized to validate the belief that LMMS would save significant resources by outsourcing production-machining effort. Figure A.2 is an example of the cost modeling analysis, which looked beyond the mere elimination of hourly machining personnel. Also considered were all support labor costs, overhead, and G&A, which had to be compared with the increased costs for administering the MOI. FFPM tools eased the identification and costing of such tasks as transportation, source inspection, and supplier certification.

Meeting Schedules

After the MOI received approval, the implementation process began. For the first 3 months of MOI implementation, daily team meetings were held with an average of 15 people in attendance. The business deputy noted that much discussion involved small groups of people, while the majority of the attendees did

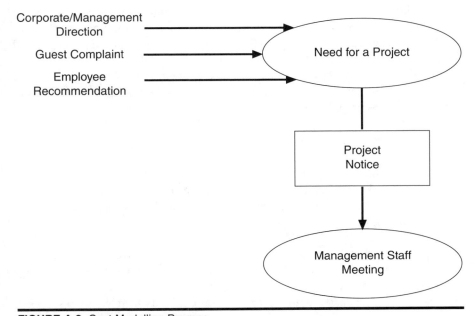

FIGURE A.2. Cost Modelling Process.

not participate. The deputy recommended that splinter meetings be called as needed, with the requirement of only a weekly team meeting. The use of e-mail and telephones greatly facilitated this process improvement.

With the elimination of the daily MOI meetings, the business deputy recognized that he could perform his assigned tasks in less than the 40 hours a week budgeted for the position. As a result, he volunteered for several other special assignments, allowing for a more even distribution of assignments within the finance and business operations community.

Contracting Process Improvement

The business deputy was concerned about the proposed plan for establishing contracts with machined parts suppliers. The original plan called for a 2-month contracting cycle as follows:

1. Each program provides machined parts requirements (quantities and need dates) to the business deputy (BD).
2. BD consolidates/forwards list to manufacturing engineers (ME), who pull specifications/drawings needed to send to suppliers for quotes.
3. ME forwards list to materials and processing (M&P) engineer to ensure the correct M&P instructions accompany the package.
4. M&P engineer forwards the package to quality assurance (QA), who supplies quality codes and packaging instructions in the package.
5. QA forwards the package to the buyer, who assembles the packages and sends them to the MOI lead buyer in Denver, Colorado.
6. The MOI lead buyer in Denver consolidates the LMMS packages with packages from other companies in the sector and sends them to the supplier for quote preparation.

The business deputy noted the following faults in this procedure:

1. Programs could not obtain machined parts in less than several months.
2. The workload required for quote package preparation is unstable. Each person must process as many as 100 parts in 1 week, and then have no related effort for 7 weeks.

FFPM concepts were used in developing a procedure that allowed the different MOI team members to perform their tasks concurrently. This greatly reduced the stress and time required to prepare quote packages. In addition, exceptions were made to the rule that packages could only be released to suppliers in 2-month intervals. These changes made the MOI more attractive to programs and MOI team members. Suppliers, too, were much happier not having to prepare quotes for 100 parts at once; they also benefited by the load leveling.

SELF-STUDY/DISCUSSION QUESTIONS

1. What are some of the negative impacts of outsourcing?
2. When overhead is allocated to labor hours or labor dollars, how does outsourcing affect overhead rates?
3. What are some of the positive benefits of outsourcing?
4. What operations in your company could conceivably be outsourced? What are the pluses? Minuses?

*Free value-added materials available from the
Download Resource Center at* <u>www.jrosspub.com</u>.

CASE STUDY B: PERKY PETS — COMMERCIAL MANUFACTURING PROJECT

INTRODUCTION

Perky Pets is a fictional case study based on real-life manufacturing goals and objectives. Therefore, it offers valuable insight into the application of financially focused project management (FFPM).

THE COMPANY

Perky Pets, Incorporated is a manufacturing company that started out as a family business. Joe, the father, had recently retired and taken a vacation trip to Antarctica. During this trip, he became acquainted with several penguins and made the following observations:

1. Penguins are fairly intelligent.
2. Penguins have webbed feet.
3. Penguins cannot fly.
4. Penguins have scale-like, barbless feathers.
5. Penguins have flipper-like wings.

6. Penguins are likeable.
7. Penguins are perky.

"Penguins are adorable!" thought Joe. Whenever he saw one, he wanted to pick it up (a small one) and squeeze it. "What an idea for a product," Joe mused. "Everyone will want one!"

Joe met with his sons and together they formed "Perky Pets, Incorporated."

THE PRODUCT

Penguins have many unique properties to consider during the product development phase. A major physical limitation the penguin product imposes is the fact that penguins require cool climates to survive.

The Perky Pets engineering team developed a state-of-the-art helmet-type cooling device that straps onto the penguin's head. The total product is the penguin and helmet sold as a unit called Penguin-in-a-Helmet. The product will be marketed as an impulse item sold at grocery stores throughout the U.S. and Canada.

Manufacturing Process

Fabrication and shipping of the cooling helmets require the following steps:

1. Various suppliers provide Perky Pets with both penguin and nonpenguin manufacturing components. Penguins are obtained in the most humane fashion possible. Effort is made to ensure that penguins are collected in family units. This avoids the trauma that could be experienced, particularly in the case of young penguins that may be separated from their parents. Research suggests that by avoiding such trauma as parental separation, penguins are more likely to maintain their perkiness.
2. Components are inspected on receipt via appropriate sampling plans. Nonpenguin components that pass receiving inspection are forwarded to the manufacturing areas. Penguins are placed in specially designed penguin quarters, where trained penguin counselors work to ensure the penguins remain healthy and perky. Components that not meet inspection criteria are returned to vendors.
3. Nonpenguin components are then used to assemble the helmets.
4. The final manufacturing step is strapping the helmet onto the penguin, ensuring a snug but comfortable fit.
5. In the shipping area, final test and checkout is performed.
6. Cases of Penguin-in-a-Helmet are shipped to the stores, where it is hoped that anxious customers will make purchases.

7. The quality engineering organization is actively involved with each step by:
   a. Developing and issuing specifications to the supplier and receiving department.
   b. Assisting in preparation of in-process manufacturing and inspection instructions.
   c. Providing guidance for those performing final checkout, packaging, and shipping of Penguin-in-a-Helmet.

Marketing

The successful sale of the product is based on an emotional response to the perky personality of the penguins. Major marketing messages were designed to present the picture of people enjoying a partnership with the perky pet. The marketing plan is fairly straightforward, as follows:

1. Advertisements have been run in many magazines targeting grocery stores.
2. Direct mailings were made to major grocery store chains throughout the U.S. and Canada.
3. Sample products were sent to magazines and newspapers throughout the sales region and favorable reviews were being given.
4. Press releases were also sent to magazines and newspapers.
5. Representatives of the Perky Pets executive board participated in the following activities:
   a. Demonstrating the product at grocery store conventions
   b. Making guest appearances on popular television and radio talk shows
6. The Perky Pets web site became extremely popular with Internet surfers. Many links were established, and the site had over 200,000 hits in its first month of operation.

First and Second Weeks of Sales

What was the result of this extensive marketing plan? Penguin-in-a-Helmet was an overnight success!

As shown in Figure B.1, eager buyers were storming grocery stores to buy their own Penguin-in-a-Helmet. The customers were happy, grocery store management was happy, and Perky Pets was overjoyed. Perky Pets made the cover of *Time* magazine. The *Wall Street Journal* hinted that Perky Pets was planning to go public. Orders for Penguin-in-a-Helmet increased tenfold in the first week. The future indeed seemed rosy.

FIGURE B.1. Penguin-in-a-Helmet Happy Customers. (Reprinted with permission from Cappels, T.M., *Financially Focused Quality*, CRC Press, 1999. Copyright CRC Press, Boca Raton, Florida.)

Third Week of Sales

During the third week, another phenomenon materialized. The encouraging start was about to be slowed substantially by an obstacle — a rather significant obstacle. Perky Pets began to experience a failure mode.

Failure Mode

Sales slowed considerably, and Perky Pets had to establish a warranty service organization. The penguins stopped behaving in a perky manner. They became lethargic, almost catatonic. After only a few of days of perkiness, the penguins entered into a stupor.

"Either fix this penguin or give me my money back!" was the jeering cry of dissatisfied Penguin-in-a-Helmet customers across the continental U.S. and Canada. It was clear from the expression of the Perky Pets warranty service representative (Figure B.2) that the company had to take immediate corrective action.

FFPM

Fortunately for Perky Pets, Incorporated, the executive board had already embraced the concepts of FFPM and used it to incorporate a financial viewpoint in the corrective action process.

FIGURE B.2. Penguin-in-a-Helmet Failure Mode. (Reprinted with permission from Cappels, T.M., *Financially Focused Quality*, CRC Press, 1999. Copyright CRC Press, Boca Raton, Florida.).

As described below, a financial viewpoint is involved from the identification of the failure through closure of quality engineering corrective actions affecting the manufacturing process.

Project Identifiers

Failures are obviously identified by the customers in this case. A little boy cries out to his mother, who is ironing in the next room: "Mommy! This penguin isn't working right! It's broken! Can you fix it?"

The mother rushes in and sees the penguin lying prostrate on its back. Its wide, unblinking eyes are glazed, its body motionless. The lad buries his tearful face in his mother's embrace. "Oh mommy," he sobs. "Can you fix it?"

The mother picks up the failed product and drives to the Penguin-in-a-Helmet warranty service organization. On her arrival she is asked to take a number from the little machine. It seems there are quite a few people in line ahead of her.

The first individuals in the company to be designated as project identifiers are the warranty service representatives. They perform the following tasks:

1. Complete the project notice (see below).
2. The project notice is attached to the defective Penguin-in-a-Helmet and forwarded to the quality engineering organization, which is designated the process improvement coordinator.

The above procedures are fairly routine for any situation, regardless of the company's corrective action procedure. FFPM requires the warranty service organization to perform the following added function:

3. A copy of the project notice is forwarded to the finance organization.

Project Notice

When filling out the project notice, special attention should be given to the description of failure. Warranty service representatives do not have formal veterinary training, and as such may not be able to write a medically accurate description of the failure. It is important, though, that the project notice contain a reasonable assessment of the symptoms, as follows:

> The Penguin-in-a-Helmet discontinued normal operation. Not only did it stop being perky, it stopped reacting to external stimuli. It ceased to eat, sleep, or breathe. Cause: unknown.

Quality Engineering

Quality engineering functions as the process improvement coordinator and performs the following tasks:

1. Receives failed Penguin-in-a-Helmet.
2. Receives project notice.
3. Performs requisite analyses and makes contact with other failure analysts as needed to determine the cause of penguin failure.
    a. The penguins failed due to heat exposure.
    b. The penguins failed because the cooling helmets were not functioning properly.
    c. The cooling helmets were not functioning properly because:
        i. The gas used in the helmet cooling mechanism had not been adequately purified.
        ii. After a few weeks, contaminated gas clogged the expansion valve, resulting in the loss of cooling.
        iii. Loss of cooling resulted in an unacceptable increase in penguin body temperature, causing the failure.
4. Using a financially focused approach, analyses are performed to identify which actions are the most cost effective, and the product support organizations are notified to perform the following:
    a. A supplier representative relocates to the city where the gas supplier's factory is located. The representative works to help improve the supplier's gas purification process.

b. Inspectors on the loading dock are required to tighten inspection criteria on all deliveries, including an increase to 100% inspection of gas.

c. Additionally, because management is concerned about unfavorable publicity and threats from several animal rights groups, inspectors on the loading dock are also required to perform 100% examination of penguins to ensure every one is perky on arrival, as illustrated in Figure B.3.

The following activities are required to ensure a financial focus:

1. Process improvement cost analyses are generated in the corrective action selection process. The cost analyses for implemented corrective actions and process improvements are forwarded to finance.

2. The cost analyses quantify the increased costs by contrasting the before and after costs:

   a. The costs associated with 100% inspection of gas vs. the prior costs of sampling.

   b. The costs associated with 100% examination of penguins vs. the prior costs of sampling.

   c. The costs of having a supplier representative work with the gas supplier. Previously this cost did not exist.

FIGURE B.3. Perky Pets Increased Inspection. (Reprinted with permission from Cappels, T.M., *Financially Focused Quality*, CRC Press, 1999. Copyright CRC Press, Boca Raton, Florida.)

3. A process improvement follow-up plan is developed to perform the following checks after 1 month from the implementation date:
   a. If receiving inspection finds that the gas is consistently meeting the increased purification standards, the on-site supplier representative may relocate back to Perky Pets international headquarters.
   b. Also, if the gas is consistently meeting the increased purification standards, receiving inspectors may revert to the less costly technique of sampling.
   c. Similarly, if pressure from animal rights groups drops to an acceptable level, the 100% penguin examination requirement may be lifted, with a reversion to sampling.
4. Finally, when the failure mode has been corrected, quality engineering issues the process improvement closure notice, which formally ends the process improvement cycle and ensures unnecessary process changes are discontinued.
5. The closure notice is forwarded to performing organizations.
6. The closure notice is forwarded to finance.

Financial Administration

As usual, finance performs the routine financial functions of any manufacturing concern, but in addition has the following financially focused responsibilities:

1. Receives and logs in the project notice, awaiting corrective action input.
2. Receives the process improvement cost analyses for implemented process improvements.
3. Monitors actual costs incurred by performing organization to ensure that they are in line with the anticipated changes in costs.
4. When actual costs vary from what is anticipated based on the cost analyses, finance investigates the variance with performing organizations, attempting to bring discrepancies to management attention.
5. Cost deltas resulting from the corrective action are incorporated to update budgets and prices as follows:
   a. Prices are updated to reflect cost increases. The price for which a product sells must be high enough to at least allow the manufacturer to break even (unless a company is being operated as a tax shelter). To ensure an adequate profit margin exists, finance considers immediate price increases to offset increased production costs.

   b. Organization budgets are adjusted for increased scope of work mandated by corrective actions imposed by quality engineering. In times of extremely tight budgets, management may expect a department to perform added requirements with existing resources. This often requires creative utilization of manpower.
6. Finance receives the process improvement follow-up plan and prompts quality engineering to ensure it is carried out as planned.
7. Finance eventually receives the process improvement closure notice and on receipt of the closure notice performs the following:
   a. Monitors actual costs incurred by performing organizations to ensure the discontinuance of any corrective actions that are no longer required (e.g., 100% inspection of gas).
   b. Files the closure notice, follow-up plan, and cost analyses for future reference.
8. Finance continues to monitor, track, and prompt quality engineering on open corrective actions.

Product Support Organizations

The product support organizations perform the following functions for failures in which a financial focus is used:

1. Observe failures and complete project notices.
2. Forward project notices and failed hardware or penguins to quality engineering.
3. Perform corrective actions and process improvements as designated by quality engineering.
4. Modify, reduce, or discontinue corrective actions and process improvements as specified on the process improvement closure notice.

The Supplier of the Contaminated Gas

The supplier has the responsibility to meet the contractual specifications for gas purity. Perky Pets Incorporated sent a supplier representative to assist with process improvement. The process changes that take place may result in an increased cost to deliver the gas to Perky Pets. This being the case, Perky Pets is hoping that the gas supplier does not use FFPM tools in its process improvement procedures, because if it did, any increased cost could immediately be passed on to Perky Pets. Without FFPM, the supplier may not recognize a need to raise prices for quite a while.

PERKY PETS SUMMARY

The benefits of FFPM are clearly presented in this model. They are summarized below:

1. A high-quality corrective action plan is implemented, leading to timely recovery from the failure mode.
2. The selected corrective actions were also the most cost effective available.
3. The company was immediately able to analyze impacts to production costs, providing the opportunity to adjust prices if appropriate.
4. A follow-up plan was established to ensure that the corrective action had been effective, providing the following benefits:
   a. If process improvements were not effective, immediate recognition of this fact enables quality engineering to generate alternative steps in a timely manner.
   b. If process improvements were successful, imposed steps can be reconsidered and, if possible, their magnitude reduced or eliminated. In this case, for example, the effort of working with the supplier to improve its gas purification system was successful, and 100% inspection of gas was no longer required. If it is no longer needed, it should not be done.
   c. The finance organization provides added impetus for quality engineering to perform the follow-up function. Finance keeps a log of open corrective actions and continues to prompt quality engineering for closure notices.

Perky Pets, Incorporated: A model case providing an ideal showcase for FFPM.

SELF-STUDY/DISCUSSION QUESTIONS

1. What could be the vision statement for Perky Pets? Mission statement?
2. Evaluate the performance of Perky Pets in the following areas:
   - Product development
   - Manufacturing process
   - Supplier relations
   - Marketing
   - Warranty service
3. What similar products can you imagine as potential moneymakers for Perky Pets? What problems might be encountered, and how could FFPM be used to resolve them?
4. Explain how FFPM tools led to improved financial results. What unfavorable financial impacts would/could have been incurred had Perky Pets not implemented FFPM?

CASE STUDY C: IMPLEMENTING FINANCIALLY FOCUSED PROJECT MANAGEMENT IN SOFTWARE ENGINEERING

INTRODUCTION

This case study is based on the technical paper "Profitable Software Quality,"[66] presented at the First World Congress on Software Quality, 1995, San Francisco. The paper was written and presented by Robert J. Herbert, Litton Applied Technology, and Thomas M. Cappels, University of Phoenix and Lockheed Martin Missiles and Space. This is a factual case study that illustrates the application of financially focused project management (FFPM) in a major software development project.

In modern software development, the process for implementing changes to the baseline configuration is made via a problem-reporting corrective action system. All changes to the items in a configuration baseline are identified on a problem/change report (PCR) and are processed through this system. All the concepts of FFPM are exhibited in this process.

On the AN/ALR-67 Project at Applied Technology, a division of Litton Systems, Inc., a problem-reporting corrective action system is in place. This method, also known as the PCR process, is used for all changes in requirements, problems, or enhancements to AN/ALR-67 capabilities. By adapting the FFPM process, substantial improvements to the PCR process were achieved.

This case study reviews related financially focused concepts and demonstrates how they have been applied to the AN/ALR-67 project. The resulting process improvements effectively transform the existing PCR process into a software FFPM system, saving millions of dollars while maintaining high quality standards.

FFPM OVERVIEW

FFPM focuses on the financial implications of every function involved in delivering products. This overview summarizes those FFPM components now and/or potentially incorporated into Litton's Applied Technology Division. The three FFPM components are (1) identification of the need for FFPM; (2) coordination, analysis, and selection of the new process or corrective action; and (3) follow-up and closure of the need identified in (1).

Identification of Need

FFPM begins with identification of any situation for which there is the potential for improvement (e.g., change in customer requirements, failures). Note that all employees/customers are encouraged to initiate the FFPM cycle. FFPM tools and techniques assist by ensuring a financial perspective is applied to the questions that arise at this stage of the cycle:

   a. Is the need identified truly needed and/or wanted?
   b. Is the current process cost effective?
   c. Do employees feel all their activities contribute favorably to the product?

Coordinate/Analyze/Select Process/Corrective Action

FFPM requires that process improvement coordination be performed by someone with a true financial perspective. In software engineering, it is usually not practical to include in the process an actual member of the financial community, so often a member of management coordinates these activities and ensures that the appropriate employees have a general understanding of the financial considerations of corrective action. An effective tool for providing such information is training recommended by FFPM.

As part of the routine coordination process, experts are consulted as options are generated, and eventually a revised process or corrective action is selected. The FFPM approach ensures the following:

a. That it is even practical to pursue the need identified in the first stage.
b. The appropriate amount of resources is expended in understanding the process, with effective meetings and management involvement.
c. That a comprehensive cost analysis is generated for those options with merit.
d. That cost is given appropriate weight in the final selection of process change or corrective action.

Follow-Up and Closure

The FFPM process ensures effectiveness, calling for revision, modification, and formalization of procedures to enhance profitability:

a. Ensures proper implementation of selected corrective actions and procedures.
b. A variance-reporting mechanism allows effective feedback on unanticipated costs.
c. Software engineering easily communicates cost data to the financial community for timely updates to proposals and pricing.
d. Selected corrective actions and process improvements are re-examined after the fact for elimination or reduction in scope to ensure every activity yields full benefit.

BACKGROUND OF PROJECT TO WHICH FFPM HAS BEEN APPLIED

The AN/ALR-67 is a countermeasures subsystem that provides Navy pilots situational awareness about the hostile and friendly radars in the environment. The AN/ALR-67 system is hosted on the F/A-18, AV-8B, A-6E, and F-14 aircraft. The AN/ALR-67 system's software is a highly complex real-time embedded software package that requires quality and reliability. These high standards of quality and reliability demand that the change control process for the AN/ALR-67 system also be of superior quality. With shrinking Department of Defense budgets, it was apparent that, while quality is important, it must be balanced with cost. Litton's Advanced Technology Division adopted the FFPM philosophy of high quality at minimum costs.

Advanced Technology Division's Problem-Reporting Corrective Action System

A software configuration control board (SCCB) controls the Advanced Technology Division's PCR process. The SCCB consists of the project's lead software engineer, the project's lead system engineer, a software quality engineer, project management, and a software configuration management engineer. Throughout the PCR process, the SCCB integrates the concepts of FFPM. The following is a description of the Advanced Technology Division PCR process. Figure C.1 charts the flow of configuration control for this process.

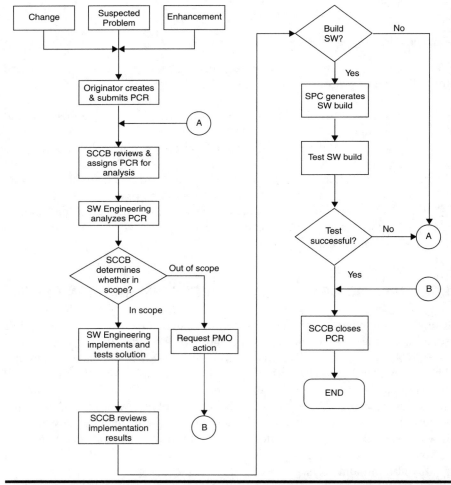

FIGURE C.1 Flow of Configuration Control. (Reprinted with permission from Cappels, T.M., *Financially Focused Quality*, CRC Press, 1999. Copyright CRC Press, Boca Raton, Florida.)

Process Steps

1. An originator identifies a change, problem, or enhancement on a PCR form and submits the PCR along with supporting documentation to software configuration management. Software configuration management reviews the PCR for completeness, assigns a PCR number, enters the PCR information into a log, and distributes the agenda for an SCCB meeting.

2. During the SCCB meeting, the SCCB chairperson:
   - Consciously performs cost trade-offs on the PCR impact.
   - Redirects the nonsoftware PCRs.
   - Screens for duplication.
   - Decides priority and suspense dates.
   - Determines if the PCR impacts the current product baseline and may assign an analyst to the PCR.

3. Assuming the PCR is assigned, the analyst:
   - Assesses the problem, as well as the cost and risks for recommended solution.
   - Looks at interim fixes or possible workarounds.
   - Explores alternative solutions.
   - Recommends solutions.
   - Identifies all affected areas on the PCR.
   - Submits the PCR to software configuration management to schedule an SCCB analysis review.

4. At the SCCB analysis review, the SCCB chairperson:
   - Reviews the PCR analysis and recommended solutions.
   - Approves or disapproves the analysis.
   - Determines whether additional walkthroughs and/or testing requirements are required.
   - Coordinates with areas identified.
   - Schedules the implementation of the recommended changes and assigns an implementor.

5. If the PCR is out of scope, the PCR is submitted to the program management office for disposition. The SCCB will initiate an engineering change request or order for a PCR that impacts the product baseline(s). The PCR will remain open until the configuration change control board returns the engineering change request or order disposition. Software configuration management documents the disposition/assignment in the SCCB meeting minutes and updates its PCR log. If the SCCB rejects a PCR, it is returned with comments to the originator and closed by software configuration management.

6. If the PCR is in scope, the assigned software engineer:
   - Implements the recommended solution per schedule.
   - Performs all minimum amount of testing, and notifies software configuration management that the PCR is ready for the SCCB implementation review.
7. At the SCCB implementation review, the SCCB chairperson:
   - Reviews a version difference report by comparing changed files to the baseline.
   - Reviews the PCR with the version difference report.
   - Ensures the appropriate portions of the software development folder have been updated with the change files. If all the items are complete, the chairperson submits the folder and attachments to software configuration management for incorporation into the developmental configuration and authorizes a software build to be made.
8. If the software build is not authorized, the SCCB returns the software development folder, PCR, and supporting documentation to the implementor for corrective action.
9. If the software build is authorized, software configuration management incorporates the changed files into the baseline and generates a software build.
10. The implementor installs the software build while witnessed by a software quality engineer and performs appropriate software qualification tests.
11. If the testing is not successful, the implementor returns the PCR and support documentation back to the SCCB chairperson for corrective action and disposition. If new problems are encountered during the testing, PCRs are generated and submitted to software configuration management.
12. If the test is successful, software configuration management prepares the PCR for SCCB closure review. The SCCB chairperson reviews the recommended closure report and authorizes the PCR closure contained in the report. The SCCB then reviews, signs, and authorizes closure or approval of the PCR. Software configuration management updates the PCR log, files the closed PCRs in the software development library, and documents them in the SCCB minutes.

FFPM APPLICATION TO THE PCR PROCESS

Litton's Applied Technology Division's software development organization successfully applied FFPM to its PCR process. This section provides an in-depth explanation of how it was achieved in three FFPM stages: (1) identification of the need for FFPM; (2) coordination, analysis, and selection of the new process; and (3) follow-up and closure of the need identified.

Need for FFPM Identified

In this implementation, management in Litton's Applied Technology Division's software development organization first familiarized itself with FFPM by undergoing FFPM training. This training was accomplished in two ways. First, employees met with FFPM practitioners to gain an understanding of FFPM tools and techniques. Second, FFPM publications were studied to gain a basic understanding of financial concepts and to learn about FFPM case studies that had yielded substantial savings.

Litton management recognized many similarities between several case studies and the operations in the software development organization. Recognizing the potential value of applying FFPM concepts and techniques, management asked its engineers to review each step of the PCR process. At each step, employees were to question the cost effectiveness of the process and attempt to validate that all their activities contributed favorably to their software product.

The responses confirmed management's belief that the potential existed for process improvement in the PCR process. Thus, stage two of the FFPM process began.

Coordination, Analysis, and Selection of Process Improvement

The lead software engineer was assigned responsibility as the FFPM coordinator. As such, he was tasked with determining the causal/beneficial relationship each procedure made to the bottom line. The goal was to determine whether steps could be eliminated that would reduce cost and still maintain quality.

Previously in the process, Litton was using a form called a secondary problem/change report (SCPR). This was another PCR that was written at the completion of the analyst's review of the PCR and prior to the SCCB analysis review. This additional form was allocated for each affected computer software component identified by the analyst. The idea was that these SPCRs would be closed as each computer software component was corrected so changes could be submitted to the developmental configuration baseline prior to having the problem completely solved.

FFPM algorithms led to significant improvements in and substantial savings for the PCR process. To derive the data for this FFPM analysis, a financial analyst either performed time studies or queried company databases to determine an historical basis for average hours spent per PCR and per SPCR.

The analyst also required access to data allowing the determination of the average direct labor rate of employees administering the reports. Finally, factors were determined to ensure that appropriate allocated costs were included for generating an overall average hourly rate. Such costs may include overhead, G&A costs, and pooled direct costs such as computer systems or common services.

The total annual cost of PCR processing was calculated at $14.7 million. And yes, Litton's process was critical to maintaining high quality and reliability in its software, but FFPM was called on to see if the same high levels of quality could be maintained at a lower cost.

The vast majority of costs resulted from the administration of the SPCRs. After several weeks of close study by the engineers and management in the group, a few changes were made in the processing of the PCR, and the SPCR was totally eliminated from the process!

Calculations proved that the "after FFPM cost" was only $3.5 million, or a savings of over $11 million. Savings resulted from the discontinuance of SPCR processing. Also, even after including a few additional steps in PCR processing, the overall impact to the time required for PCR processing dropped, because there was no longer a need to track individual computer software components and the corresponding SPCR.

Follow-Up and Closure

After a few months of trying the modified process, it was formally recognized that the SPCR processing was indeed not cost effective. In fact, it was very expensive. The additional form increased the software engineer's documentation by as much as fivefold. One case was documented where five PCRs generated an additional 25 SPCRs. In addition, Litton found that all the PCRs and their SPCRs were closed at the same time. In fact, closing these PCRs simultaneously was inevitable because of the nature of the problems the PCRs were identifying.

Typically, if a problem affects more than one computer software component, the problem lies in the communication between the components. When this occurs, the only way to determine if the problem has been corrected is to implement a complete solution and test the components together. This means that the components must be implemented, tested, and therefore submitted for closure at the same time!

The SPCR handling did nothing for the process except add cost to the product. Accordingly, the SPCR form and all associated tasks were formally deleted from written task descriptions and job instructions.

Future Improvements

Litton is continuing to seek new ways to improve its process. Currently, Litton is undertaking the complete rewrite of the AN/ALR-67 software to make it more maintainable. During this development, improvement of Litton's current PCR process was initiated. Litton is concentrating on computerizing the PCR process. Currently, the PCR is filled out by hand and then placed on the flat database called Filemaker Pro, which is hosted on a Macintosh computer. Potential areas of improvement and cost savings are in how the information flows to people involved in the system. There is a lot of paperwork and disconnects because individuals do not receive or lose their paperwork.

Currently Litton is implementing its PCR process on a workstation that is connected to a dedicated Local Area Network. The PCRs and the forms will be on a relational database and an event promotion system is being developed. The relational database will be used to generate metrics so Litton can begin measurement of its overall software development process.

It is envisioned that PCRs will no longer be written by hand. Instead, when a PCR is written, the originator will type the problem into the PCR form on the network. The PCR then will be sent via e-mail to software configuration management. Software configuration management then will be able to generate the SCCB agenda on-line and notify the SCCB members by e-mail.

As each PCR goes through each step of the process, it will be promoted by the on-line PCR system to a new state, and electronic notification will be used to maintain communication with all affected parties. Litton anticipates that this system will greatly reduce the load on software configuration management personnel who currently are busy enough with paperwork.

CONCLUSION

This case study has demonstrated a successful FFPM application to software development, with substantial savings for Litton's Applied Technology Division. Effectively eliminating waste in business will ensure that every effort will positively impact society.

SELF-STUDY/DISCUSSION QUESTIONS

1. How does the FFPM approach utilized at Litton differ from the approach used in a manufacturing environment? A service industry?
2. What circumstance, if any, could justify the continued use of secondary problem/change reports? Why do you think they were used in the first place?

Free value-added materials available from the
Download Resource Center at www.jrosspub.com.

CASE STUDY D: TIARA PLAZA HOTEL

INTRODUCTION

The goal of this project is to make improvements in the Tiara Plaza Hotel courtesy car service. This case study provides an application of financially focused project management (FFPM) to the service industry.

There are three major components of FFPM for hotel operations:

1. The project identifier (segment I)
2. The management staff meeting (segment II)
3. The hotel controller office (providing the financial viewpoint)

FFPM IN HOTEL OPERATIONS: OVERVIEW

Figure D.1 presents the FFPM process flow.

Project (Failure or Opportunity) Identifier (Segment I)

The FFPM cycle beings when a project has been identified. The project can originate from either corporate headquarters, hotel management, or, most frequently, after a problem has been noted. In hotel operations, a failure may take many forms, such as:

1. Case of food poisoning occurs in a hotel restaurant or at a banquet.
2. There is a power failure.
3. Guest rooms are not made up fast enough to accommodate check-in of guests.

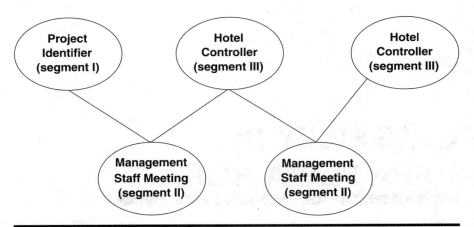

FIGURE D.1. FFPM Overview: Hotel Operations. (Reprinted with permission from Cappels, T.M., *Financially Focused Quality*, CRC Press, 1999. Copyright CRC Press, Boca Raton, Florida.)

4. Hotel guest is taken to airport in hotel courtesy car and arrives late for flight.
5. Wake-up calls are not made as promised.
6. Reservations are lost.
7. Hotel rates are misquoted.
8. The band in the hotel lounge is too loud and keeps guests awake.
9. Appliances in hotel rooms not operating properly.
10. The list goes on and on.

The formal FFPM procedure used for a manufacturing environment includes reference to two different but similar forms, generically referred to as the project notice or the project recommendation. Similar forms are easily adapted to hotel operations. This case study deals with a specific failure, and therefore, the project notice is used.

There are numerous ways that failures are brought to management attention, including the following:

1. Guest complaints and observations
2. Nonmanagement complaints and observations
3. Management complaints and observations

When a failure is identified, the FFPM project identifier (segment I) performs these steps:

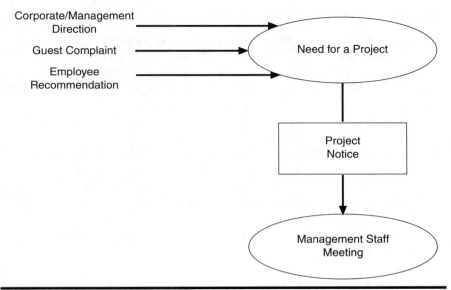

FIGURE D.2. Project Initiation: Hotel Operations.

1. Generates the project notice.
2. Forwards the project notice for review at the management weekly staff meeting. If the failure is of significant urgency, a special meeting may be called (Figure D.2).

Management Staff Meeting (Segment II)

The supervisors of all hotel departments attend the staff meeting. As a result, management of all potential failure solvers is in attendance.

The following actions are taken in regard to the project notice:

1. The notice is reviewed with attendees.
2. Potential causes are discussed.
3. Potential corrective actions and process improvements are generated.
4. Corrective action and process improvement cost analyses are determined for the proposed steps.
5. Implementation of the most cost-effective process improvement is assigned to appropriate department supervisor.
6. Corrective action/process improvement follow-up plan is developed.
7. The cost analysis corresponding to the selected corrective action and follow-up plan is forwarded to the hotel controller's department.

Hotel Controller Office (Segment III)

The hotel controller and staff provide the focus for including consideration of financial impacts with the corrective action cycle. Although FFPM is a mindset that should be instilled in the minds of all company employees, the involvement of an individual specifically trained in the science of finance is particularly beneficial. The hotel controller is such an individual.

The hotel controller office (segment III) performs the following tasks:

1. Attends and provides input to the management staff meeting (segment II)
2. Updates pricing policies and budgets utilizing the cost analysis
3. Tracks corrective action expenditures to the cost analysis
4. Prompts organization supervisors to comply with the requirements of the follow-up plan
5. Prompts the generation of the corrective action/process improvement closure notice

Management Staff Meeting (Segment II)

Final actions to close the corrective action cycle are taken as follows:

1. When it has been determined that the process improvement has successfully eliminated the failure, the closure notice is issued to formally approve or modify process improvement procedures.
2. Responsibility for implementation of any closure notice activities is assigned to the appropriate department supervisors.

Hotel Controller Office (Segment III)

The hotel controller office continues tracking costs and prompting closure of open project notices.

FFPM IN THE TIARA PLAZA HOTEL

The Tiara Plaza Hotel is a full-service hotel, with two restaurants (coffee shop and fine dining), a lounge that features live music into the wee hours of the night, several ballrooms, many meeting rooms, and 400 guest rooms. It is located in San Mateo, California, about 10 miles south of the San Francisco International Airport.

The Front Office

Hamid manages the front office of this large, independent hotel. His department is comprised of the following functions:

1. The front desk (cashier and registration)
2. Reservations
3. PBX (switchboard) operations (including wake-up service)
4. Night audit (close the financial books each night)
5. Bellstand, which includes:
   a. Bellpeople
   b. Courtesy car service

Project Identifier

Manager Hamid has been quite concerned of late, because he has been receiving numerous complaints about the Tiara Plaza courtesy car service. It is the responsibility of the courtesy car service to pick up hotel guests when they arrive at the San Francisco International Airport and shuttle them to the hotel for check-in. Also, the hotel courtesy car transports guests back to the airport after they have checked out.

The hotel is 10 miles from the airport and the trip can take anywhere from 30 to 60 minutes round trip, depending on the traffic. Traffic becomes very heavy during the morning and evening rush hours.

The most common — and most serious — complaint stems from the inflexible hours of service operation. The courtesy car only leaves for the airport on the hour, which often results in the following situations harmful to guest perception of hotel service:

1. Guest is very nervous during the trip to the airport and arrives just barely in time for the flight.
2. Guest arrives at the airport too late for the flight.
3. Guest becomes very upset and has to call a cab to ensure that he or she gets to the airport on time for the flight.

Complaints arising due to the above situation most frequently are made directly to the courtesy car drivers, but occasionally are addressed in letters to hotel management.

All employees having contact with hotel guests are instructed on how to record guest complaints or their observations regarding hotel operations. Project notices are completed and contain the following information:

1. Name of employee completing the project notice
2. Date of complaint
3. Name of guest/employee with complaint/observation if different from (1) above
4. Nature of complaint/observation

The notices (complaints) are filled out by courtesy car drivers and given to the front office supervisor so that the issue may be addressed at the management staff meeting.

Hamid knows the courtesy car issue will be on the agenda for the next staff meetings and, as such, meets with bell captain Bongo to get any additional pertinent information.

Bongo has been the bell captain for 4 years. The bellstand has recently had a big turnover in personnel. As a result, courtesy car drivers are sometimes required to help check guests in, and bellpeople are sometimes needed to make trips to the airport. Bongo apologizes profusely to his boss, as Hamid heads off to the meeting.

Management Staff Meeting: Segment II

At the management staff meeting (Figure D.3), a time slot is always scheduled for discussion of complaints and corresponding project notices. Front office manager Hamid initiates discussion on the complaints related to the courtesy car service. He begins by giving an introduction to the policies and procedures of courtesy car operation, and then summarizes the complaints.

Other department managers participate in the ensuing discussion. Coffee shop manager Yolanda speaks of a guest who dashed away from a half-eaten breakfast without paying. "He seemed fine until he heard the announcement that the hotel courtesy car was leaving for the airport," Yolanda explained. "It was only then that he learned the courtesy car leaves on the hour, and NOT at the whim of the guests."

Depending on the degree of the problem, process improvements and corrective actions may be determined at the current meeting. In this case, however, it is decided that a comprehensive analysis is needed, and a report should be prepared.

A specific statement of the problem will be required. A determination of the probable causes must be made and several corrective actions and process improvements recommended.

In addition, those making the process improvement recommendations are asked to prepare corrective action and process improvement cost analyses for each. Individuals are assigned responsibility for these inputs, due at the next weekly meeting. Until that time, bell captain Bongo will be given the authority

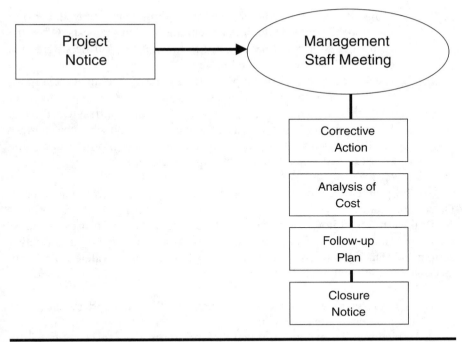

FIGURE D.3. Management Staff Meeting.

to hire a taxi if needed to satisfy guest transportation requirements. The hotel controller points out that the payment to the taxi driver will come out of the hotel petty cash fund, which is an overhead expense.

One week later, at the next meeting, the following data are presented:

- Statement of problem: Guests frequently miss flights or must hire a taxi at their own expense. Some bellpeople even charge guests to take them to the airport in their own cars, since the courtesy car may only be driven on the hour. Because of insurance ramifications, management forbids this action, and when detected, the bellperson is subject to disciplinary action. Guests also complain that after a long flight, they often must wait on the curb at the airport for as much an hour before they are picked up by the next scheduled courtesy car. Thus, the problem has been stated clearly.
- Next, probable causes are determined.
  1. Cause A: Hotel policy is inadequate. The courtesy car is only allowed to leave on the hour. A guest arriving for the courtesy even 1 minute late may have to wait 59 minutes until the next departure or pickup.

2. Cause B: Though the hotel policy regarding departure to the airport may indeed be adequate, it is not communicated to guests. Often the complaint is "I could have gotten to the courtesy car departure area earlier had I known the hotel policy."
3. Cause C: In the case of people waiting to be picked up at the airport, the PBX operator (who receives calls for airport pickups) does not successfully communicate guests' needs to the courtesy car drivers. When a guest does not need a ride to the airport, and when the courtesy car driver is not aware that someone is at the airport waiting, the courtesy car does not make the trip to the airport.

So the problem has been stated, and potential causes have been offered. Discussion follows.

Brainstorming follows in an attempt to determine which causes are most likely and, then, what the probable root causes and corresponding corrective actions are. During this discussion, the cost analyses are considered. Probable discussion points may include the following:

1. Why are many guests under the impression that the courtesy car leaves the moment a guest needs it?
2. Why are all guests not informed that the courtesy car leaves only on the hour?
3. Has there been any benchmarking performed? Do other hotels offer courtesy car services that leave at the whim of the guests?
4. Possibly some bellpeople intentionally mislead guests so that they can drive the guests to the airport in their own car, and charge an amount that would easily exceed the usual tip.
5. Perhaps the hotel courtesy car policy of every hour on the hour is not adequate. It is true that many hotels located within 5 miles of the airport have full-time courtesy car drivers who constantly drive back and forth and thus have a car leaving almost every 5 minutes. But a round trip to the airport from this hotel averages one-half to one full hour. It would require six to ten courtesy cars in operation simultaneously to match the frequency offered by these other hotels. The cost of concurrent operation of six to ten courtesy cars would be quite high. Would this be practical and cost effective?

A potential policy change could result in maintaining the hourly departure time but allow courtesy car departures for pickups at the airport as needed. Such a policy change would eliminate guests waiting for an hour at the airport. Perhaps the current courtesy car policy is valid and sufficient, as long as the policy is presented clearly to hotel guests. Three process improvements are then identified as follows:

1. Possible corrective action A: Revise policy.
2. Possible corrective action B: Take steps to ensure guests are properly informed of hotel policy.
3. Possible corrective action C: Allow bell captain to hire a taxi every time a courtesy car is needed but none is available.

Discussion regarding these potential corrective actions focuses on two elements: (1) the quality of service and (2) the cost of service. As the pros and cons of each action are discussed, special consideration is given to the cost impacts.

It is agreed to adopt, to some extent, all three of these process improvements. The following steps are designated, and responsible managers assigned:

1. Courtesy car policy is revised to allow immediate pickups of guests at the airport. The PBX operator is directed to ensure courtesy car drivers know when a guest is at the airport for pickup. This is coordinated with registration and cashiers at the front desk. If the PBX operator is unable to make telephone contact with a courtesy car driver, the operator may assign the responsibility of contacting a courtesy car driver to an employee at the front desk. In this case, the front desk personnel would keep an eye out for the first bellperson to return to the lobby. If no bellperson returns within 5 minutes of the call, the PBX operator will page a bellperson to come to the front desk.
2. No revision is made to the policy of making departures on the hour.
3. Bell captain Bongo holds a meeting with all bellpeople and courtesy car drivers to ensure that they understand the policy. Attendees are also instructed to frequently inform guests of the policy. Such informing should be performed as part of the service when picking someone up at the airport or when assisting a guest checking into a room.
4. Bellpeople are instructed to include the following as part of the check-in service:
   a. Escort guest to room.
   b. Set bags on luggage racks.
   c. Point out the location of ice and vending machines, and offer to get ice.
   d. Inform guest of any required safety information.
   e. Announce restaurant and lounge hours of operation.
   f. Explain procedure for getting wake-up calls.
   g. Offer to set the guest up with a rental car or sightseeing tour.

    h. Clearly tell guest that the courtesy car leaves for the airport every hour on the hour. Suggest that the guest call down 5 to 10 minutes early so the bellperson can come up and assist with checkout, and ensure the driver will be ready to go on the hour.

    i. Provide miscellaneous other information.

    j. Entertain questions.

    k. Hand guest the room key.

    l. Accept tip graciously.

5. Bellpeople and courtesy car drivers will be cross-trained to be able to perform either task when necessary and understand the policies of both functions.

6. A large sign is prepared and posted at the bellstand and at the courtesy car departure area. The sign announces that the courtesy car departs every hour on the hour.

7. The PBX operator will make announcements over the hotel public address system 15, 10, 5, and 1 minute prior to courtesy car departure for the airport.

8. And even after all these actions are taken, the bell captain (or acting bell captain) is still authorized to hire taxis for guests whenever it is felt that a guest was not adequately informed of departure times.

Lastly, cost analyses are finalized for the chosen actions. The analyses contain the following data:

1. Cost of performing the new task, such as having the courtesy car operate on a will-call basis for airport pickups: Costs are stated in two elements:

    a. Labor costs, stated in terms of hours and fractions thereof

    b. Nonlabor costs, itemized by expenditure

2. Costs related to the previous policy: This is the cost of just having one airport trip each hour.

3. The cost delta: Subtracting the prior costs from the new costs results in the cost impact of the corrective actions.

The hotel controller office will often work with the corresponding hotel department in preparing the cost analyses. This collaboration ensures a more accurate estimate of costs.

When more than one corrective action can solve a specific problem, a comparison of cost analyses will help determine the most cost-effective solutions. In this case study, the comparison was made before selecting and implementing corrective actions.

With a full understanding of the cost ramifications, management considers the costs involved in implementing the process improvement, and contrasts this against what the hotel will gain (or not lose) in respect to customer satisfaction.

There needs to be agreement that the costs involved will result in an equal or greater return in income.

Development of Corrective Action Follow-Up Plan

The meeting attendees generate a follow-up plan for each unique corrective action or process improvement. The follow-up plan allows the company to increase profitability in three ways:

1. If the process improvement/corrective action did not fully satisfy the cause of failure, follow-up action in a timely manner can lead to the generation of an effective alternate process improvement.
2. If a process improvement has proven to be successful, follow-up action can alert staff meeting attendees that this process may be useful at other hotels or for other applications. For example, the technique of using the hotel paging system may be adopted to make other helpful announcements.
3. By following up, processes that are no longer needed can be readily identified. For example, after 3 months, if the only guests requiring special airport taxi rides are those who carelessly oversleep, perhaps the on-call taxi service should no longer be allowed.
   - The cost analyses and the follow-up plan are provided to the hotel controller office.
   - Finally, when it is determined that a particular process improvement is no longer required (as in the taxi example above), and that failure has been corrected, the closure notice is generated. The closure notice officially completes the FFPM process by modifying and/or formalizing the process improvements into routine procedures.
   - The closure notice is provided to the hotel controller office.

Hotel Controller: Segment III

As shown in Figure D.4, the responsibilities of the controller increase in an FFPM environment. The controller receives the cost analyses, follow-up plan, and closure notice from the management staff meeting. The primary additional tasks follow:

- Considers changes to pricing (e.g., room rates) and budgets based on the cost analyses.
- Analyses of cost: When pricing a new product or contract, the controller relies heavily on historical data. It is advantageous to alert the controller to the cost impacts of new corrective actions. The controller's office considers revising prices to ensure that any additional operating costs are included.

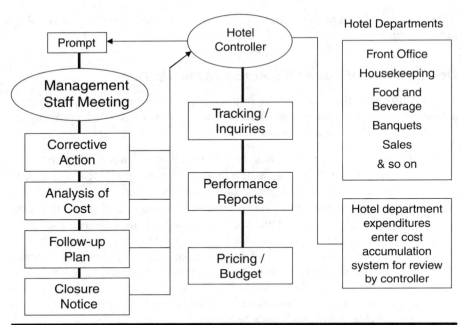

FIGURE D.4. Hotel Controller. (Reprinted with permission from Cappels, T.M., *Financially Focused Quality*, CRC Press, 1999. Copyright CRC Press, Boca Raton, Florida.)

■ Prompts management regarding the cost analyses, follow-up plan, and closure notice. The controller is in the ideal position to prompt management when expenditures are not in line with the cost analyses. Perhaps the performing organization has misunderstood the corrective action and is not performing properly. The controller, in reviewing cost data, can identify this situation and work with management toward the cost effectiveness of corrective actions.

■ Finally, the controller should ensure that management is adhering to the follow-up plan, issuing alternative corrective actions or closure notices in a timely manner.

HOTEL SUMMARY

The key to the successful cost-effective resolution of the courtesy car failure is not in any one FFPM tool. The important factor is the overall financially focused mindset. Every member of Tiara Plaza management is required to examine cost impacts of process improvements and allow such considerations to heavily affect the final selection process.

FFPM, as outlined here, presents the Tiara Plaza with the means to:

- Determine the existence of specific problems
- Take timely and appropriate corrective action to ensure such problems are resolved
- Ensure the most economical implementation of corrective actions through cost comparisons, corrective action revisions, and cancellations/ formalizations
- Anticipate increased operating costs in preparation for salary and wage negotiations, and revise pricing policies

It has been proven that effective use of FFPM tools can enable companies to increase productivity and profitability. This case study exhibits just one of the many potential applications of the FFPM approach to process improvement and corrective action.

SELF-STUDY/DISCUSSION QUESTIONS

1. Would you recommend initiating formal financial training for employees in hotel operations? Why or why not? Which employees, if any, would receive such training, and by what method?
2. Describe the FFPM activity that might take place for complaints about broken ice makers or vending machines, including identifiers, potential and probable causes, potential corrective actions, cost analyses, implementation, and follow-up and closure.
3. Describe the FFPM activity for complaints about coffee shop employees, about the time it takes to prepare and serve dinner in the dining room, or lost reservations.
4. What other problems in hotel operations have you experienced? How could they be resolved using FFPM?

Free value-added materials available from the
Download Resource Center at www.jrosspub.com.

REFERENCES

1. Project management skills highly sought-after, *Business Times*, April 27, 2001.
2. Cappels, T.M., *Financially Focused Quality*, CRC Press, 1999.
3. Romberg, D., Project management tools cannot guarantee success, *Computing Canada*, **24(42)**, 29, 1998.
4. Romberg, D., Project management tools cannot guarantee success, *Computing Canada*, **24(42)**, 30, 1998.
5. Genesis 6, Bible.
6. Web helps city streamline project management, *American City and County*, **117(3)**, 16, 2002.
7. De Meuse, K. and Marks, M.L., Eds., *Resizing the Organization: Managing Layoffs, Divestitures, and Closings*, Jossey-Bass/Pfeiffer, 2002.
8. Pitagorsky, G., How to manage projects, *CMA — The Management Accounting Magazine*, **70(10)**, 15–18, 1996.
9. Cappels, T.M., *Full-Cycle Corrective Action: Managing for Quality and Profits*, Quality Press, 1994, 202.
10. Leemann, T., Managing the chaos of change, *Journal of Business Strategy*, **23**, 5, 2002.
11. Hauschildt, J., Realistic criteria for project manager selection and development, *Project Management Journal*, **31(3)**, 10 and 23, 2000.
12. Lechler, T., *Erfolgsfaktoren des Projektmanagements*, P. Lang, 1997
13. Hicks, D., If you meet a technology guru in the road, kill him!, *IIE Solutions*, **30(9)**, 16, 1998.
14. Parachin, V.M., Integrity — the most important trait to cultivate, *Supervision*, **63(2)**, 2002.
15. Gray, C.F. and Larson, E.W., *Project Management: The Management Process*, McGraw-Hill/Irwin, 2000, 224, 227, 231–233.
16. Jassawalla, A.R. and Sashittal, H.C., Cultures that support product-innovation processes, *Academy of Management Executive*, **16(3)**, 42, 2002.
17. *Jakarta Post*, June 22, 2002.
18. Meredith, J. and Mantel, S., Jr., *Project Management, A Managerial Approach*, John Wiley & Sons, 1995, 171–172.

19. Gido, J. and Clements, J., *Successful Project Management*, South-Western College Publishing, 1999, 111–115.
20. Ammeter, A. and Dukerich, J., Leadership, team building, and team member characteristics in high performance project teams, *Engineering Management Journal*, **14(4)**, 2002.
21. *Incentive*, **175(9)**, 16, 2001.
22. Alpert, A., 6 keys to effective communication, how to empower your sessions with listening and speaking techniques, *Massage Magazine*, **90**, 2001.
23. Shinn, L.J., Financially focused quality, *Association Management*, **51(1)**, 1999.
24. Kirkman, B.L., Rosen, B., Gibson, C.B., Tesluk, P.E., and McPherson, S.O., Five challenges to virtual team success: lessons from Sabre, Inc, *Academy of Management Executive*, **16(3)**, 2002.
25. Hawn, C., Fear and posing. *Forbes ASAP*, **169(7)**, 22, 2002.
26. Parviz, F.R., From the Editor, *Project Management Journal*, **31(4)**, 2000.
27. Bates, W.S., Improving project management, *IIE Solutions*, **30(10)**, 1998.
28. Solomon, M., Project portfolio management, *Computerworld*, March 18, 2002.
29. U.S. Army Corp of Engineers, AGC/USACE Partnering Revitalization for the Next Millenium, http://www.agc.org/Partnering_Project/History.asp.
30. Patterson, P., A Study of International Business Partnerships in SE Asia, http://www.smallbiz.nsw.gov.au/textonly/forms/Dept-State-Dev2.ppt.
31. Armstrong, R., About Win/Win Negotiations, http://www.rvarmstrong.com/AboutWinWinNegotiations.htm.
32. Institute of World Affairs, Preparing for Negotiations, http://iadc.iwa.org/en/Unit7.htm.
33. Darst, B.A., The Basics of Commercial Contracting, http://www.fedpubseminars.com/seminar/bcc1.html.
34. Cappels, T.M., *Full-Cycle Corrective Action: Managing for Quality and Profits*, Quality Press, 1994.
35. Asner, M., Bid or no-bid?, *Learning Curve*, November 1997.
36. *Community Banker*, **10(3)**, 18, 2001.
37. Sant, T., *Sell!ng*, June 1999.
38. Gray, C.F. and Larson, E.W., *Project Management: The Management Process*, McGraw-Hill/Irwin, 2000, 301.
39. Perrons, R., What Is a Make-Buy Decision? http://www-mmd.eng.cam.ac.uk/csp/One_Page_Summary/MvB.htm.
40. Abdomerovic, M., Show it simply, *Project Management Journal*, **31(4)**, 2000.
41. Meredith, J. and Mantel, S., Jr., *Project Management, A Managerial Approach*, John Wiley & Sons, 1995, 218.
42. Gray, C.F. and Larson, E.W., *Project Management: The Management Process*, McGraw-Hill/Irwin, 2000, 89–115.
43. Gido, J. and Clements, J., *Successful Project Management*, South-Western College Publishing, 1999, 221–240.
44. Production Scheduling from Asprova Corporation, http://www.asprova.com/en/home/index.html.
45. Ten Step Project Management Process, http://www.tenstep.com/7.0ManageRisk.htm.

46. Microsoft Technet, http://www.microsoft.com/technet.
47. Illustrative Explanation of Earned Value, http://www.acq.osd.mil/pm/evbasics.htm.
48. Meredith, J. and Mantel, S., Jr., *Project Management, A Managerial Approach*, John Wiley & Sons, 1995, 568 and 571.
49. Travelers Insurance Companies, Management Guide to Product Quality and Safety, 1973, 90.
50. Hormozi, A.M., McMinn, R.D., and Nzeogwu, O., The project life cycle: the termination phase, *SAM Advanced Management Journal*, **65**, 45, 2000.
51. Paul, L.G., Know when to bail out, *Network World*, **15(9)**, 46–47, 1998; Project management from start to finish, *Modern Materials Handling*, 46, 1991.
52. Bounds, G., The last word. *IIE Solutions*, 41–43, 1998.
53. Meredith, J. and Mantel, S., Jr., *Project Management, A Managerial Approach*, John Wiley & Sons, 1995.
54. Bommer, M. and Pease, V., Mitigating the impact of project cancellations on productivity, *National Productivity Review*, **10**, 453–462, 1991.
55. Mandell, M. and Murphy, B., Wake-up strategies for tired R&D projects, *High Technology Business*, **9**, 22–25, 1989.
56. Dobson, J. and Dorsey, R., Reputation, information and project termination in capital budgeting, *Engineering Economist*, **38**, 143–152, 1993.
57. Slevin, D. and Pinto, J., Balancing strategy and tactics in project implementation, in *Project Management, A Managerial Approach*, Meredith, J. and Mantel, S., Jr., Eds., John Wiley & Sons, 1995.
58. Ware, R., People before technology, *Journal of Systems Management*, **41**, 20, 1990.
59. University of Phoenix Accounting and Finance data through February 2000.
60. Ott, E.R. and Schilling, E.G., *Process Quality Control*, Quality Press, 1990, 172.
61. Cound, D.M. and McDermott, T.C., *The Handbook of Industrial Engineering and Management*, Prentice Hall, 1971.
62. Laroche, L., Managing cross-cultural differences in international projects, *Engineering Dimensions*, **19(6)**, 1998.
63. Smetana, H., Challenges of Global Project Management, PMI Presentation, April 15, 2002.
64. Webb, A., Project management, *Project Manager Today*, May 1996.
65. Cappels, T.M., *Full-Cycle Corrective Action: Managing for Quality and Profits*, Quality Press, 1994, back cover.
66. Herbert, R.J. and Cappels, T.M., Profitable Software Quality, The First World Congress on Software Quality, San Francisco, 1995.

INDEX